# THROW YOUR VOICE

# THROW YOUR VOICE

## Suspended Animations in Kazakhstani Childhoods

### Meghanne Barker

CORNELL UNIVERSITY PRESS   ITHACA AND LONDON

Thanks to generous funding from the University College London, the ebook editions of this book are available as open access volumes through the Cornell Open initiative.

First published 2024 by Cornell University Press

Library of Congress Cataloging-in-Publication Data

Names: Barker, Meghanne, 1981– author.
Title: Throw your voice : suspended animations in Kazakhstani childhoods / Meghanne Barker.
Description: Ithaca [New York] : Cornell University Press, 2024. | Includes bibliographical references and index.
Identifiers: LCCN 2024002594 (print) | LCCN 2024002595 (ebook) | ISBN 9781501776458 (hardcover) | ISBN 9781501776465 (paperback) | ISBN 9781501776472 (epub) | ISBN 9781501776489 (pdf)
Subjects: LCSH: Chekhov, Anton Pavlovich, 1860–1904. Kashtanka.—Social aspects. | Children—Kazakhstan—Social conditions—21st century. | Children—Institutional care—Social aspects—Kazakhstan. | Puppet theater—Social aspects—Kazakhstan.
Classification: LCC HQ792.K3 B375 2024 (print) | LCC HQ792.K3 (ebook) | DDC 891.72/3—dc23/eng/20240205
LC record available at https://lccn.loc.gov/2024002594
LC ebook record available at https://lccn.loc.gov/2024002595

*To Honoré, my sensory trap, who animates me*

# Contents

List of Illustrations ix

Acknowledgments xi

Note on Transliteration xv

Introduction 1

**1.** Getting Lost 27

**2.** Meeting a Stranger 53

**3.** Jumping through Hoops 78

**4.** Getting Comfortable 101

**5.** Losing a Friend 123

**6.** Going Home Again 147

Coda 168

Notes 171

References 195

Index 221

# Illustrations

1. The Wolf and the Kid Goats    2

2. The Children Play the Wolf and Kid Goats    3

3. Kashtanka at the Doorstep    28

4. Kashtanka at the Doorstep as a Puppet    29

5. In the Classroom    38

6. Letter to Mamochka    45

7. Nurlan Plays the Helicopter    48

8. Kashtanka Meets a Stranger    54

9. The Children Fix Me    70

10. The Girls Care for Dolls    73

11. The Gander and Cat Rehearse    79

12. The Puppets Make a Pyramid    80

13. The Children Dance in Tutus    82

14. Kashtanka Lies on Her Mattress    102

15. Olzhas Tucks Spider-Man into Bed    118

16. Liuba Cuts Out the Cat Head    120

17. Kashtanka Runs from a Broom    124

18. Maral Loses the Gander Puppet    124

19. A Girl Gets All the Balloons    130

20. Erlan Gets a Stuffed Lamb    145

21. Kashtanka Makes Her Debut    148

22. Marlin Kisses the Children Goodbye    159

23. The Artists Make a Circle of Embraces    164

# Acknowledgments

Hope House and the puppet theater welcomed me into fantastic worlds, which I attempt to reanimate on these pages. Any errors and shortcomings are my fault, and omissions are unintentional.

The children of Hope House made every day of research an experience of wonder, surprise, and humor. They were the best children, and I wish them every happiness as they near adulthood. I am grateful to their parents for letting me get to know their children during my two years there. The directors, teachers, and other staff were patient and welcoming, showing me how to teach and care for children. I have used pseudonyms here, but I cannot thank them enough.

At the puppet theater, I thank all the staff and crew who made room and time for me. The actors and directors let me into their daily lives, sharing knowledge, jokes, food, and drink. Thank you to Sabila Mendigalikyzy Abueva, Kuba Adylov, Orazaly Akzharkyn-Sarsenbek, Araylym Dosbatyrkyzy Baiyrbekova, Gulvira Zhumakankyzy Beysembieva, Asemgul Kalikankyzy Chaelganova, Natasha Dubs, Kulzhamilya Aiypkyzy Ilyasova, Kuralay Absamatkyzy Ismagulova, Maksat Nurlanuly Kamalov, Meruert Konakbaykyzy Karibayeva, Bakytzhan Shadiyarbekuly Kayuov, Shokhan Zhalgasbayuly Kulnazarov, Elmira Garifollakyzy Kumarova, Bolat Ragytuly Momynzhanov, Ulbolsyn Altynbekkyzy Momynzhanova, Gulim Rakhimova, Elvira Maratbekkyzy Suleimenova, Altay Batyrbekuly Tauekelov, Maral Zeynelkyzy Tauekelova, Tolkyn Orynbaykyzy Tleulieva, Rauan Tauratkyzy Ukarova, Anton Alekseevich Zaitsev, Aydyn Keneskaliuly Zhakypbayev, and Erkesh Kaztaykyzy Zhunisova. I thank Vladislav Rafaelevich Berkin, who is missed. The women of the props department, whom I have anonymized, nurtured my meager sewing skills and patiently mended my mistakes over tea and talk.

I learned as well from puppet artists at Zazerkalye Theater, from puppetry professors and students at the Elebekov Republic Estrada and Circus College and at the Zhurgenov Kazakh National Academy of Art—particularly Maisa Omarbekovna Utebaeva and Serik Makulbekov—and from puppeteers and directors I met at puppet festivals and theaters in central Asia, Europe, and the US, including Lena Gousseva, Heather Henson, Raven Kaliana, Gaspare Nasuto, Michel Rosenmann, and Nargis Rozikova. Assiya Khairulina and the Women's League of Creative Initiatives, the Eurasia Foundation, and the SPOON Foundation gave insight on issues of childhood in the region and connected me to essential research partners. Erika Alpert, Aina Begim, Eva-Marie Dubuisson, Helen Faller, Erika Pelta Feldman, Rustem Kubeyev, the Lukashova family, Lisa Sang Mi Min, Masha Vlasova, and Alex Warburton all proved indispensable fieldwork friends at different moments. Elmira Shardarbekova gave invaluable support as a language, research, and translation assistant.

I was able to complete this research thanks to generous funding from the Foreign Language Area Studies Fellowship, Fulbright-IIE, and the National Science Foundation Graduate Research Fellowship Program. At the University of Michigan, I received support from the Center for Russian, East European, and Eurasian Studies, the Department of Anthropology, and Rackham Merit Fellowship.

From Tovah Klein and Patricia Henderson Shimm, I learned to pay attention to children. At the University of Michigan, my professors, classmates, and friends helped me form the ideas behind this book, and many have proven precious interlocutors in years hence. Thanks especially to Jeff Albanese, Gillian Feeley-Harnick, Anna Genina, Alysa Handelsman, Judith Irvine, Deborah Jones, Lavrentia Karamaniola, Webb Keane, Ujin Kim, Jason de León, Jane Lynch, Bruce Mannheim, John Mathias, Erik Mueggler, Mike Prentice, Elana Resnick, Joshua Shapero, Perry Sherouse, Puninder Singh, Thomas Trautmann, Chip Zuckerman, and everyone at Ling Lab. The mixture of tough questions, good ideas, and patient encouragement from my PhD committee gave me skills I continue to hone: Susan Gelman encouraged cross-disciplinary engagement in childhood. Michael Lempert taught me to analyze interactions. Krisztina Fehérváry first turned my attention to the role of materiality in postsocialist childhood and has remained a trusted reader and listener ever since. From Alaina Lemon, my adviser, I learned creativity and courage.

The interdisciplinary intellectual community I found as part of the Harper-Schmidt Society of Fellows at University of Chicago helped to shape the form and scope of this book. William Mazzarella's generous mentorship resonates in each chapter. Constantine Nakassis has been a great source of help and inspiration regarding the relationship between linguistic anthropology and visual culture. I received excellent feedback on drafts of chapters and discussed my work with my colleagues in the Society of Fellows, as well as from the Department of Anthropology, the Department of Comparative Human Development, the Slavic Department, the Mass Culture Workshop, and the Semiotics Workshop. I thank especially: Nicholas Baer, Nadine Chan, Julie Chu, Jennifer Cole, Michele Friedner, Susan Gal, Grigory Gorbun, Britta Ingebretson, Sarah Johnson, Katie Kadue, Natacha Nsabimana, Eugene Raikhel, and Adam Spanos.

Over the years, I have benefited from presenting and discussing my work at Academia Sinica Institute for Ethnology (Taipei), UCLA Discourse Lab, the Yale University Slavic Colloquium Series, NYU Shanghai Humanities and Social Sciences Colloquium, University of Indiana Department of Anthropology, University of Hong Kong Department of Sociology, and the Sense and Semiosis Workshop, funded by the Wenner-Gren Foundation, at University of Chicago. Conferences where I have presented materials include the Annual Meetings of the American Anthropological Association in 2011, 2014, 2015, 2016, 2017, 2018, and 2019; the Michicagoan Graduate Student Conferences in 2011 and 2015; Interdisciplinary SSRC Field Development Workshop on "Youth and Social Stability in Eurasia" in 2011; "Kazakhstani Art: A National Foundation with Universal Values" at the Republic Estrada-Circus College named for Zh. Elebekova in 2013; "Scientific Heritage and National History: Young Scientists' Contribution" in Almaty in 2013; the ASEEES-CESS Joint Regional Conference in Astana in 2014; "Language, Indexicality, and Belonging" at Somerville College, Oxford University, in 2016; the Princeton University Symposium, "Pedagogy of Images II: Depicting Communism for Children" in 2017; "Seen but not Heard? The Spatial, Emotional and Material Sites of Childhood and Youth from Antiquity to Modernity" at University of Sussex in 2017; ASEEES Conventions of 2014 and 2018; SOYUZ Symposium 2018; RAI Conference on "Art, Materiality, and Representation" in 2018; the Inaugural Conference of the Society of Linguistic Anthropology 2018; ASEES Regional Convention 2019; and the CESS Annual Conference in 2021. Through these and other events I have grown from provocative comments, mentorship, and exchange from many, in particular Christopher Ball, Molly Brunson, Erin Debenport, Steven Feld, Gabriella Ferrari, Ilana Gershon, Bruce Grant, Anna Grimshaw, Catriona Kelly, Paul Kockelman, Ruth Mandel, Zdenko Mandušić, Sergei Oushakine, Teri Silvio, Matilda Stubbs, Kristina Wirtz, and Chelsea Yount-André. Without Paul Manning, I would not have known how to start or where to go with animation. Aswin Punathembekar, Mary Francis, Ieva Jusionyte, and Kathleen Stewart offered generous encouragement and advice on publishing the manuscript.

I am so grateful to Jim Lance for championing this project and embracing its quirkiness. The three anonymous reviewers' careful treatment of the manuscript greatly improved it. Thank you to the whole editorial team at Cornell University Press. Ethnographic materials and parts of the arguments that unfold in this book were first developed in the form of articles published in the *Journal of the Anthropological Society of Oxford* (Barker 2017a), *Anthropological Quarterly* (Barker 2019a), *Journal of Linguistic Anthropology* (2019b) and *Russian Review* (Barker 2021). Relevant citations appear throughout. I thank the journals for allowing me to develop these materials, along with the anonymous reviewers.

In the LSE Department of Media and Communications, I developed new understandings of media, childhood, and separation from colleagues and mentors including Sonia Livingstone and Myria Georgiou. While finishing this manuscript in the Department of Education, Practice, and Society at UCL's Institute of Education, I found myself surrounded by colleagues offering a wealth of knowledge and innovative approaches to nurturing the growth of young people in different contexts. I had the pleasure of teaching students who were excited to study children and childhood with me.

Alison Cool, thank you for making me an anthropologist. Candice Haddad, Jina Kim, and Wendy Sung have shown me how to balance commitments to scholarship, social justice, aesthetic pleasure, and nurturing friendship. Tiffany Ball's twin commitments to whimsy and compassion have made scholarly life joyful. In a book full of aunts, I thank Maggie Weber for taking me to the theater and for sharing her home for many months of writing. My parents, Jeffrey and Mary Barker, have been my teachers, collaborators in dollhouse making, and constant nurturers of curiosity. Josh, Matthew, and Louis Barker taught me how to play. Justin Barker, with speed, patience, and magical illustrating powers, has transformed this text into a book.

Jean-Christophe Plantin has read this manuscript, cover to cover, more than once. Each page has improved thanks to his sound advice, jokes in the margins, soothing assurance, and his care for me and for our shared endeavor in animation. We are lucky. Honoré Lazare Dima Barker-Plantin, you teach me every day. You screamed your way out of the last puppet show we attended, but I will take you back.

## Note on Transliteration

The materials of the puppet theater, along with archival materials and most terms that emerged in the Soviet period (such as terms related to children's institutionalization), have been translated from Russian unless otherwise noted. Likewise, utterances from Hope House have been translated from Kazakh unless otherwise specified in the text. Kazakh is a Turkic language that, during my fieldwork, still relied completely on the Cyrillic alphabet that had been adapted for Kazakh during the Soviet period. I try to indicate throughout whether other transliterated or translated words are from Kazakh or Russian. I use ALA-LC romanization conventions for transliterating Russian Cyrillic. For utterances in Kazakh, I relied on the most recently available Latin version of Kazakh, published in 2021, except that I use ñ for ң.[1] Nonetheless, for Russian and Kazakh transliteration, I make many exceptions to align spellings with those most commonly found in print. I maintain the most commonly used spellings of *Kazakh* and *Kazakhstan*. I spell people's names and pseudonyms as I have seen them spelled most often. With the names of famous figures, such as *Meyerhold* or *Nazarbayev*, I chose the spellings that seemed the most common in English-language print sources, though these spellings vary.

# THROW YOUR VOICE

# INTRODUCTION

There was a game the children played, over and over: A mother goat must leave her kids to go to the market. While she is gone, there is a knock at the door, a high voice claiming, "It's your mother, let me in." The kids open the door and scream at the sight of a wolf, who growls, grabs a few of them, and leaves. The mother returns. The leftover kids tell her what happened, and she runs off to find the wolf. She frees her children and takes them home.

The children who played the game lived in Hope House, a temporary institution in Almaty, Kazakhstan. Their parents had placed them there with the promise of returning by the time their child was seven years old. The boys took turns as the wolf; the girls rotated as the mother goat. The rest of the children played kids—some captured, some spared. When they played this game outside, the kidnapped children marked their captivity by pinning their backs against a tree or a painted tire. This was their state of suspended animation, waiting for their mother to save them.[1]

This book tells a story of vulnerable protagonists, of losses and strangers, and of reunions and returns. At Hope House, teachers made daily life into this narrative, and children acted it out. Thus, when I started watching rehearsals of *Kashtanka* at the Almaty State Puppet Theater, my second field site, I thought immediately of the children. Kashtanka, the dog at the center of this story, follows a trajectory similar to that of the children of Hope House: she gets lost, enters the house of a stranger, learns to perform, and then goes home again. The story of Kashtanka—originally penned by the Russian writer Anton Chekhov more than a century before the puppet theater adapted it—serves as a narrative

1

**ILLUSTRATION 1. THE WOLF AND THE KID GOATS**   A mother goat must leave her kids to go to the market. While she is gone, there is a knock at the door, a high voice claiming, "It's your mother, let me in."

thread throughout this book, bringing together disparate sites.[2] I trace parallels between children and puppets, between teachers and puppeteers, between fictional masters and real directors. Different figures tell the same story. Different bodies—child, puppet, doll—animate the figure of the protagonist, with help from others.

Scholars and artists have offered various interpretations of the simple narrative of "Kashtanka," ranging from the psychoanalytic to the political. The first home, which both Kashtanka and the children have temporarily lost, symbolizes freedom for some and privacy for others. It is a natural state that is also a return to origins. It represents uncertainty and sentimental ties. The second home, with the stranger the protagonist finds there, is even more ambiguous. Sometimes the stranger saves the lost hero; at other times, the outsider causes the displacement—like the wolf who captures the kid goats, or the state that creates orphans through famine, war, or poverty. Can the second home be both cause and remedy for this rupture?

As readers and spectators have used Kashtanka as a symbol for a range of interpretations, different adults made the children of Hope House into symbols who could serve various political projects. The family story that Hope House offered, as a temporary institution, was one of separation and reunion, yet the

**ILLUSTRATION 2. THE CHILDREN PLAY THE WOLF AND KID GOATS** The boys took turns as the wolf; the girls rotated as the mother goat. The rest of the children played kids—some captured, some spared.

child's overall trajectory should be one of steady development. Cute faces and fragile bodies animate narratives of an optimistic future for the nation-state. The cliché that children are the future is expedient in many situations. During Nursultan Nazarbayev's leadership of Kazakhstan, the figure of the promising child assured the populace that positive growth and change were inevitable as long as citizens remained under the care of their paternalistic leader. Children are useful for constructing positive narratives linked to relationships of dependency because aesthetic tendencies surrounding them emphasize a combination of helplessness and hope. Children rely on adults to survive, and adults need children so that they can imagine continuity and improvement.

In a country that had seen no change in leadership since the dissolution of the Soviet Union, pinning hope onto the bodies of children aided the continual deferral of political change. Nazarbayev had been general secretary of the Communist Party in Kazakhstan just before the Soviet Union collapsed. He led Kazakhstan through its turbulent first years of independence. Friends of mine in Kazakhstan explained to me that Nazarbayev had made a deal with them: he could offer political and economic stability, but in return, democracy would have to wait. When I asked what they thought would happen after Nazarbayev ceased to be in power, they said they were afraid. During my fieldwork, a number of small protests were quickly quashed (Lillis 2018). The government kept opposition to a minimum, ensuring stability and postponing democracy—a state of suspension.

The children of this book serve as useful signs to various interests, but they are also real and require care. The institutions of childhood examined in the following chapters bring together personal and political stakes of providing care by employing *familiarization techniques*. Children and adults use these everyday aesthetic devices to solicit sentiment, such as when teachers dress children in costumes that emphasize their cuteness to corporate sponsors. I focus on two primary familiarization techniques: the *creative chronotope* and the *animation of intimacy*. The first consists of people making connections between fantasy and real life. For the second, people bring characters to life, producing and maintaining social relations in the process. Moreover, I identify three acts essential to the animation of intimacy: *displacement*, *destrangement*, and *projection*, discussed below. By participating in imaginings of a positive Kazakhstani future, the children of Hope House gain continued support from government and private sponsors, who sustain this temporary home, where the children wait for their families to return for them. Meanwhile, the children serve as indexical icons of potential for which these benefactors can claim responsibility.[3]

# Two Institutions of Animation in Kazakhstan

Between 2012 and 2014, I split my time between two government-run institutions for young children in Almaty, Hope House and the Almaty State Puppet Theater.[4] Despite the seeming impossibility of real change in leadership in Kazakhstan during my time there, both field sites revealed dynamic tensions regarding Soviet and Russian legacies and continued presence in Kazakhstani culture.[5] Russian was the dominant language while I was in Almaty, but Kazakh became increasingly important during my time there. Kazakh is the state language of Kazakhstan, while Russian maintains the status of an "official" language. Both institutions made use of Kazakh and Russian, but in different ways. The puppet theater had always been bilingual and offered programming equally in each language, though Kazakh productions were often translations from Russian.[6] During my fieldwork, I saw the theater stage three other new productions—one based on a French children's book and performed in Russian, one based on a Soviet animation and staged without puppets in Russian and Kazakh, and one based on a Kazakh folk tale and performed exclusively in Kazakh, but without puppets. I chose *Kashtanka* as the focus of the book because its story paralleled the children's and because its rehearsals incited the most passionate articulations of the artists' work of animation that I observed. Its Russian origin aligned with the persistent reliance on Russian and Soviet children's culture for the troupe's repertoire, which artists at the theater cited as a problem without a clear solution. It was difficult to find new Kazakh-language materials for the theater, they lamented. Archival research shows that this has always been an issue. In fact, the "new" Kazakh production staged during my fieldwork, *Aldar Kose*, was the first play that the Kazakh-language troupe performed in the 1930s. It remained the sole piece in their repertoire for the first few years of the troupe's existence.

At Hope House, most groups spoke Kazakh, with one mixed-age (and mixed-ethnicity) Russian-language group. Hope House was atypical, at the time, of residential institutions in Almaty in its stress on Kazakh language. Children of Russian ethnic backgrounds were overrepresented in the institutional systems in Kazakhstan, relative to their population.[7] I spoke Russian more fluently than Kazakh, yet the vice-director placed me in a Kazakh-speaking group because it had more girls (four, versus three boys, when I first joined them). She reasoned that this would benefit my interest in dolls and puppets. When I asked about the emphasis on Kazakh at Hope House, a teacher supposed that because the home was sponsored by the state, the children should speak the state language. Hope House's stress on Kazakh language in many ways anticipated the campaign of "Spiritual Revival" (*Ruhani Jañğyru*) launched in 2017, aimed at promoting national identity. Kazakh language—and the Latinization of Kazakh—became a focal point of this campaign. Many continued to perceive Russian as the dominant language in the public sphere, nonetheless, particularly in Almaty and for conducting business (Sharipova 2020).[8] However, Kazakh seemed to be gaining importance in Almaty during and after my time there.

At first glance, orphanages and government puppet theaters might appear as remnants of a Soviet past, destined for extinction, with public schools and family homes offering more obvious sites to study children and childhood. Yet I suspected that their link to particular Soviet histories and their ability to survive the intervening decades of transition meant that they could tell us something unique about childhood in Nazarbayev-era Kazakhstan. Each institution saw itself as potentially competing with other options for children's care or entertainment. This gave special urgency to their projects of constructing ideologies of hopeful future. Both relied on state sponsorship but sought private support as well, so their missions tied images of happy children to various interests. These institutions are ideal for studying techniques of animation because the labyrinthine bureaucracy results in a complicated participation structure. Within each institution, I found constant negotiation between institutional workers' goals in serving children, state interests in ideologies of childhood, and the stakes of private sponsors whose investment could ensure the institutions' survival in the twenty-first century. In a postsocialist state known for reliance on patronage in politics and in art, these sites remind us that such informal networks are not merely strategic, but sentimental as well.[9]

In considering these various participants in the sustenance of the institution, we should not forget the parents and children these sites were designed to serve. Parents, mostly single mothers, brought their children to live at Hope House when they were as young as six months old. More often, children arrived as toddlers. They stayed at Hope House for at least a year, often longer. In the meantime, parents and other family members visited the children, but the children could not go home for short trips. By the time children were old enough to attend school, their parents would return for them, and they would resume their life back in the first home of their families. In the meantime, Hope House needed not merely to maintain these children but to nurture their growth. Founded in the 1990s as an alternative to permanent institutionalization of children, Hope House and other temporary homes for children were something of an innovation in Kazakhstan.[10] Whether in a baby house, children's home, or state-run boarding school (dom rebënka, detdom, and internat in Russian, respectively), permanent group care served as the dominant Soviet solution to children lacking parental care.[11] Structurally, Hope House resembled these homes in many ways— grouping children by age and assigning a rotating staff of women to look after them. The collapse of the Soviet Union led to the decline of social welfare programs and an increase in income disparity in Kazakhstan, bringing new challenges to struggling parents in the 1990s.[12] Meanwhile, international and local organizations working with children in Kazakhstan increasingly questioned government reliance on institutional care for children. Hope House presented a solution to this problem, even if it resembled the structures it was meant to replace.

Hope House was a large house of concrete, painted yellow. Set uphill, toward the mountains, the air was cleaner than in the city center. The bright playground equipment, the rocks painted like ladybugs, and the child-sized statues of Kazakh nomads and camels all made clear that this was a place for children. A gate and guard kept strangers from wandering inside without permission. When I entered the building, I first passed the offices of the directors and the doctor. Hallway walls were lined with framed certificates from organizations and photographs of prestigious visitors surrounded by children or with small ones in their arms. Eventually, I arrived at a collection of plants and an aquarium, where a turtle lived. Each door bore the name of the group of children who lived inside. There were more groups farther down the hall and upstairs on the second floor.

The home eschewed certain techniques that other orphanages in Kazakhstan had adopted in order to make themselves less institutional.[13] Rather than staggering the children to recreate a family structure of older and younger siblings, Hope House grouped children by age. This was efficient for the teachers, who were responsible for keeping the children cleaned, fed, and clothed, and for offering them daily lessons. The children of my group were between four and five years old during my first year. The following year, as the eldest children in the home, they were called the "preparatory group" and moved into a different set of rooms on the upstairs floor.

Adults and children at Hope House used, in Kazakh and in Russian, the term *gruppa* to refer both to a group of children and to the collection of rooms that they inhabited together. The exact number of children and of groups varied. When I left, there were forty children living in six groups. Each of these groups had a set of rooms, adjacent to one another, in a cellular structure: a cubby room, where they kept coats, shoes, and the few toys that were not communal; a playroom that became a classroom in the morning (tables were moved to the center when in use and to the sides when not); a bedroom, with beds lining the walls and bunk beds for the eldest groups; a small dining room, where the children ate all their meals; and a small kitchen with a sink, though the cooking was done in a central kitchen. Besides these, the children moved to other parts of the home for various lessons. There was a music room, a computer room, a Montessori room, a sensory room with colorful lights and soft furniture, a large room for physical education, and an indoor swimming pool (which they only used during summer, they said, and I never saw it in action). Rooms had large windows with bright curtains. Toys were kept in neat order on shelves, taken down with teacher permission.

The children had new clothes that they wore for special visitors. Two unrelated children might wear matching shirts or coats because multiple identical items had been donated when new, sometimes directly from shops. The rest of the time, children wore the same outfit a few days in a row, which was common in Kazakhstan. Their everyday clothes were clean, colorful, and in good condition. Numbers sewn or drawn onto each article designated its owner, but clothes would be passed down as one child grew up or went home. One boy, whom I call Olzhas, had to wear pink snow boots because those were the ones that fit him, but teachers otherwise maintained binary gender distinctions in children's dress and appearance. One teacher regularly trimmed the boys' hair with an electric razor. The girls' hair was left to grow long. Teachers and aides kept it clean and neat, and fixed elaborate braids for special occasions.

These details bear mentioning, in case the mention of the postsocialist orphanage evokes images of dirty children in rags. The labor undertaken by teachers and aides to maintain the children's appearance formed a fundamental part of their care work. At other orphanages I visited, young girls' hair was kept short because it required less maintenance from overburdened caregivers. The material provisioning of the adults indexed other types of care the home provided. Nonetheless, as we find in chapter 4, sometimes people worried that the material care ensured at Hope House threatened to replace the sentimental care that the family home offered.

Funded through a combination of state funds and private donations, Hope House offers an ideal site for examining the ways particularly vulnerable children become incorporated into nation-building projects and the promotion of private brands. Other remedies existed for children in need of care in Kazakhstan, including foster care, adoption, and temporary homes for single mothers to live with their young infants. Just under a third of the 33,682 children classified as "orphans and children without parental care" in 2013 lived in some form of residential care. Discourses surrounding institutionalization within Kazakhstan frequently highlight the idea that a child deserves to grow up in a home, with a family. Representatives at organizations that work on issues of children's institutionalization expressed dismay, during my fieldwork, that most children in residential care were "social orphans," meaning that they had at least one living parent. Local pedagogues and international organizations alike argued that more work should be done to keep these children with their living parent. Kazakhstan has seen a general decline in children growing up in orphanages and an increase in local parents wishing to adopt, yet the problem was far from eliminated. The parents of most children living in residential care in Kazakhstan had been deprived of their parental rights, rather than having given them up. The children of Hope House were thus atypical even of these nonnormative trajectories of childhood.[14]

Hope House offers a unique lens for watching ideologies of helplessness and hope play out through exchanges of gifts and performance. It acts as a node bringing together the interests of state and private sponsors, along with visitors from the press, volunteer groups, and the parents themselves. Unlike run-down, overcrowded Eastern European orphanages that featured prominently in Western news stories in the 1990s (Cartwright 2005), Hope House's vast network of sponsorship meant that they could show off shiny playground equipment, their abundant staff, and, above all, the children, in bright, new clothing. Costumed as baby chicks or as Kazakh warriors, the children sang, danced, and recited poems that ensured spectators that they were a worthy investment.

Hope House also fostered intimate familiarizations between children and their temporary caregivers. In each group, two women shared primary responsibility for the children's upbringing. I refer to them as "teachers," for they held pedagogical degrees and taught lessons every morning, but their title could also be translated as "caregivers."[15] These women worked alternate shifts of approximately ten hours, though they sometimes came in on their days off for meetings and other special events. This meant that they worked long, irregular hours, but they were paid better at Hope House than they would have been at a school, they told me.[16] A helper or aide worked twenty-four-hour shifts, every three days.[17] Teachers often wore dresses and even heels as their indoor shoes (for we all needed to remove our outdoor shoes before entering the *gruppa* and other classrooms). Aides wore flip-flops and clothes they could get dirty. They cleaned, served food, occasionally minded an active child one-on-one during lessons, and watched the group when a teacher had a meeting. It was they who stayed with the children overnight and went home the following morning. Besides the teachers and aides, adults employed at the home included a director and vice-director, a pedagogical director, a psychologist, a music and physical education teacher, and a rotating staff of doctors. The only men who worked at the home were guards and drivers, who occasionally took the children on field trips in a large van.

The children left the confines of this world rather rarely, especially during the cold winter months, yet they were acutely aware of the outside. Teachers emphasized the certitude of the eventual family reunion and the joyfulness of the child's ultimate departure. The sociologist Erving Goffman characterizes total institutions—prisons, monasteries, and asylums—as encompassing all spheres of inmates' lives. He argues that they are not set up to replace the world outside of them, but rather, "They create and sustain a particular kind of tension between the home world and the institutional world and use this persistent tension as strategic leverage in the management of men." He speculates that orphanages might be excluded from his list of total institutions. Children who are born into such environments, he imagines, could know no home culture, except "by some process of cultural osmosis even while this world is being systematically denied" (Goffman 1961, 13). Without an understanding of "outside," he reasons, the tension between the two worlds cannot be upheld.

Hope House actively cultivated a tension between the children's home and the "home world." Media, materialities, and practices cultivated by the teachers all worked to establish an imagined and anticipated outside. This "outside" was also an "inside"—a private family home where children would not sleep in a numbered bed with seven peers, rotating staff, and regular visits from strangers. Teachers at Hope House nurtured the children's understanding of their family homes as their first and eventually permanent homes, thus figuring Hope House as temporary. They taught the children to take for granted that a family home awaited them, even as children's memories of the first home likely faded. It was a future that the employees, parents, state, and private donors were all working quite hard to make possible.

State institutions such as Hope House and the puppet theater generate affect-saturated relationships, in addition to power relations and subjects. Institutions—total institutions such as asylums, prisons, boarding schools, and orphanages, along with schools—have received intense focus as sites for exercising power and producing subjects. Michel Foucault outlines the structural, material, and discursive techniques whereby such powers make diffuse the process of subject formation, yet acts of submission and resistance also produce new pleasures.[18] In state institutions, power works through affective means, and affect exerts power. Interest in institutions at the end of the twentieth century has perhaps given way to attention to infrastructure in the twenty-first; it is in the latter that we can find increasing discussion of affect (Knox 2017). Madeleine Reeves (2017, 713) describes *infrastructural hope* as the "simultaneity of the social and the material in the coming-into-being of infrastructural forms." Institutions, too, come into being through a convergence of structures, actors, objects, acts, and feelings. Hope House and similar sites can thus act as sites of institutional hope.

Outside perceptions of institutions such as orphanages tend to strip them of affect, portraying them as sensorial and sentimental wastelands. At the same time, institutions such as orphanages have at particular moments been infused with discourses of hope—for preserving the children themselves, for rescuing family members (e.g., pulling mothers up from the slavery of domesticity), and for saving the nation. Positive imaginings of the future, so often tied to images of Kazakhstani children, helped to sustain loyalty to "Papa," as President Nazarbayev was called, and to his political leadership that had not changed since Kazakhstan declared independence in 1991. Former First Lady Sara Nazarbayev's highly publicized work with children's institutions such as Hope House suggests a mutual dependency between the First Couple and children lacking parental care. Children's reliance on government care helped to constitute a greater Kazakhstani family, held together through state bureaucracy.[19]

This book emphasizes children's culture as public culture. Humanities scholars have offered brilliant analyses of images of childhood, while anthropologists and sociologists have let us into the "private worlds" of children that otherwise go unnoticed. Rather than emphasizing differences between ideas about childhood and children's lived experience—and then focusing on one or the other—I study them together. Adults' beliefs shape children's own fantasies, and children's experiences often include animations of adults' projections.

Hope House was created during the first years of Kazakhstan's post-Soviet independence. The puppet theater was established in 1936, during another tumultuous period. It sounded absurd, when I first learned of it, that the Soviet government would found a puppet theater in Kazakhstan during the same period that Stalin was using the Kazakh steppe as a site of forced deportation, collectivization, exile, and imprisonment. Famine had recently ravaged the Kazakh population (see chapter 1). Of course, the puppet theater was hardly a consequence of these tragedies. Enthusiasm for puppetry had been bubbling up among artists in Moscow and St. Petersburg since the turn of the twentieth century.[20] The government created puppet theaters all over the Soviet Union during this period, including in Alma-Ata, the Soviet name for the city which became capital of the Kazakh Soviet Republic in 1927. The puppet theater was founded at a time when Alma-Ata was still developing the basic infrastructure necessary to support its rapid growth and activity.[21] The puppet theater led a modest existence during its first years, without a building of its own. Traveling to factories and collective farms, the young theater was charged with entertaining and socializing both the (adult) masses and the children of Soviet Kazakhstan. Gradually, it came to focus on the latter. While children's performances at Hope House elicited the affections of visiting adults, the puppet theater animated objects in order to educate and socialize children on how to be good citizens. As an institution, it also cultivated sentimental ties and hopeful imaginings.

The Almaty State Puppet Theater was part of a pan-Soviet project of establishing, institutionalizing, professionalizing, and bureaucratizing the puppet theater over the course of the twentieth century. Despite the massive changes that occurred after 1991 all over the former USSR, post-Soviet states largely continue to support these puppet theaters. By the time I arrived to begin my long-term fieldwork in Almaty in 2012, the theater employed more than thirty full-time puppet artists, most of whom had finished a three- or four-year program specializing in puppetry. They were adept at manipulating a range of puppet forms: rod puppets (with sticks controlling elaborate puppets from below, perhaps the most typical puppets of the Soviet tradition), hand puppets, marionettes (according to the artists, the most difficult forms), and tabletop puppets, including Bunraku-style puppets, in which three humans work together to bring one puppet to life. They had tiny puppets and giant ones over ten feet tall. They voiced animals and humans, adults and children. They danced and sang. In certain shows, human transformed to puppet and back again. The puppeteers had spent years studying their craft and did not invite me to try it. Even the students I met, in their last year at the two art schools I visited, were spending all their days rehearsing for their final show, making it impossible for me to learn puppeteering skills with them without getting in the way. My participation in the theater's activities thus took place backstage, with the seamstresses in the props department.

At the theater, I asked how everyday animations of objects for children could inform our understanding of childhood and theories of animation. Political discourse denigrates the puppet as a symbol of absolute passivity controlled by a single puppet master. It is common, in Russian as in English, to disparage an individual for being a mere "puppet" (*marionetka*). However, the puppet makes a more useful metaphor if we consider its place at the center of a complex network of social, material, and sentimental relations, such as that of the postsocialist puppet theater. Besides the puppeteers, permanent staff included props artists, carpenters, costume designers, technicians for light and sound, assistants responsible for procuring various necessary supplies, and a number of administrators. Various authors and authorities, not all of whom were physically present, made up the theater's participation framework.[22] Like the performances of the children, each show at the theater was the product of a coordinated effort of a range of interests, visible and invisible. Directors were often charged with voicing the state, even if they subtly used the puppet to question dominant acceptance of the political regime. Puppets, like dolls, offer insight into the agency of objects. This comes through most clearly when they break down, when they fail or refuse to behave as the puppeteer or child expects. The Kashtanka puppet, her torso of rope covered with segmented foam, was lithe and sinewy. Sometimes her body got twisted. The plastic dolls of Hope House sometimes made the children cry when they failed to sit or stand. This invites us to compare the manipulations of puppeteers with those of the children at Hope House, whose use of objects in play proved less prone to prolonged episodes of fantasy but more open to creative reinvention.

The Almaty State Puppet Theater inherited missions of pedagogy and socialization from its Soviet years. Shows lacked explicit political content. The troupe focused on instilling positive moral virtues in their young audiences, drawing from folk tales of Kazakh, Russian, and international origins, along with the occasional play about obeying traffic lights to make their pedagogical value obvious to supervisors. The theater offered shows each weekend and some weekdays in Russian and in Kazakh. The puppeteers visited schools, hospitals, and shopping malls, with occasional travel abroad to puppet festivals. When I arrived, the theater had maintained most of its repertoire from decades past. However, a massive renovation of the theater building shuttered the theater during most of my first year of fieldwork. This *kapitalnyĭ remont* motivated the city's Department of Culture, which funded the theater, to insist that the troupe overhaul its repertoire and artistic vision. Artists needed to rearticulate their relevance in the twenty-first century for new audiences of children. New media and private venues competed for the children's attention. The building's renovation meant that the puppeteers spent a winter rehearsing in a cold room in the city zoo. Practicing for months without a space where they could perform, the theater company spent much of my first year with them in a state of suspended animation as well. They worked to reinvent themselves in time for the building's reopening.

The actors themselves often criticized their theater—along with the classic theaters around the city—as being too "Soviet." To call something "Soviet" in independent Kazakhstan could be positive, if referring to the quality of fabric or the stability of a retirement fund (Begim 2018). Here, however, it suggested that the theaters were old fashioned in style and in repertoire. The puppet theater stood out to me as Soviet in the bureaucratic norms it had inherited. Costume and puppet makers, their ateliers in the back of the theater, could not begin their work until money to buy the material had been secured. This often meant weeks of sitting around followed by a mad rush to complete costumes, sets, and the puppets themselves in time for a premiere. Yet it also enabled dozens of full-time, permanent, salaried staff, unlike the pared-down troupes I met at festivals. A French director reluctantly performed in a two-person production so that they could afford to travel to Tajikistan. An Australian couple, who were using a world puppet tour to double as their honeymoon, marveled at the size of the Almaty troupe and the stability of their salaries, however modest.

In addition to having a model of theater that was bigger, more bureaucratic, and less flexible than the private troupes I met from non-postsocialist countries, the Almaty State Puppet Theater used forms of puppetry that were also Soviet, in their own way. Despite the variety of puppets and the inclusion of traditional Kazakh folktales in the repertoire, Kazakh puppets were conspicuously absent from the theater. Traditional Kazakh puppetry, *orteke*, usually consists of a wooden, hinged animal, such as a goat, on a pedestal, with strings below connecting it to a musician. Often, the strings wrap around the musician's fingers, so that when they strum the *dombyra*—a traditional Kazakh instrument that resembles a lute—the animal begins to dance. In the twenty-first century, this tradition risked extinction. In my first year there, the puppet theater's director organized a festival of traditional puppetry, but his troupe only performed for the opening ceremony. The revitalization of *orteke* appeared more often in institutions supporting traditional arts and music rather than puppetry.[23] The puppet theater, instead of looking to revitalize *orteke*, sought to update its offerings for new generations.

During the renovation, new directors arrived. Under pressure from the city to make a profit from ticket sales, the administrative director imagined an American "art business," a model whose main component seemed to be increasing ticket prices so that the public would appreciate the theater's work. Economic and artistic concerns overlapped as the theater began planning new plays for the first time in decades. In my second year of field work, the Almaty State Puppet Theater staged a production of *Kashtanka*. Though the story had been adapted for puppet stages and animations countless times and had been enjoyed by Soviet and post-Soviet audiences for decades, new directors brought unconventional methods to the theater. Conversations between actors and directors leading up to the premiere provided a metadiscourse on animation that I had been unable to draw from the artists in early attempts to interview them. Complicated relationships unfolded—between directors and actors, and between actors and instruments of performance, which included both puppets and their own performing bodies.

Hope House and the puppet theater barely met. The puppet theater troupe told me they frequently performed for children's homes and hospitals around the city, and occasionally they did. The directors at Hope House assured me the children often visited children's theaters around the city, and they did, but these points of contact were fewer than I anticipated. Instead, I made myself a node between these sites. The only time the children at Hope House visited the puppet theater was through a visit I arranged for them, for a New Year's celebration that involved few actual puppets. The two sites competed for my attention. Spending time at one, I risked missing an important event at the other. Working in two languages created its own challenges. My Russian was always better than my Kazakh, and I used it as a crutch, though I only spoke Kazakh with the children. Lessons and plays were easy to follow, for they were slow and repetitive, as teachers made use of exaggerated, lilting prosody. The children were adept at making their needs and feelings known to me, and I turned to teachers for translation when necessary.

Though I was able to get to know the children quite well by staying with the same group from fall 2012 through spring 2014, I had little access to information about the parents or the children after they had gone home. Experienced anthropologists of the region had warned me that gaining access to a postsocialist orphanage would be difficult, perhaps impossible. I was wary of pushing my luck. When parents visited their children, I did not wish to intrude on the brief time they had together, so my understanding of their circumstances was minimal, as described in chapter 1. If my discussion of the visiting "sponsors" is vague, this corresponds with the lack of attention teachers and children gave to such details (see chapter 3). The clothing and gifts of such guests varied, yet these visits set off a consistent interchange of gifts and performances.

The children played with dolls. The artists animated puppets. Beyond this expected correspondence across the two sites, a surprising one emerged as I realized how often the children rehearsed and performed for adults, just as the theater entertained children. Both offered insight on techniques and ideologies of performance and on the imagining of child and adult audiences. I made props and puppets backstage at the theater. Teachers asked me to make masks and other props for children's performances. I was tasked with making art projects that should look as if the children had made them, so that I too played a role in animating the figure of the ideal child.

I worked to situate the sites within the larger context of Kazakhstani childhood. During my first summers of fieldwork in 2010 and 2011, I met with representatives of organizations, state and nonstate, local and international, who concerned themselves with issues of childhood welfare in Kazakhstan, such as UNICEF and the Committee Protecting the Rights of Children in Kazakhstan. I volunteered and held internships at local and international organizations involved in issues of childhood and institutionalization. I volunteered at kindergartens in the city to get a sense of pedagogy outside the children's home. I visited other theaters and participated in puppet festivals in the region, along with child-focused initiatives at restaurants and shopping malls that gave a range of perspectives on the publicness of childhood in the city. My archival work on the puppet theater traced its origins from a roving troupe to the institution it became. When I returned to Kazakhstan to teach in Astana during the summer of 2017, I used the opportunity to visit the memorial museums of KarLag (*Karagandinskiĭ ispravitel'no-trudovoĭ lager*, Russian for "Karaganda Correctional Work Camp") and ALZhIR (*Akmolinskskiĭ Lager' Zhen Izmennikov Rodiny*, Russian for "Akmolinsk Camp of Women of Traitors of the Country"). These offered a broader historical perspective on the role of forced deportations and imprisonment during the first decades of Soviet Kazakhstan in breaking up families and creating orphans, while also producing narratives of fostering, adoption, and reunion.

Hope House and the puppet theater are unique institutions, yet they offer broader insight regarding Kazakhstani childhood. In their construction of pedagogical fantasies, teachers, puppeteers, and children referenced fairy tales and figures from Soviet, Kazakhstani, and transnational popular juvenile culture— from *Buratino* to Aldar Kose to Kung Fu Panda. Both sites maintained a commitment, established during the Soviet period, to using central institutions to promote proper childhood as key to the nation's future. These parallels helped me theorize the role of fantasy in maintaining political ideologies and intimate social relations, as they played with slippage between animate and inanimate, human and nonhuman, subject and object. Children and puppets were particularly prone to ambiguities between such categorizations. Children sometimes resembled the puppeteers in their play, but adults also treated children like puppets and encouraged them to mimic the cuteness of dolls. Puppeteers insisted that if they did their jobs well, child audiences hardly noticed them. Teachers at

Hope House similarly strove for a certain invisibility as they treated the children's eventual return to their families as inevitable.

## Familiarization Techniques

This book examines what I term *familiarization techniques*. Drawing from early twentieth-century theorizations of art as aiming for "defamiliarization," I look at everyday aesthetic devices that cluster around particular institutions. These techniques invite involvement by creating shared worlds of fantasy and of cocreated figures. The Russian art historian Viktor Shklovsky, in his influential 1917 article "Art as Technique," introduced the principle of *ostranenie* ("defamiliarization" or "estrangement") to argue that artists make the familiar strange in order to help audiences see the world in new ways.[24] Puppets, hovering between animate and inanimate, can easily become strange objects in performance. In the early twentieth century, the Russian director Vsevolod Meyerhold took inspiration from the puppet theater to stress a purity of form that would give greater space for (human) actors' interpretations and for viewers' projections.[25] This insight echoes puppet artists' beliefs about the particular effectiveness of puppets. By pushing viewers out of modes of habituation, estrangement can make tacit knowledge explicit and can offer a new perspective to see unrealized possibilities.

My call for attention to "familiarization" is not a rejection of such insights, but rather attends to the continual dynamics of distancing and approximation. The political potential of creativity, as theorized by the Soviet inventor Genrich Altshuller, has offered twenty-first century scholars of central Asia a creative alternative to the historically mainstream Soviet focus on dialectical materialism. Altshuller's pedagogical school emphasizes imagination as a collective endeavor and underlines the radical political potential of fantasy in offering a vision of the world as it could be otherwise. Rather than making the familiar strange, queer and feminist scholars of the region have taken up science fiction (which Altshuller also penned) in order to explore political alternatives, "presenting the unfamiliar as if it were familiar."[26] The book traces dynamic movements between the native and the alien, me and not-me, animate and inanimate, and distancing and approach. Children present a special case for exploring tensions between the familiar and the strange, as evident in writing on the uncanny (Jentsch [1906] 2008; Freud [1919] 1953). I look at familiarization techniques within my field site that serve as a provocation for engagement, while attending to moments when uneasy boundaries between known and unknown produce aversion.

Familiarization techniques offer a way to consider the personal and political use of ideal figures. I use the term "figures" as a capacious category that, as Goffman described, can include real and fantastic individuals. A figure can also be a general type, such as the ideal, cute child within a particular cultural context.[27] The figure of the ideal child in Kazakhstan plays a central role in the book, with the bad child looming in the shadows. This book tracks the ways adults and children alike draw viewers into children's worlds and create intimate ties. Scholars have debated the uses and dangers of media that makes a spectacle of suffering (Boltanski 1999; Chouliaraki 2006). A focus on mass media representations of pain assumes a stark divide between those making the images and those featured as the victims. However, people make art from their own misfortune and cite ideal figures in their everyday acts. Animations of ideal childhood contribute to nation-building projects and public relations campaigns, while ensuring the care of certain vulnerable subjects. Meanwhile, children and adults create and maintain delicate relationships of familiarity with one another, often mediated by objects and images.

My research sites, filled with puppets, play, and performance, drew me to two specific familiarization techniques—the *creative chronotope* and the *animation of intimacy*. The first connects different worlds, real and imaginary. The second traces lines between participants as they bring to life a particular figure. The creative chronotope offers a way to understand how the narrative worlds of others become part of one's own. As used here, it follows connections between the real and the represented, showing how people make use of narratives outside their own direct experience. In studying the animation of intimacy, I follow the ways people transpose energies, voices, and points of view across bodies. These acts—of throwing voices and pulling strings—give rise to and sustain social relations.

The chronotope brings together space and time as an organizing principle, as set forth by the Russian literary theorist Mikhail Bakhtin (1981), who introduced the term in the 1930s. Bakhtin was interested in the chronotopes of novels, each genre following a particular logic surrounding the hero's relationship to space and time. The chronotope has proven useful for unpacking understandings of space-time relations within everyday life and in spoken utterances.[28] The relationship between space and time received constant attention in Soviet projects of industrialization and innovation, in which lands perceived as "peripheral," such as central Asia, were ever in need of the capital's modernizing influence (Bissenova 2016). Looking at the role of children in nation-building projects, this book examines Kazakhstan's fantasies of futurity and the movement of human capital produced by these modernizing projects.

While social scientists have found the notion of the chronotope productive for thinking about relationships between space and time in society, Bakhtin cautions us from confusing representation and reality. These should be treated separately. However, he almost immediately backtracks, warning against taking the difference between the two as "absolute and impermeable," for they are "indissolubly tied up with each other and find themselves in continual mutual interaction." Like an organism in its environment, real and represented would die without each other. Bakhtin (1981, 254, emphasis in original) proposes a "*creative* chronotope inside which this exchange between work and life occurs, and which constitutes the distinctive life of the work." By "work," he refers to the work of art—the novel. I follow this exchange between plays—and play—and those experiences we call everyday life.

The children, teachers, and puppet artists of these two institutions were experts in making use of the creative chronotope. People use represented worlds for themselves, while real humans come to represent ideal figures to others. Artists, teachers, and children inserted themselves (or were inserted) into narratives, creating comparisons across chronotopes. The puppeteers devoted their lives to conjuring fairy tales. They asserted that children believed their puppets were really alive. Children at Hope House not only brought to life the worlds of folk tales and cartoons, but they also lived with the daily fantasy of the world outside. Children and the adults around them, through play and performance, with objects and actors, participated in projects of creation and projection that moved between lived life and representation.

This book offers a creative chronotope in its form by working through the representations and experiences of people I met across these sites. It juxtaposes the worlds of a children's story, a theater, and a group of children into a shared narrative. I pull together elements of Kazakhstani childhood that include tragic memories and nostalgic reanimations of Soviet childhood. Beyond my primary sites, I look at histories of forced deportation and imprisonment throughout the Kazakh steppe. Such events scatter families. Residue of this past resonates in ways that are not always articulated in official discourses, but are nonetheless felt.[29] Movement between these worlds, real and represented, involves not only a world of words. In looking across narrative worlds, the project is intertextual in nature, but this intertextuality has an intersensory texture. Language is never merely about words and their meanings, but makes use of sound symbolism and indexical ties to the real.[30] Accordingly, I consider not only texts and narratives but a mix of aural, visual, and tactile elements. David MacDougall's (2006) concept of "social aesthetics" describes sensory coherence within institutions—through color palettes, uniform movements, and predictable soundscapes.[31] People make use of sensuous, poetic parallels across human and nonhuman bodies. In attending to the social aesthetics and everyday poetics of childhood in Kazakhstan, this book highlights the sensory and sentimental aspects of environments that get overlooked in trying to define a group or a place. It treats child-hood as a project of worlding, of "burrowing into the generativity of what takes form, hits the senses, shimmers" (K. Stewart 2010, 339). Though the institutions where the book unfolds—the home and the theater—appear closed and con-tained, fantasy offers an infinity of worlds within their gates and walls.

I treat children and artists as equals in offering insight on the anthropology of art and creativity, countering consistent marginalization of the anthropology of childhood.[32] The children of my field site expertly traversed creative chrono-topes, cultivating intimacy through their animations of cuteness.

Throughout this book, the performances of children, their everyday play with objects such as dolls, and the artistic work of puppeteers are all projects of ani-mating intimacy as a key familiarization device. I define animation as an inter-corporeal act of bringing a figure to life. Animated bodies—of dancing children or childlike objects—act as focal points that bring together animators and spec-tators, authors and sponsors. Teri Silvio (2010, 427) defines animation as "the projection of qualities perceived as human—life, power, agency, will, personal-ity, and so on—outside of the self, and into the sensory environment, through acts of creation, perception, and interaction." Animation is an engagement with the world and a collaborative creation of individuals and selves. This shift moves away from a focus on performance, of presenting an "authentic" self to others. Anthropologists of animation instead study how multiple parties come to make a figure come to life.[33]

A move from interrogating authenticity can raise new questions about the stakes and effects of performance, rather than dismissing spectacle as void of real meaning. Laura Adams (2010, 72) describes how, in central Asia, mass spec-tacles (*spektakli*), which seemingly taught Uzbeks about traditional culture, nonetheless ignored local interests in favor of "cultural globalization grounded in Soviet internationalism." Citing Guy Debord's ([1967] 1977) writing on the spectacle, Adams underlines the emptiness of large, public performances, which failed to motivate citizens despite compulsion to participate in them. Other scholars of the region have examined performance as more than "mere" spec-tacle (just as the animated body is often more than a "mere" puppet). Despite the Uzbekistan government's promotion of the popular Soviet musical genre Es-trada, for example, local citizens cultivated their own attachments to the music, and artists contributed creatively to the form (Merchant 2009; Klenke 2019). Eva-Marie Dubuisson (2010) has argued that *aitys*—a traditional form of competi-tive Kazakh poetry—offered a unique forum for political debate in Kazakhstan, relying on claims of national tradition to protect it as a space of contestation.

These studies highlight a range of political projects in which performance plays a significant role in contemporary central Asia. This book highlights the affective dimensions of such projects. Discourses of childhood as universal and apolitical serve to augment the child's potent symbolism for the nation-state.

My interest in the *intimacy* of animation begins with a familiar argument, for anthropologists, that the individual as a discrete unit is a fiction. Anthropologists working in a range of contexts have consistently worked to upset Western-centric emphasis on the individual (Strathern 1988), tracing the distribution of agency across bodies and to nonhuman actors as well.[34] Culture and language are not objects that fully formed adults transmit to passive blank slates, but are part of a continuous creative exchange that transforms people and practices in the process.[35] Christina Toren (2012) has argued that we place intersubjectivity— and, thus, children—at the center of anthropological inquiry, as this helps us to understand the ontogeny of each person as a microhistorical process. Children's development is a site not of cultural reproduction, but of historical change.

Nonetheless, the independence of the adult acts as a compelling fiction. Our perceived ability to change our lives is necessary for projects of self-cultivation, which we might align with Western cultures of exercise and self-improvement (Sloterdijk 2014). Too easy a contrast between the ideal of the Western liberal subject versus the passive, simple *Homo Sovieticus*, however, overlooks complex and evolving relationships between individuals and structures in Soviet and post-Soviet societies.[36] The project of the self was also a key part of Soviet ideals of *kul'turnost'*, which began as an external process that one eventually internalized, with these "inner commitments . . . to be regarded as the true identity of the individual. One should now take care of one's soul, the name for which became the Bolshevik consciousness."[37] The Soviet self needed to be cultivated for the good of society, yet the internal aspect of the individual was hardly ignored. For children and for those charged with their care, adults might covertly exert control in ways designed to make children seem agentive but without actually allowing them to decide their fates. Adults put words into children's mouths (or hands, in Soviet propaganda) and steered them subtly toward normative behavior, despite discourses of "self-management" in early Soviet schools and correctional institutions for children (Maslinsky 2020; Weld 2014). Contemporary debates among Russophone scholars reveal the methodological and ontological difficulty of trying to uncover or incorporate children's voices, agency, or subjectivity— hardly a simple task regarding adults (Kozlovskaya and Kozlova 2020).

This book follows the work that children and adults put into creating the child as an individual. The properly performing subject was a goal at both the theater and at Hope House. Discourses of personal responsibility became central to reforms at the puppet theater during my fieldwork, yet this was always directed toward the collective good of the theater. At Hope House, teachers held the children up as future leaders, though eventual independence could only occur if children left their institutional upbringing. This book asks how it is we come to create and sustain belief in both the independently animated other and in our own self-sufficiency, alongside the many acts of manipulation, modeling, and motivating through which we make one another up.

Acts of animation are not inherently deceitful or violent, but can involve, instead, a combination of control and care. Three processes prove essential to the animation of intimacy in my sites: displacement, destrangement, and projection. Displacement is a defining moment in *Kashtanka* and at Hope House, as well as being a key technique for animation. Animation is not about embodying a character or "taking on" a role, but instead often involves a process of disembodiment.[38] Puppeteers manipulate a body outside of themselves. Ventriloquists throw voices so that they can be attributed to other sources, transposing the locus of articulation, so often tied to conceptions of self and of agency, outside one's own body (Keane 1999). Adults can resemble ventriloquists when they manipulate children or project their own hopes or nostalgic notions onto them, yet the children have also experienced displacement through their placement in Hope House. As they lived with frequent reminders that this was not their first or final home, the children learned to imagine the future that awaited them. Displacement, by definition, unsettles, yet this act can lead to new encounters and is often necessary for creating eventual unity between initially disparate parts.

The redistribution of social relations is often mediated through semiotic and material processes. Scholars of childhood have often charted a rise of consumer culture as a trend toward media and consumer goods usurping the fragile agency of children or their caregivers.[39] Moral panic over children's consumption often assumes a white, middle-class family with a disposable income for such goods. Studying a wider range of class and racialized backgrounds shows that children are surprisingly creative in their uptake of consumer goods. Children and families engage with media objects and technologies in a variety of ways, whether interacting with print, television, or digital cultures.[40] The children of Hope House show how the objects animated in play simultaneously create opportunities for connection with one another while anchoring relations with absent parents.

In order to explore processes of approaching others while still recognizing distance or difference, I use "destrangement" as a more expansive term than "attachment" (discussed in chapter 2). If estrangement creates distance to invite surprise, the inverse renders the stranger unexpectedly familiar. Destrangement is a dynamic movement. Often ambivalent, it opens participants to momentary flickers of contact and resonance.[41] It includes the various techniques through which humans make inorganic objects worthy of affection. This occurs when children and puppeteers speak to an object as if it understands, when they cradle it in their arms or feed it fake food. Teachers and directors bring fiction closer to everyday life through acts of comparison. Puppet makers destrange through design—making limbs and eyeballs that can be moved and covering wood or metal bases with foam to make them look soft to viewers, adding bright fabrics to catch children's eyes.

A third party—a spectator—completes an act of animation. Audiences project life onto the bodies of moving puppets. This is the secret to animation—that we are the ones doing the animating, while puppet makers are busy thinking about how to drag their puppet's leg across the table in a way that will make it seem heavy. Projection highlights the act of spectating in allowing oneself to be drawn into the fantasy. Animation, moreover, draws something out of the viewer and onto these bodies. Projection implies space between the viewer and the object that allows for multiple interpretations. The directors of *Kashtanka* interpreted the story as one of a dog who chooses independence over safety, and thus protest over political stability. The narrative itself, nonetheless, keeps any such reading implicit. Directors could stage the play with this political metaphor even though they worked at a government-sponsored puppet theater in a country where authorities increasingly clamped down upon protest. Because it remained open to alternative projections, *Kashtanka* continued to be staged at the theater even after original directors and cast had left.

Children become objects of both intercorporeal and temporal forms of projection. Adults, especially those who have invested time and energy, see themselves in the children they rear. Because of this, children often become reflections of adults' insecurities and hopes about the future, while also being steeped in adults' nostalgia for their own imagined childhoods. Children and youth become icons of futurity as part of larger ideological projects.[42] At the beginning of the twentieth century, utopian visions of ideal societies abounded in artistic and political movements (Buck-Morss 2000). Early Soviet planners envisioned a system of children's homes that would save children from improper socialization and would mold them into model Soviet citizens.[43] War and famine meant that ambitious ideals of collective child-rearing, based on scientific principles, had to be shelved, however, as orphanages overflowed with needy children in the 1930s and 1940s. The institutional system never regained its romantic visions.[44] By the end of the twentieth century and into this one, hope and optimism became objects of inquiry as their continued viability came into question.[45]

Childhood itself is a political site in the sense that questions of power, agency, and rights sit at the center of children's experiences. In addition, children participate in political projects in which they might seem to be mere symbols—and thus pawns or puppets—of adults in power. At Hope House, hosts and visitors touted the promise that these children represented—for the restoration of the family and the prosperity of the nation-state. The trajectory of loss and recovery helps restore the narrative of progress, which proves crucial to state ideologies and to expectations surrounding human development. This book shows the usefulness of anchoring positive narratives for the nation-state to the bodies of children, whose growth is visible and tangible.

## Overview of the Book

The chapters to come follow the story of Kashtanka and trace articulations between the action happening at the theater, onstage and off, with interactions at Hope House—during lessons, in playtime, and in performances for visitors. Parallels across sites and stories reveal the dangers and possibilities of animating intimacies in response to conditions of loss.

## Chapter 1. Getting Lost

*Kashtanka, a dog, finds herself alone on an unknown doorstep.* This chapter is about displacement. Often considered a tragic moment, it is also required for the lifegiving act of animation, as puppet artists transpose voices, energies, or souls into other bodies. This chapter relates the events that separate Kashtanka from her first master to the disruption experienced by the children at Hope House. Historical upheavals in Kazakhstan during the first half of the twentieth century, meanwhile, mark it as a place of displacement, particularly the massive forced deportation of minorities and prisoners under Stalin. While memorial museums in Kazakhstan work to make sense of this past, at Hope House, simple stories connect children to the persons and places they have lost. In a language lesson at Hope House, Nurlan narrates a trip to the toy store with his mother, a simple pleasure that has been denied to him these past few years, but which children are taught to imagine. Nurlan shows that, like puppeteers, he is savvy in making use of mediating objects. A broken toy becomes a flexible instrument that allows him to connect with other children and with me. With talk and toys, Nurlan anticipates and enacts movement, separation, and reunion.

## Chapter 2. Meeting a Stranger

*Kashtanka is taken in by a kind man who feeds her and gives her a new name.* This chapter shows how strangers—often feared, in folk tales and in psychological literature—can nonetheless become familiar, through acts of destrangement. At the puppet theater, the new stage director, Kuba, works with actors on a moment in the play when a stranger finds and falls in love with the dog. Meanwhile, Kuba works to get closer to the troupe, though he and his techniques are new and alien. This chapter examines twentieth-century psychological studies of attachment and their treatment of the stranger as a source of anxiety or comfort. Observations of children growing up in orphanages were key to the development of such studies. From the beginning, ideal attachment has been designed to stand in contrast with the development of children in residential institutions. The children at Hope House show, nonetheless, that they are adept at forming bonds with different adults, with one another, and with the inanimate objects of their care. Two girls, Toghzhan and Näziliia, offer quotidian acts of destrangement to their dolls—painting them, feeding them leaves, and rocking them in hats. They allow roles and relationships to remain ambiguous until I ask for a label. Caregivers at Hope House emphasize that they are not mothers, but it turns out the children see acts of care as equivalent, regardless of such distinctions.

## Chapter 3. Jumping through Hoops

*Kashtanka learns that her new master is a clown and that the other animals are trained performers.* This chapter shows how humans and nonhumans animate ideal figures in performance. Performances promise to transform actors and audiences alike, yet they often create slippage between categories of person and thing. Kuba, in his work at the puppet theater, pushes the puppeteers to treat their own bodies like performing objects, akin to the puppets they animate. Cute figures slip between person and thing, a common trope in the children's performances and in animations, such as the Soviet-era Cheburashka, whose popularity endured in Kazakhstan. At Hope House, the children put on tutus and wigs to perform as dancing dolls and as puppets brought to life. These acts train children to slide between performing object and cheerful child. Their round faces offer a combination of vulnerability and potential, allowing adults to project hopes onto them.

## Chapter 4. Getting Comfortable

*Kashtanka acclimates to her new home, but the monotony of material satisfaction weighs on her.* This chapter explores ambivalence surrounding material provisioning. The comfort of things threatens to replace intangible qualities such as personal rights or social relations. A simple renunciation of the material world is hardly possible, however, especially where children are involved. Scholars and parents fret endlessly over the agency that objects, such as dolls, exert over children. The directors of *Kashtanka* articulate the political message of their play: that the dog must reject the satisfaction that the new home represents to return to a life of freedom, and that Kazakhstani citizens must likewise refuse the political status quo. At Hope House, teachers remark that they give the children everything, but that nothing can replace a mother's love.

Both sites express a wish for the correct materials and objects. They condemn the wrongful treatment of things. Puppet makers' labor largely goes unnoticed until the director explodes over a malfunctioning dog leg. At Hope House, Saltanat Apai, a teacher, describes the toys as secretly animate, liable to get broken and become the laughingstock of their toy peers. She calls on the children to protect the toys from such abuse. When she compares toys to children, she suggests the children's own susceptibility to damage. Objects ideally become recipients of proper care, rather than sources of satisfaction that stand in the way of social ties.

## Chapter 5. Losing a Friend

*Kashtanka's companion, a gander, dies one night.* This chapter shows how positive narratives of promising children are nonetheless haunted by uncanny figures of permanent loss. It begins with the disturbing deanimation of a puppet in a death scene, reminding us that the uncanny unsettles because a figure has crossed a boundary thought to be impermeable. This chapter examines two traversals that give rise to anxiety—the movement from alive to dead and the shift from human to animal. A visiting puppeteer animates Death before an audience of sick children, with the conviction that children are more capable of confronting the topic than adults realize. Children's fragility not only leads to fears regarding their exposure to unpleasant topics, however. It also incites anxiety over their precarious position as marginally human. By analyzing depictions of Eastern European orphans—from news stories to horror films—this chapter shows how improperly socialized children get made into cautionary tales. In these portrayals, such children not only lose the potential they were supposed to exhibit, but they also become evil or wild. At Hope House, Erlan, a boy struggling to cope with his precarious family situation, risks embodying the fears that adults project onto institutionalized children.

## Chapter 6. Going Home Again

*Kashtanka makes her debut at the circus. Her first master discovers her, recuperates her, and takes her back to her first home.* This chapter shows how awareness of impending loss motivates multiple acts of framing. The much-anticipated return gives rise to new rifts. This chapter notes the ephemeral nature of performance, of the children's time at Hope House, and of childhood itself. Kashtanka steps into the frame of the circus ring only to jump out of it and into the arms of her first master. At the puppet theater, a rupture between the director and actors requires a ritual of healing. At Hope House, technologies of framing mitigate absence, before and after the children return home. Before the departure of Marlin, a boy in the group, with his father—and before my own—teachers weigh us down with gifts and delay our departures by requesting letters to leave traces of our time together. Mediating acts and objects offer the means for teachers to see their work articulated back to them.

Across sites, this book shows how adults and children construct a hopeful narrative, one that repairs broken kin ties and averts threats to progress. This second home—of suspended animation—is nonetheless a lively world of activity. Institutions of childhood employ familiarization techniques to connect fairy tales to children's lives and to tether children's animations of cuteness to optimistic projections for the nation. Hope House, aware that some children risk exclusion from such cheerful visions, worked to ensure that their children would be considered worthy emblems of promise. Like the puppeteers who become invisible when the puppet successfully comes to life, the women so actively involved in these projects got little credit for their efforts. Just as Kashtanka eagerly resumes her old life, the children's ideal trajectory would smoothly return them to family life, without always acknowledging the work that has gone into this—the hands that have been pulling strings, the voices that have been thrown—to animate this story of loss and recovery.

# GETTING LOST

*A young, reddish dog—a mix of dachshund and cur—very foxlike in face, ran up and down the sidewalk and looked uneasily from side to side. Occasionally she stopped and, whining, lifting first one chilled paw and then another, tried to account to herself: How could it have happened that she got lost?*

*. . .*

*If she had been human, she probably would have thought: "No, it is impossible to live like this! I must shoot myself!" But she thought about nothing and only wept.*

Kashtanka's puppeteer, Bolat, walks onstage at the Almaty State Puppet Theater with the short-legged, long-bodied dog, in puppet form. A tall, thin young man with black hair and a close-trimmed beard, wearing blue pants with suspenders and a black shirt, Bolat narrates Chekhov's lines to the audience, speaking about the dog as if she were not there, as if the long rods attached to her back did not render her body an extension of his. "She remembered quite well," Bolat tells us of Kashtanka, "how she had passed the day and how, in the end, she had found herself on this strange sidewalk."

The next scene replays the events of the day: Kashtanka follows her master, a carpenter (played by a human actor, Vlad). The two traverse the city to meet the carpenter's clients, the carpenter stopping at taverns along the way to "fortify" himself. As her master gets drunk, the world around Kashtanka turns chaotic. With each toast, the carpenter curses his dog; she howls in response. She works to keep up as they make their way through a market, where sellers shout their wares. The noise culminates in a military parade, made up of mere boots in the hands of the puppeteers, pounding on wooden boxes. The carpenter salutes the parade, while Kashtanka barks furiously, eventually kicked out of the way. The parade so distracts the dog that she fails to note when the carpenter wanders offstage. Kashtanka finds herself alone. She sniffs but cannot pick up her master's scent. Now here she is, on an unknown doorstep, cold and shivering (see Illustration 4).

This chapter examines tropes of displacement—in puppetry, at Hope House, and in Kazakhstan's history—to reveal a recurrent ambivalence surrounding such movements. The rift is painful, yet it creates the possibility of new connections and

**ILLUSTRATION 3. KASHTANKA AT THE DOORSTEP**    *If she had been human, she probably would have thought: "No, it is impossible to live like this! I must shoot myself!" But she thought about nothing and only wept.*

a promise of restoration. Animation has a unifying effect, while forced movement breaks social relations. These two types of displacement seem quite different. Yet, rupture is necessary for novel recombination. Projection in time and place offers hope during periods of disconnection. Reminders of the children's lost homes reinforced their understanding of their condition in Hope House as a temporary one. Rather than dwelling on the moment of loss, they learned to anticipate the moment of recovery, and thus to understand the present as a state of waiting for a desirable future. At another scale, Kazakhstan has been the site of major rupture and loss for families, due to exile, imprisonment, and forced resettlement. The worst took place under Stalin, but Kazakhstan's characterization as the middle of nowhere extends before and after this period. Portraying the country as empty steppe helped justify acts of exile and forced settlement. These acts led to familial separations and losses through death, making the orphaned child a salient figure. Those living with temporary loss exist in a state of waiting, a part of the self elsewhere. Shared histories of loss motivate others—of return, of healing, and of reunion.

Displacements examined in this chapter were difficult at best, and often catastrophic. The work of the puppeteer involves a displacement of energy, a transfer of voice from one's own body into that of the puppet enabling animation. Puppeteers spoke of animation as a transposition of self into the puppet, of the puppet becoming an extension (*prodolzhenie*) of self. There can be more or less

**ILLUSTRATION 4. KASHTANKA AT THE DOORSTEP AS A PUPPET**   "She remembered quite well," Bolat tells us of Kashtanka, "how she had passed the day and how, in the end, she had found herself on this strange sidewalk."

distance between animating and animated bodies: Kashtanka's rods are detachable, and Bolat sometimes holds the dog in his arms. Other puppets in this play have short handles in the backs of their heads, and puppeteers never hide when manipulating them. With various situations of proximity or distance between the puppet and puppeteer, the puppet should become the focal point, though it is the puppeteer who does all of the work—or at least a great deal of it.

Puppetry involves a dislocation of voice and of self that can result in movements of pure grace by presenting an animated body unencumbered by the
human ego. The German writer Heinrich von Kleist ([1810] 1982, 212) describes
the marionette theater in a famous short essay, which takes the form of a fictional dialogue between the narrator and a dancer, who is a fan of puppetry. The
dancer of Kleist's essay argues that puppetry creates a spiritual connection between human and marionette, for the line of gravity between the two "is nothing less than the path of the dancer's soul; and he doubted whether it could be
found except by the puppeteer transposing himself into the center of gravity of
the marionette; or, in other words, by dancing." The line of gravity, extending
from the body of the puppeteer into the body of the puppet, serves to empty the
soul from the human body into an unthinking puppet.

The transposition of the puppeteer's soul into the marionette is not a total emp-
tying out. Nor does the puppeteer exercise total control in manipulating the puppet. Instead, puppetry creates a dance between these two bodies. Such situations
necessitate new forms of participation. This is their constitutive encounter (Mazzarella 2017, 9). Mutual participation remakes puppet and puppeteer—though
only with the help of the spectator, who recognizes this movement between them.
Thinking about displacement in the context of animation invites us to consider
the productive potential that movement brings, along with the pain of loss. This
movement creates new dependencies, as the interdependence that always existed
becomes more apparent. The loss of taken-for-granted social connection necessi-
tates new relationships.

## Every Stage is a World

The first scene of *Kashtanka* sets the stage, showing the audience what kind of
world this play will be—its rules, logic, and mood. It is, in many ways, a temporary world. The stage is rather bare, the sets simple and modular, the main piece
of furniture a doorway on wheels, with art nouveau curves, made of light ply-
wood that has been faintly sprayed with pastels. There is a moon that always
hangs in the back. The style is simple and muted in comparison with other sets I
have seen at the theater, which often layer bright patterns one on top of the other.

The sparse set emphasizes the loneliness of Kashtanka at the beginning. This
first scene presents the dog as a passive heroine, with the events of the day happening to her: she followed her master, the boots distracted her, and she got lost.
Kashtanka resembles the hero of a Greek romance, in that the dog's reactions,
thus far, appear as *"enforced movement through space,"* while she *"endures* the
game fate plays,"* continuing to be the same dog (Bakhtin 1981:105, emphasis in

original). Bakhtin describes heroes of the Greek romance as moving through adventures unchanged. Kashtanka and the children face the challenge of returning to the place from which they came with their relationship intact, though the children will inevitably have grown. In each world—the institution of Hope House as a world without parents, the stage of *Kashtanka* as a cold doorstep on a winter night, the land of Kazakhstan as a naked steppe—characters lack something that leaves them at once vulnerable and open to new encounters. The types of encounters that will follow depend on the kind of worlds these will turn out to be and on who else will populate them. Worlding does not merely describe a world but makes it, often in response to others.[1]

The theater, as a world, is a kind of doubling of reality, a frame parasitic on the "real." It offers viewers the opportunity to observe and perhaps note coincidences between the staged action and spectators' own lives. Antonin Artaud sought an "alchemical" theater that would show the audience a different reality, a theater that would offer a spiritual double: "not of this direct, everyday reality . . . as empty as it is sugar-coated—but of another archetypal and dangerous reality, a reality of which the Principles, like dolphins, once they have shown their heads, hurry to dive back into the obscurity of the deep" (Artaud [1938] 2010, 48). Artaud's theater promises to show us a world that is real, but barely visible. It is neither idle fantasy, nor does it reproduce the banality of the mundane. Artaud wants the theater to do more. He wishes for the theater to infect the spectator, as in a plague. He promises that such a theater "infinitely extends the frontiers of what is called reality" (13). Offering new possibilities of creativity, it requires artist and spectator to embrace this blurring of boundaries, which renders vulnerable all involved.

Theater in the early twentieth century in Europe (including Russia) sought not only to create distance through theories of alienation, as discussed in the introduction, it also worked to use such techniques to erase common distinctions. Puppets, dolls, and other objects that come to life—automatons and robots—prompted artists and scholars to explore porous divisions between humans and the nonhuman figures that resemble them. Puppets slip between categories of animate and inanimate when people treat objects as if they are alive. Children slip between these categories when people treat them like things. Ernst Jentsch ([1906] 2008) sparked interest in the uneasy movement between animate and inanimate in his discussion of the uncanny. He defines the uncanny as a state of "psychical uncertainty," and suggests that dolls, automatons, and wax figures are especially likely to produce an uncanny effect because they create uncertainty about whether they are alive or dead, animate or inanimate. Nonetheless, the uncanny can occur in a host of situations, and the same situation will not be uncanny for everyone. Jentsch's essay is productive for considering relationships between humans and nonhumans, whether these nonhuman others take the shape of puppets or online avatars.[2] Freud ([1919] 1953) treats the uncanny as a feeling that arises when we are confronted with something that is not merely "uncertain," but which is, more specifically, an uneasy combination of familiar and strange. Ultimately, he connects the paradox of the familiar/strange to repressed fantasies and fears. In the process, he imagines a wider range of phenomena as causing uncanny effects—such as repetition, coincidence, dismembered limbs, and the appearance of a double.

The puppet often acts as a double to a human counterpart. The unclear boundaries between bodies (and between classifications of human and puppet) trouble certain viewers. I have heard puppeteers admit that they find puppets uncanny not when animated but when placed on display. For them, it is the deanimation that disturbs. This becomes important in chapter 5. Like dolls, robots, and other objects made in human likenesses, the puppet comes to life at certain points and leaves at others. It serves as a point of comparison for people who are, perhaps, insufficiently independent or inconsistently animate. The puppet can give rise to pathos, fear, or a mix of the two.

The puppet, as a model for intersubjectivity, need not be so frightening. Kleist treats it as a choreographed exchange of spirit. And yet these representations of power relations expose ambivalence surrounding relationships of care and control. To treat persons as things—and thus to render them malleable and even disposable—can lead to instances of profound violence. Something both Artaud and Freud suggest in their theories of doubling is that each new representation threatens to remind us of something we wanted to forget, suggesting a trace of something troubling on the seemingly blank slate of the child, on the empty stage, or in the naked steppe.

The worlds of the puppet theater and Hope House unfold within other borders, with complex histories of crossing and moving within these boundaries.[3] While writers and political leaders underscore the vastness of the Kazakh steppe, this notion of boundlessness—and emptiness—has lent itself to projects of fixing or disrupting flows of bodies across and within it. Nonetheless, powerful landmarks connect Kazakhs to ancestors of spiritual importance. Like borders, landmarks are open to contestation and require work to establish and maintain.[4] The nomad and the yurt serve as potent signs of Kazakh identity that celebrate mobility. Contemporary artists and queer theorists in central Asia draw from the legacy of the nomadic past and the Silk Road in reimagining the region, identifying with the possibilities presented by movement (Kudaibergenova 2017; Shatalova 2016).

Movement and settlement were often violent acts in the past two centuries in Kazakhstan.[5] Authorities under the Russian Empire tried various strategies to settle and civilize the Kazakh nomads, with measures ranging from spreading Islam to sending Cossacks and other non-Kazakhs to settle in the best land. By the time of the first Soviet census, a fourth of all Kazakhs were sedentary, and more than 65 percent lived seminomadic lives. The Soviets took a more aggressive tack on settling the nomads of Kazakhstan, forcing herders to take up work on collective farms and stripping *bais* (or beys) of wealth and power by diminishing their livestock (Kindler 2018, 16). Those who would not give up their stock fled to neighboring areas in Mongolia and the western Chinese province of Xinjiang, beginning in the winter of 1927–1928 and continuing into the 1930s (Pianciola 2001).

Meanwhile, the Kazakh steppe became the site of gulags for suspected enemies of the people, along with the destination for forcibly deported "special settlers" (*spetspereselentsy*) of various ethnicities—Koreans, Germans, Chechens, Poles, Balkars, Meskhetian Turks, and others. They, too, were placed on collective farms in the 1930s.[6] The upheavals imposed on people's ways of life, without proper resources or planning, led to famine between 1930 and 1933, with an estimated 1.5 million deaths, or a quarter of the republic's inhabitants (Cameron 2018; Kindler 2018). The Kazakh population suffered the most, with estimates that the famine killed 38 percent of the total Kazakh population (Pianciola 2001). Starvation caused further flight to neighboring areas, and Kazakhs became a minority population in their own republic (Cameron 2018).

During this period, children were among the most vulnerable. Personal accounts include a childhood memory of a boy's younger sister being sacrificed to a pack of hungry wolves in order to save the rest of the family. The mortality rate in orphanages in some places was estimated at more than 80 percent (Kindler 2018). Numbers do little justice to the scope of children's misfortunes during this time because so many were never registered. Children's homes were overcrowded, underfunded, dirty, and disease filled. Funds and food allotted to them sometimes disappeared (Green 2006). Children and adolescents were deported to remote villages in large numbers to live in the abandoned houses of former *kulaks* and largely had to fend for themselves.[7] As the famine wore on, children were at greater risk of falling victim to cannibalism, more often than not from their own family members (Kindler 2018).

There is, then, a dramatic history of forced movement and settlement to and around Kazakhstan. Nonetheless, a persistent imagining of the land as unsettled—or uninhabited—has played a key role in the region's identity. The Kazakh steppe is often designated in literature on the region as the "empty steppe" or the "naked steppe" (*goli step*, in Russian). Fyodor Dostoevsky, after his imprisonment, was sent to the town of Semipalatinsk, in East Kazakhstan, for mandatory military service. Before leaving Omsk in 1854, he writes in a letter, "I am now going to a veritable desert, to Asia, and there, in Semipalatinsk, it seems to me that all my past, all memories and impressions, will leave me."[8] Dostoevsky anticipates an emptiness so powerful that it will prove contagious. From stories of exile to a 2016 news report on a former Guantanamo detainee sent to the same city, narratives abound of Kazakhstan as cold and lifeless (Walker 2016). These overlook and erase histories of people moving through the steppe. Inhabitants of cities such as Semipalatinsk are treated as unworthy of mention. Figuring Kazakhstan as a blank canvas or empty stage justifies using the space for grand projects and projections. Nuclear testing and space launches could be conducted in the steppe and concealed in the Soviet period.[9] In independent Kazakhstan, a new capital could be erected, seemingly, in the middle of nowhere, even if this project remade a city that had already seen multiple makeovers.

# An Unknown Moment of Separation

Chekhov, via Bolat, declares that Kashtanka's despair at being lost on a doorstep was such that if she had been human, she would have shot herself. The dog puppet puts her tail to her ear as if it is a gun. This line elicited laughter from those watching rehearsals. I immediately thought about the children of Hope House, however. I never saw the moment when they found themselves at the doorstep of the home, so to speak.[10] This is only a manner of speaking, of course. Parents who wished to leave a child at Hope House had to sign a contract, promising to return in one to three years. A parent could extend the contract until the child was seven, old enough to start their first grade of elementary school. Unlike Kashtanka, the children at Hope House and their parents never lost one another accidentally. It was a planned, controlled loss, a temporary relinquishment to prevent a permanent one that would have come with placing the child in a regular children's home (*detdom*). The children of my group had come to Hope House, for the most part, in the first or second year of their lives. Many were already in their fourth or fifth year there when I met them. For Kashtanka, the events leading up to the moment on the pavement are all still quite vivid, but as the play progresses, dreams will reveal an increasingly muddled memory of the past. The children may have forgotten the moment they were left, yet they needed to understand this—they had lost a home and family, but they would be recovered.

When I visited one traditional *detdom* in Almaty, I asked a worker how they discussed the children's loss of family. She replied, "We don't. It's too sad." Rather than focusing on the moment of displacement, Hope House offered a counternarrative—of a happy ending to the loss. How and why the children found themselves at Hope House in the first place were questions that went largely unanswered during my time there. Lacking permission to interview parents, and not wishing to impose on their time with their children on the days they visited, I could only glean their circumstances from their occasional visits that happened to overlap with mine, from our few conversations and from what the teachers chose to tell me. My general understanding was that these were mostly single mothers with limited financial means. The only father who visited was a single father. Most of them were working, and they likely lacked relatives living close by, such as grandparents, who could provide free childcare before the children started school.

These were women who would have benefited from the robust Soviet system of free nurseries and kindergartens. Politics and policies surrounding motherhood shifted over the twentieth century in the Soviet Union. The plan for ideal early Soviet orphanages was part of a Bolshevik promise to liberate women from domestic slavery, yet this was followed by measures under Stalin to revalorize motherhood, in large part because of the demographic crisis the Soviet Union faced after civil war, famine, and World War II.[11] This period also saw a recriminalization of abortion (Michaels 2001). Under Khruschev and Brezhnev, a complex scene emerged: On one hand, Soviet women worked at among the highest rates in the world, and Khruschev briefly expanded the building of residential boarding schools to free working women from childcare responsibilities. At the same time, discourses arose through parenting manuals and other media to promote "intense motherhood," placing all the burden on women to anticipate children's every physiological and emotional need and to prompt their mental development through carefully designed tasks (Chernyaeva 2013). Thus, the late-Soviet woman ideally fulfilled two roles—of worker and of ideal mother. In early post-Soviet years, economic crisis led to a renewed demographic crisis throughout the former Soviet republics, though Kazakhstan's fertility decline was less severe than Russia's (Agadjanian et al. 2008; Becker and Hemley 1998). In the twenty-first century, gender inequality regarding childcare has persisted due to "the neo-liberal approach to welfare provision, conservative social norms, and limited agency of civil society to influence the policy agenda" (Dugarova 2019, 385). Care and education of preschool children has especially suffered in independent Kazakhstan, which lost 70 percent of its preschool establishments with independence (Heyneman and DeYoung 2004). In Almaty, this problem has proven acute and persistent, with frequent reports in the popular press that tens of thousands of children await a place in a public preschool/kindergarten. Such reports continued years after my fieldwork ended, despite regular government announcements of various interventions.[12] The lack of care and educational facilities for young children increased the burden on single mothers, who must also deal with pronounced gender disparity in wages, while the post-Soviet welfare benefits available to single mothers shrank to the extent that many found the benefits not worth the bureaucratic process required to attain them.[13]

The general circumstances that would lead one to place a child in Hope House were fairly clear, but these conditions did not explain how a parent finally decided to place a child at Hope House or how the parent dealt with it afterward. When some mothers visited, the pain of the repeated separation was apparent on both ends. Children clearly looked forward to a parent's visit and sulked when another child received family and they did not. One mother told me that her ability to adjust to the situation surprised her. When she first placed her daughter there, at less than a year old, both cried at every visit. It got easier for them. When I met this mother, she only visited every few weeks, usually on holidays.

Some agreed with this mother that it was easiest if everyone got used to the situation as quickly as possible. The psychologist on staff at Hope House told me she preferred for parents to leave their children when they were too young to understand what was happening. They would grow up with no memory of where they had come from. This was possible when they came in the first year or so. The later they were left, she said, the more problems they had. She worked with the children by offering intersensorial soothing. She brought them into a "sensory room," a room filled with disco lights, fake-fish aquariums, and soft furniture. She played gentle music and told them to relax. The day I visited this session, they were restless, wanting to jump on the soft furniture instead of lying peacefully. Rather than working through the past through talk or play therapy, the sensory room offered a way to help children manage unpleasant emotions by providing a calming space. Here, they could arrange their bodies as they wished rather than sitting up straight in hard chairs and keeping their hands neatly folded on desks. Lights and projections simultaneously tranquilized and stimulated.

This suggests an ideal of healing that contrasts, for example, with the nursery school in New York where I worked before starting graduate school. There, directors encouraged teachers to narrate our perceptions of the children's inner emotional states as models for them to follow. A child's separation from the mother or father for just a few hours brought distress that we were taught to help articulate for the toddlers in our care. The directors instructed all of us, as teachers, to repeat, "Mommy's gone away, but she's coming back," as many times as deemed necessary for the child to stop crying and to be able to play. We were taught to make explicit connections between the children's games of making things disappear and reappear and the separation we were supposed to be helping them process, much like the fort/da game Freud describes.[14]

This suggests a contrast between a sensory versus linguistic approach to dealing with the loss, yet language was crucial to Hope House's approach as well. Even if the younger children had little memory of their first home, teachers at Hope House modeled narratives of return. They reminded the children that they had lost something they should want to recover, though not by discussing the loss itself. Staff made efforts to help children feel good without necessarily aiding their articulation of negative emotions, instead orienting the children toward the moment of reunion. Whereas the teachers at permanent orphanages in Kazakhstan avoided the topic of loss altogether, at Hope House teachers could at least assure the children that their mother or father was coming back.

One morning, in the fall of my second year, I filmed a lesson at Hope House on expressions of time. The group was between five and six years old, named the "preparatory" (daiyndalyp) year, linking their identity with the near future. Because they needed to go home by the time they were old enough to start school, they were preparing for both. Some children I had observed the previous year had already left, and certain children in this group would be leaving sooner than others. In the lesson, they first discuss their daily routine at Hope House—what they do in the morning, afternoon, and evening.[15] Next, their teacher, Saltanat Apai, introduces words used in time phrases: buryn, keıın, deıın. She points to the animal illustrations she has put on the magnetized board and begins, with her booming yet lilting pedagogical voice, "Buryngy ötken zamanda," her voice trailing with the last syllable (See Illustration 5). This phrase, like "Once upon a time," commonly begins folktales in Kazakh.

"What was there?" she asks.

Nurlan offers the same lilting prosody as he offers, "Ayu (a bear)."

Ainura offers, "Animals."

Saltanat Apai asks, "What folktales (ertegı) do we know?"

Ainura guesses, "Bauyrsaq!" She is correct. Named after small balls of fried bread, it is the Kazakh version of the Russian folktale, "Kolobok," about a Gingerbread Man–like runaway ball of dough. Saltanat begins retelling the story but moves on without finishing it. Her second example is also a Kazakh adaptation of a Russian folktale, this time about a turnip, and the various household members—human and animal—who come together to pull the giant vegetable from the earth.

Saltanat offers a third example, this time not from a folktale: "For example, 'Once my mama came and brought me a toy.' For example, you can say."

Ainura raises her hand to offer her own sentence. She stands up to say, "Once my uncle Talgat came and brought me toys." It didn't matter that Ainura's example was almost the same as Saltanat Apai's. Teachers encouraged imitation and repetition.[16] Whether or not the visit from her uncle had ever taken place was also beside the point. Teachers invited children to recall and invoke parents and other family members as visitors who left gifts, by which they were to be remembered, whether or not these recited memories were true. Ainura's mother had placed her there when she was still a baby, just under a year old. Her mother, a teacher, lived and worked in another city and could not visit often. A teacher

**ILLUSTRATION 5. IN THE CLASSROOM**   Saltanat Apai points to the animal illustrations she has put on the magnetized board and begins speaking with her booming yet lilting pedagogical voice.

once complained that it was a shame that Ainura's mother could not see how good she was, the star pupil.

Saltanat Apai's example and her encouragement of similar sentences from children made the family present in a lesson ostensibly about language and time. Even for children who rarely saw their parents, teachers and other staff at Hope House made it clear that they were not replacing the children's mothers. They went by *Apai*, their first names preceding this title (e.g., Gulym Apai). Children and adults alike used *apai* in Kazakh as a term of respect for teachers or for older women of authority, though it also translates as "aunt" in certain parts of Kazakhstan. The Russian-speaking group did not call their teachers "Aunt" (*Tëtka*) (though this is what they called me). They used, for the teachers, the women's first name and patronymic, another sign of respect. Helpers and teachers alike were addressed with *siz*, the formal second-person singular term of address in Kazakh (or *Vy* in the Russian group), and not the more personal *sen*. Teachers corrected the children if they neglected to address me in the same way.[17]

Permanent children's homes, in contrast, did work to replace the family home, to a certain extent. Children referred to all of the personnel—who were almost exclusively women—as "Mom" (*Mom*), along with the woman's first name.[18] At one where I volunteered, where the children were all of preschool age, and some were just toddlers, the children immediately started calling me "Mom"—along with a young man who was volunteering with me.[19] The director of this home, a bubbly woman with wavy blonde hair, overflowed with enthusiasm I little expected from an orphanage director. She had tried teaching at a school, she said. But those children had families. At the *detdom*, she was their family, and so she had returned.

Families need not consist of "blood" relations. They need not be limited to a "nuclear" model of parents and children, nor is the primacy of the mother-child dyad universal, as anthropologists have shown us.[20] Group care is not always a deviant alternative to having a family but can be interwoven into social and economic relationships.[21] Ethnographic accounts of post-Soviet orphanages have approached them as a problem to be solved, and have concentrated on the social, economic, and political contexts that cause institutionalization.[22] This leaves us with a number of questions regarding children's experiences within such homes.

Instead of replacing mothers, Hope House fostered children's imaginings of the family home, with special emphasis on the mother. It was most often she who had promised to return. In order for Hope House to preserve the primacy of the mother, they had made their own institution into a home devoid of mothers, however full of aunts. I explore the complexity of the relationship between the children and the caregivers of Hope House in chapter 2. It is important to show here that Hope House made it clear to the children that mothers and fathers existed, but did not exist at Hope House. These simple narratives helped make Hope House into a space in which a key event is a parent's visit.

On the day of the language lesson, after learning the term "once," the next word to be learned is *kein*, a term describing a general period of "later." One of the boys, Nurlan, sitting in the front row that day, offers an example. He speaks quickly, as if nervous his turn will be taken away: "Apai, later we're going outside."

Saltanat Apai doesn't correct his sentence, but offers another: "For example, you and your mother are at the toy bazaar, yeah? You're at the store. You say to your mom, 'Mama, buy me this thing and give it to me please.' You say to your mom. In your mama's pocket there's no money left. 'My child, *later* I'll buy it for you, OK?' She says. What word did she say? *Later* let me get it,' she said. What word does she use?"

Saltanat Apai ventriloquizes the children's mothers, so that in practicing their use of this word, they can also imagine an interaction with her.[23] While the example of "once" encouraged the children to imagine a past interaction with a family member bringing them a gift, Saltanat now invites them to imagine a "later" in which they have returned home. Rather than being discouraged by his initial error, Nurlan tries again, "Apai, let me say it. I go with my mom to the store. 'Mama buy this for me.' My mama says there's no money. 'Then *later* I'll buy,' she said."

During my first year of observing the children, Nurlan was one of the quiet ones. He was the sidekick to Maksat, who had, during my summer absence, gone home with his mother. Since then, Nurlan had emerged as more confident. The teacher never explicitly corrected Nurlan's first use—"later we'll go outside." I asked my research assistant afterward if this was really an incorrect use of the word, or if the teacher just wanted to give them another example. My assistant explained that in the first example, *keiin* did not fit because they could be sure that they would go outside later, and it would happen soon. *Keiin* was for a less defined future. In this case, the example modeled for them was based on a number of things that would be happening at an ill-defined later time. Later, they would go home to their mothers or fathers. Later, at some point, they would go with their parent to a toy store, and they would ask for something. And at that time, the teacher imagined, there was a good chance their parents would lack the money to buy their child the thing they wanted. Even in anticipating their return, then, the children rehearsed an acceptance of continued anticipation. But what is a deferred toy, next to a mother?

In the same day's lesson, Saltanat Apai discussed another key moment—of the children's departure—by asking them to name the children who had lived in this group of rooms the year before. Those children had all gone home. They lived now on the outside, with their families, while teachers prepared these children to do the same.

# Model Prisons

Memorial museums often attempt to recreate a past world. Themes of family separation and loss figure large in those found in Kazakhstan, particularly those that preserve the history of the Soviet gulags that occupied a large section of the steppe. Just outside of the capital city is the museum dedicated to ALZhIR. The women imprisoned there were guilty by association: the prison camp, which operated from the 1930s to the early 1950s, housed women whose brothers, fathers, or husbands had been accused as enemies of the people. ALZhIR was one gulag in a vast network of Soviet prison camps in Kazakhstan. KarLag, the museum dedicated to the Soviet gulag system in Kazakhstan, is housed in the former central administrative office of the camps, located just outside the city of Karaganda. Like other former prisons rendered museums, ALZhIR and KarLag converted total institutions into displays for visiting tourists to pass through.

The inmates gone, memorial museums of former prisons vary in their approach to filling the space. Mannequins often remind visitors of the living bodies once held there.[24] ALZhIR features a life-size diorama of an interrogation room that visitors can enter. An officer sits behind the desk with an unevenly sculpted face and dull, asymmetrical eyes that stare straight ahead. His mouth hangs partly open, as if he is about to speak. His ear seems disproportionately large, yet his hat does not reach down to its tip, as if the head were generally too big for it. Here is the replica of a man once asked to animate the Soviet government.[25] To the officer's left stands a woman, her face mostly obscured, in the picture I took at the time, by her hair and by the scarf she wears over it.

Smaller models in the museum offer an overview, in miniature, of the entire camp, of the watchtowers and the trucks. Toy-sized figures comprise scenes of women sweeping the ground and working the fields while officers watch over them. Miniatures create an interior temporality of the subject, according to Susan Stewart (1984, 66), always "tend[ing] toward the tableau rather than toward the narrative, toward silence and spatial boundaries rather than toward expository closure." Both the miniature and the reconstructed interrogation room act as tableaux, yet the former allows visitors to see an entire scene and to imagine it unfolding, as if from afar. Stewart writes of doll houses, which are associated with childhood, so it is not surprising that she argues that the miniature provokes nostalgia. The geographer Natalie Koch (2010) examines miniatures of Astana's new cityscape to argue that these create a utopian space that disallows political discourse; thus the miniature depoliticizes. However, the miniatures of ALZhIR—featuring not only buildings but tiny human figurines—might do something different. They could, instead, remind the viewer of the distance and disregard with which central planners seemed to treat the populations suffering in the Kazakh steppe during this period. Glass prevents visitors from picking up the tiny women or moving them, yet in creating a likeness to the miniature playthings of children, it is possible to imagine the ease with which one could handle, crush, or dispose of them.

The persistent presence of disappeared persons can haunt those who are left. In Siberia, Eveni children tell ghost stories of severed arms that are part of the history of the region's gulags; those imprisoned there, and those forced to report fugitives, haunt new generations with the notion that the land is cursed, so a better future can only be realized by escaping.[26] Nonetheless, haunting can allow individuals to imagine and sustain connection to those they have lost. Media can help vivify the dead as characters, though these reanimated deceased remain "partial and fragmentary . . . evoked rather than represented . . . expanding into a multiplicity of different versions to which shifting attachments can form" (Hales 2019, 189). Even as we argue for the reality of haunting, it is also an act of imagination, of projection, of animating a relationship to an absent other.

In addition to recreations, the museums at ALZhIR and KarLag offer copious traces of those who were sent there, similarly partial and fragmentary. There are photographs of the prisoners themselves, of various activities at the camp, and of the prisoners' children, waiting to be shipped off to the orphanage. These appear amidst artifacts such as an album of a woman's embroidery samples. Susan Sontag ([1977] 2001, 71) notes that photography makes us into collectors. Photographs, as fragments of space and time, are akin to quotations, pulled out of context. Exhibited images and objects compete for the visitor's attention. Even if they are presented as equivalent to one another, nothing compels the viewer to give each artifact attention. However, with these scraps of embroidery, accounts of the camps' agricultural successes, and photographs and descriptions of educational and cultural activities, the exhibit seems keen on showing the visitor that inmates did not merely survive, but made life possible for others.[27]

Both museums include the camera as an instrument of interrogation, along with the mug shot–type photographs that such cameras apparently produced. As Sontag notes, "The industrialization of photography permitted its rapid absorption into rational—that is, bureaucratic—ways of running society. . . . Photographs were enrolled in the service of important institutions of control, notably the family and the police" (21). The camera in the room with the photographs behind it helps underscore these photographs as products of bureaucratic inventory. While the museums furnish a context for understanding the power relations surrounding the production of these portraits, the photographs themselves remain difficult to read. A woman who looks defiant may have been wide-eyed with terror. Sontag repeatedly emphasizes that photographs disallow understanding, however much they invite "deduction, speculation, and fantasy" (23). She worries that photographs, in this way, pretend to produce knowledge but actually foster sentimentality.

We can accept that the photographs provoke sentiment but follow, nonetheless, the attitudes or actions that such encounters produce.[28] The photographs of inmates in the interrogation room—looking squarely at the camera, and then in profile—invite the visitor to make eye contact with them at the moment when the gulag photographer captured their image. The meeting of gazes, however imagined, animates. Roland Barthes (1982) traces movement from his own eyes to those of Napoleon's brother, in a picture, which enables Barthes to feel a connection to Napoleon. Sontag (2004, 61) notes, on viewing a photograph of the condemned, that the viewer "is in the same position as the lackey behind the camera." The photograph creates a mutuality of regard, this eye contact itself somehow proving contagious. It excites Barthes but sickens Sontag.

At ALZhIR and KarLag, I snapped pictures of a few of the mug shots, the ones I found most compelling. The face of a young woman with dark hair stayed with me. In profile, she looks elegant; straight on, she seems tough. With dark eyes and a full lower lip, she seems to flare her nostrils expressly for the camera. I spent time projecting a story onto the woman's picture—or onto the image that haunted me. Such a projection could tell me little about the woman whose face had provoked it. When I returned to the photograph later, I realized her name was scrawled at the bottom—Inna Aronovna Gaister. It was astonishingly easy to find her life story. She lived mostly in Russia but made three significant trips to central Asia in her youth. Born in 1925, she was twelve when her parents were arrested. Her father was quickly executed while her mother was sent to ALZhIR. Inna saved up money to visit—her first trip to the region. During World War II, she and her remaining family members were evacuated to Uzbek SSR. Inna's third trip to the region began in 1949, on the day of her thesis defense, when she was arrested and sent to live in exile in Kazakhstan. Having heard of Borovoe, a resort area just north of where her mother had been kept, Inna requested to be sent there. It was then that her mug shot must have been taken, the one now on display at KarLag. In 1953, she was able to return to Moscow to stay.

The photograph does not tell me any of this. Without the inscription at the bottom, I never would have been able to connect the face in the photograph to this biography. Nonetheless, it was the photograph, the eyes, that initiated my response to it, that invited speculation and a certain amount of fantasy in wondering about her. As Barthes (1982, 20) asserts, it is not that a photograph is animate, but that "it animates me: this is what creates every adventure." It prompted me to search, and I was lucky enough to find out more. In a 2005 interview, she credited her husband for healing her after she returned from exile, but admitted that she continued to live in constant fear. In 2009, she slipped and fell under a city bus in Moscow and died.[29]

# The Capacity to Call

The women at ALZhIR were ballet dancers, theater directors, doctors, and teachers. It was their identity as wives, sisters, and daughters—their kin ties to enemies— that caused their sentences of deportation and hard labor. The museum often emphasized their status as mothers, nonetheless. Children could only stay with their mothers at ALZhIR for their first few years before they were sent to orphanages. In a letter on display at ALZhIR, a child who has been separated from his mother writes to her. The author of the letter assures his mother he is fine. He works to maintain a connection, despite their separation:

> Hello dear mamochka why do you write me letters. mamochka you don't know where is papa. Mamochka I am studying in the second grade. Mamochka I was sick for a very long time with ringworm. Mamochka I am alive and well. Mamochka, you wrote that you don't have paper. mamochka I am sending to you(?). mamochka, I miss you very much. There's nothing more to write.[30]

The letter is unsigned, but the gendering of the past particles and adjectives indicates that the author is a boy. If he is in second grade, he would have been around eight years old. The first line is a puzzle, as if the child forgot to negate the writing of letters, for the mother's reasons for writing would seem obvious, if it had happened. Later, the child mentions that the mother lacks paper, which raises the question as to how the boy knows this. Nonetheless, it seems he is sending her paper so that she might be able to reply. Rather than the parent offering a modest gift to the child (as occurred when parents visited Hope House), the child sends a small gift to his mother. It is paper that she will, presumably, return to him in the form of a letter, so his gift offers the promise of a sustained relationship via correspondence.

Despite many uncertainties, I can be sure of the letter's addressee. She is *Mamochka*, "Mommy." The boy has taken care to write her name at the beginning of every line, a kind of incantation. Barbara Johnson describes poetic authority as "the capacity to call." Her description of the power of apostrophe, the poetic calling out to an absent party or to a personified object, is fitting here. She argues, "He doesn't even have to say anything about X; he merely has to 'ring' it. In fact apostrophe can be mere sound, amplified by the laws of sound waves, 'redoubled and redoubled' or 'sounding and resounding'" (Johnson 2010, 9). The phatic (attention to channel), emotive (attention to speaker), conative (attention to addressee), and poetic (attention to form) inhere in the repetition of the name, *mamochka* (Jakobson 1960). Various senses work in concert to make this word appear on the page, through the visual, aural, and haptic acts of reading and writing. For a child in the second grade, writing would still be new enough to require special care. He writes with blue ink. His handwriting is fairly unsteady, and there are a few errors. Writing becomes a way of performing a "kinetic melody" of the repeated word, as the Soviet psychologist Alexander Luria (1973, 32) described. We can imagine a hand—a small hand—gripping a pen, moving it over the paper, *ringing* this woman's title, again and again, through contact between the instrument and the paper that will bear its trace.

She was, of course, not the only *mamochka* at ALZhIR. According to the displays at ALZhIR, small children of the women were sent to a special orphanage, *Mamkin Dom*, "Mama's House," where they died by the thousands. They were buried in a cemetery nearby, *Mamochkino kladbishche*, "Mothers' Cemetery," named not for the inhabitants, but for the women who, when free, would presumably come to visit their children's graves. The museums of KarLag and ALZhIR are full of stories of children and mothers. To the boy writing the letter, however, his is the one Mamochka. He is careful to interpellate her as such, no fewer than nine times in the course of his brief, but careful, epistle.

Unlike a photograph, the letter offers the mother a narrative, however compact, of suffering and rehabilitation, for the boy was sick (*bolel*), but is now alive (*zhyv*), and healthy (*zdorovyï*). At the bottom of the page, the child has drawn a long house with shingles on the roof and three chimneys with smoke coming out (See Illustration 6). Between the chimneys the child has written, in large block letters, *3i KORPUS*, or "3rd building." Just to the right of the last chimney he has written, "Mamochka this is my building" (*Mamochka eto moi korpus*). He does not write, "This is my home."

**ILLUSTRATION 6. LETTER TO MAMOCHKA**    "3rd Building. Mamochka this is my building."

# Lost Memories and New Opportunities

The perceived emptiness of the Kazakhstani steppe helps outsiders (and government planners) to overlook and erase evidence of those who were there before—whether natives or exiles—and of those who remain after exiles have gone home. This is a common trope of settler colonialism—figuring the land as wild, untouched, or virginal, and either ignoring the previous presence of humans or aligning them with the wilderness, waiting to be tamed. Just as histories of particular groups or places disappear, intimate memories can slip away as well. Literary analyses of Chekhov's story of "Kashtanka" have argued that it is all about issues of memory.[31] On her first night away from her first home, Kashtanka remembers the carpenter and his son, Fedyushka, vividly. After a month, however, "in her imagination appeared two vague figures, not quite dogs, not quite people, with physiognomies friendly, dear, yet unintelligible . . . and it seemed to her that she had somewhere sometime seen them and loved them" (Chekhov 2017, 26–27). As memories become more dreamlike, the faces of the first master and his son transform.

The amount that the children at Hope House recalled of their time at home with their parents was unclear. According to research on "infantile amnesia," children's memories of specific events (their anecdotal memory) in their first years will recede gradually.[32] As five-year-olds, the children of Hope House might remember their first year or two with their families, but they would not be expected to keep these memories by the time they were twelve or thirteen (Madsen and Kim 2016). Moreover, within Hope House, the loss of the parents wasn't acknowledged as a memory in the past. Caregivers instead treated children as living in an ongoing state of missing, which was then enveloped in a narrative of healing via return.

At Hope House, the children's play frequently made use of breakage to give way to something new, revealing an ability to cope with loss and to exploit the new possibilities that rupture presents. The day I filmed Nurlan giving the model sentence in class about the deferred toy his mother would promise him, he was far more outgoing on the playground than I had ever seen him before. In the video I captured outside that day, he is at first in the background. However, he quickly attracts my attention because he is holding a toy helicopter by its tail and bowing across it with a stick. The helicopter's rotor system is missing, and he has turned it into a musical instrument—perhaps a violin, or perhaps a *qobyz*, a traditional Kazakh instrument praised for its sad sound. Aruzhan, a girl new to the group and to my camera, asks me to turn the viewfinder around so that she can see herself inside of it. When I comply, she says "wow" and calls Nurlan over. Nurlan now performs more loudly. He plays for the camera. He throws down his bow and turns the helicopter to a horizontal position. He begins strumming it with his hand: it is suddenly a guitar or a *dombyra*. He moves the helicopter from his left hand to his right, making it vertical again, but continuing to strum (See Illustration 7). He picks the bow back up, switches from one hand to the other, the whole time singing what was nonsense to my assistant and to me: "Ala bali pa pa aha la la ua fa fa fa . . ."

Zhamilia, one of the twins, wants to play with Nurlan. The two of them go to the cupboards in the group's outdoor playhouse to seek other instruments. Outside, children are freer to take whatever toys they want from the cupboards in their playhouse and do with them what they please. Among these toys are broken vehicles, train tracks that lack a train, and dolls and stuffed animals that are dirty or maimed. Sometimes, the busted objects invite more inventive uses than when they were intact, as it becomes less obvious what their shapes are meant to resemble. In chapter 4, a teacher imagines damaged toys as creating social conflict between the toys themselves. Here, however, the children exploit breakage as an opportunity to alter signification, to discover new dimensions of iconicity. As Nurlan does this, it becomes an invitation for other children to do the same. This enables parallel play to unfold that would have been impossible if they had focused on differences between things.

Nurlan finds an object that once held other parts. Probably once a drawing board, it is now just a piece of blue plastic, with grooves in the middle where other parts have fallen off, and a small hole in the corner. Zhamilia has a miniature pinball game. Back behind the playhouse, Nurlan props one foot on a toy tractor, which he uses as a kind of footstool. He and Zhamilia hold their respective plastic rectangles vertically, in their left hands. They beat them with their right. Nurlan sings a song that is nonsense. Their teacher, Saltanat Apai, stands nearby and rehearses a text with another boy for an upcoming performance. She does not tell them to stop playing, but she leads the other boy by the hand around the corner of the playhouse. Nurlan falters in his song. The boldness he displayed earlier with the helicopter seems to have diminished, perhaps because he sensed his teacher's annoyance at their impromptu concert in her own practice space. Zhamilia also loses her nerve, banging on her toy a couple of times but then transitioning from playing it as an instrument to playing with it as a pinball game. She watches the parts move around inside as she pushes the buttons. As Nurlan stops his own song with an "oy," he smiles shyly. He holds the blue piece in front of his mouth and then brings it up to cover his whole face. With this, the frame of their play as fellow musicians is broken.

This loss of footing leads Nurlan to reorient to a new game.[33] He notices a small hole in the corner of the rectangle and puts his eye up to it. He says "Meghanne Apai," his voice high and singsongy, and he waves to me. Zhamilia

**ILLUSTRATION 7. NURLAN PLAYS THE HELICOPTER** Nurlan throws down his bow and turns the helicopter to a horizontal position. He begins strumming it with his hand: it is suddenly a guitar or a *dombyra*.

rises and stands in front of Nurlan, working to reestablish his attention to their music. Nurlan looks at her through the hole, as Zhamilia again turns her toy vertical and bangs on it a few times. Nurlan lowers the blue plastic from his face and says something to Zhamilia that I cannot make out. Zhamilia drags her instrument on the ground and walks away from him, Nurlan calling to her as she leaves, "I'm like Meghanne Apai!"

"You're like me?" I ask.

Having shifted the frame of play—albeit with the same object—he has moved from the music-making endeavor he shared with Zhamilia to a project of image making that aligns him with me. He confirms this move by switching from Kazakh to Russian to answer, "This is my camera" (*eto moia kameru*). I normally spoke Kazakh with the children, but Nurlan was beginning to speak a bit of Russian. He practices with me. He makes grammatical mistakes that he would not make in Kazakh. He says to me, "*Snimite kamera*," by which he could either mean that he wants me to film (*snimite s kameroĭ*) or that he wants me to lower the camera (*snimite kameru*). Since I am already doing the former (filming him), I do the latter as well: I squat down to his level. He counts, in Russian—*raz, dva, tri*—pushes an invisible button on his blue rectangular camera, and lowers it from his face. He turns it around and points to a rectangular hollow space within his instrument. My picture is there, in that empty space, according to his game, and he shows it to me. He gets up so that I can show him the pictures I have taken of him in return. The clip ends. After Nurlan has looked at the footage of himself, he says to me, "And you'll take this to America and show it to people and tell them, 'This is my friend Nurlan.'" I tell him that this is what I will do, even if I will change his name.

Before, my camera blocked an easy mutuality of gaze because it came between my eyes and those of Nurlan and Zhamilia. At the same time, it oriented them toward my camera and toward me as a spectator, even as their playing together created alignment through the parallelism of their actions. Nurlan's shift from playing with Zhamilia to mimicking me enables him to establish a mutuality of mediated gaze. This corresponds to Mazzarella's (2017, 5) description of constitutive resonance as "a relation of mutual becoming rather than causal determination." Nurlan is not merely captured by me, but I am also captured by him. Nurlan's act creates a moment of equivalence with our shared gaze and capturing, and with the photographic artifacts produced afterward which we show to each other.

My apparatus enables a durability of Nurlan's image that the blue plastic rectangle cannot. At the same time, the tenuousness of the blue plastic as a technology for image making serves Nurlan, for he can continue to transform it by noting its similarity to other objects. Its ambiguous iconicity enables a flexibility so that he can shift away from this game to begin a new one. Nurlan takes the piece of blue plastic and holds it in front of him with both hands. He says he is driving a bus, and we are going to America. We make it just a few feet before Nurlan notices an insect on the ground. He calls Zhamilia over to look at it. The earlier loss in alignment between Zhamilia and Nurlan gets regained, but again proves fleeting. Saltanat Apai announces that it is time for them to go inside. It is time for me to go home for the day. Here, instability and ambiguity enable Nurlan to shift in his alignments toward various games and toward different people. He moves away from me, ending what had been a meaningful moment of connection with him, but this is also a return to Zhamilia, with whom he had played at the beginning of the afternoon when they chased insects. She had sought to reconnect with him in their brief musical career together. At the end of their time outside, he called back to her.

# Reworlding Kazakhstan in the Twenty-First Century

The echoes of past displacements in present-day Kazakhstan are in some cases more recognizable than others. In postindependence Kazakhstan, under President Nazarbayev, policies were introduced to welcome back the Kazakhs who had fled (or whose ancestors had gone) to Mongolia, China, and other neighboring areas during forced collectivization, offering financial incentives to these returnees, *oralman*, in Kazakh.[34] The notion of "return" glosses over the complexity of historical and contemporary movements, threatening to erase the historically porous boundaries between present-day Kazakhstan, Mongolia, and Western China. It suggests an imagined original object that is to be retrieved—a lost past or a lost homeland. Integration has not been easy, and in 2019, President Kassym-Jomart Tokayev proposed replacing the term *oralman*, which had become stigmatized, with *kandas*, or "compatriot."[35]

While new political conditions after the end of the Soviet Union led to new issues of borders and the authority of states on either side of them, movement continues. The notion of "home" remains potent, whether in political discourses about returning to a homeland or in the form of a particular house. As Sergey Abashin has shown in his research on labor migration from Uzbekistan to Russia, this home is loaded with moral significance for both migrants and their family members left behind; and its physical upkeep requires constant work to make and maintain, which also demands the continual coming and going of migrants in order to procure necessary resources.[36]

I visited ALZhIR and KarLag in the summer of 2017, while spending the summer in Astana. In the capital city, the narrative of building something in the middle of nowhere is a popular one, each new instance erasing the people who had been there before. This trope was key to the Virgin Lands campaign in Soviet times, and it reappeared with the movement of the capital city from Almaty to Tselinograd in 1997. The city's reinvention inspired renaming: Aqmola and Aqmolinsk under the Russian Empire and in early Soviet years, Tselinograd in 1961, Aqmola in 1991, Astana from 1997–2019, Nur-Sultan from 2019–2022, and then back to Astana. The flashy new architecture and influx of Kazakhs, who were presumed to be prioritized for government positions, brought feelings of alienation for those who had lived in the city longer. When I visited, non-Kazakh populations described feelings of marginalization, prompting many to consider leaving. Residents of the Soviet-era Right Bank continued to refer to their side of the city by its Soviet name of Tselinograd, creating a chronotopic contrast with the futuristic new neighborhoods on the other side of the Ishim River. This new side includes, nonetheless, nods to Kazakh heritage. The yurt inspired a Norman Foster–designed building, Khan Shatyr, a shopping mall with an expensive indoor beach at the top, like an oasis of warmth and capitalist indulgence in the middle of the so-called naked steppe.[37]

I was in Astana that summer to teach American student ambassadors of EXPO Astana. Exhibits and pavilions optimistically envisioned the country as a world leader in "Future Energy," the theme of the EXPO. The forward-facing chronotope established on the EXPO grounds found use mainly for elements of the past that could be conveniently integrated into messages of techno-optimism. It depicted the land as vast and full of natural resources. It exploited tropes of Kazakh hospitality to encourage multinational partnerships. The EXPO sprang up on the edge of the city, across from the new national university and next to a new shopping center, as a monument to the future. Meanwhile, ALZhIR was only a thirty-minute drive—close, by Kazakhstani standards, but without public buses or information at the EXPO about how to get there. Each site offered visitors a particular space-time. If children were poignant victims of Stalinist purges at ALZhIR, in EXPO pavilions their smiling faces promised an energy-efficient future.

Each movement—into or out of a space—affects more than just those bodies in motion. At Hope House, children's reunions with their parents were promised but temporarily deferred. Two days after Nurlan's performance for my camera and his invention of instruments, I returned to Hope House to find out that his mother had taken him home on the afternoon of my last visit. I do not know if Nurlan had known he was leaving. The children's returns and the technologies mediating their departures are the focus of chapter 6. However, writing about the loss experienced by the children living at Hope House—describing that moment when Kashtanka finds herself on the cold pavement, trying to recall how she got there—cannot easily be separated from the anticipation of return, and the second loss that this will bring.

# MEETING A STRANGER

*When soft, fluffy snow had completely stuck to Kashtanka's back and head, and from exhaustion she had plunged into a heavy slumber, suddenly the entrance door clicked, creaked, and hit her on the side. She jumped up. Through the open door came some kind of man. . . . As Kashtanka squealed and got under his feet, he could not help noticing her. He leaned down and asked:*

*"Pup, where did you come from? Did I hurt you? Oh, poor thing, poor thing. . . . Well, don't be angry, don't be angry. . . . It was my fault."*

*Kashtanka looked up at the stranger.*

This moment produced ire in Kuba, the director, during rehearsals of the puppet play. Baqytzhan, the human actor playing the stranger, walked through a doorway onto the sparse stage in a fur-trimmed coat and black top hat, almost stepping on the dog. When he crouched down to inspect her, he kept looking off to the side rather than directly at Kashtanka, no matter how many times Kuba corrected him.

"The first point of emphasis should be that it's unexpected," Kuba explained in the penultimate day of rehearsal. "And after that, the emphasis should be that you're in love with her from first sight." Kuba continued, as if the link between all these points was straightforward: "And immediately your thoughts go to the perspective that you're going to make a performance with her. That's why you name her 'Aunt' [*Tётka*]."

Baqytzhan had a broad frame, a round face, and a voice that boomed and grumbled when he voiced a bear or wolf puppet. In this scene of meeting Kashtanka, however, crouching before her, he speaks softly, warmly, asking if he has hurt her. As Kashtanka growls at the stranger, he smiles and tells her not to get angry. He says to her, "Come with me. Maybe you'll come in handy for something." Walking offstage, he continues to call back, "Let's go!" *Poidёm!*

Baqytzhan's meeting with Kashtanka celebrates the opportunities that displacement offers. The last chapter examined moments of loss and deferral. This chapter explores *destrangement*, the process of transforming a relationship of stranger into one of familiarity. In literature on "attachment," the stranger functions as a potential source of anxiety. A single, primary caregiver is supposed to

**ILLUSTRATION 8. KASHTANKA MEETS A STRANGER**   *"Pup, where did you come from? Did I hurt you? Oh, poor thing, poor thing. . . . Well, don't be angry, don't be angry. . . . It was my fault." Kashtanka looked up at the stranger.*

be the source and sign of a child's security. However, the children of Hope House prove capable of distinguishing among a complex field of caregivers whom they bring closer. This chapter asks, when someone vulnerable meets a stranger, how does the stranger win trust? What conditions will drive one to turn to an unfamiliar face, even if trust has not been won? Animation is a process of destrangement, of holding and manipulating, and of marking and remarking on relationships of belonging. Relationships often elude easy categorization, as two girls show in their doll play. Sometimes the lack of a label permits roles of care to overlap and become usefully muddled. Proximity can give rise to friction or affection. These relationships are often hierarchical and cannot be taken for granted as permanent.

*Poidëm!* The same command that her first master, the carpenter, used to call Kashtanka out of the house in the morning now compels her to follow this unknown man to a new home. The stranger is ready to take in the lost dog, yet his comment about her coming in handy raises questions regarding his intentions. Baqytzhan leads the dog away, while Bolat—the dog's puppeteer—walks close behind, holding her by the rods that extend from her head and torso. In this play, and in its rehearsal, there are many masters: the carpenter and this unfamiliar man, the puppeteer, and the director. They have various powers over Kashtanka and the other puppets. Kuba, the director, holds sway over all of them. He also keeps himself at the greatest distance, watching from the other side of the prosce- nium and approaching when he needs to show them something.[1] Bolat, as pup- peteer, is in the most intimate relationship with the dog, animating and voicing her as he handles her. At certain moments, the dog will be set free from the rods and will get thrown from one set of hands to another. The dog has no problem accepting this, of course, for the dog is a puppet. But in order for her to continue to exist as Kashtanka, each pair of hands needs to know how to handle her. They must gain at least a fleeting intimacy with her, or she will become a mere object as she is passed around.

## Destrangement Effects

I use "destrangement" to describe the transformative process of strangers be- coming familiars. I offer it as a more expansive term than "attachment." "Attach- ment" effectively evokes a bond between two people (and could, conveniently, imply intermediating materialities that connect two bodies, such as strings or rods). However, Western psychological literature has encumbered it with a rather overwhelming amount of baggage.[2] Theories of attachment have a complex rela- tionship with the institutional care of children. Attachment theory was devel- oped, in part, in response to observations of children separated from their parents, such as a study describing American children who spent their first three years in an institution (and afterward lived in foster care) as "incapable of recip- rocating tender feeling" and exhibiting only a "meager love potential."[3] Attach- ment was later used to diagnose differences between children who had spent time in Eastern European orphanages and those growing up in family homes.[4] People use descriptors of attachment style to predict future relations. I use destrange- ment to move away from diagnosis. People approach one another through varied and surprising processes. Literatures on attachment and psychoanalysis none- theless pose important questions about substitutability. Who or what can stand in for someone else, and what are the effects of this? In attachment literature, the relationship between mother and child is often treated as the basis for all relation- ships that will follow. If the child has already been diagnosed with a meager love potential, and if each new relationship substitutes the first one, all relationships are doomed before they begin (discussed further in chapter 5).

Another possibility is to treat each new relationship as an opportunity for working out the dangers and promises of intimacy.[5] Freud's writing on transference—when a patient treats the psychoanalyst like a parental figure or love object—similarly relies on substitutability, but it is not merely a repetition of a past relationship mapped onto a new body. Freud (1949a) treats transference with some ambivalence, as a process that is dangerous but inevitable. The psychoanalyst understands how to use transference to help the patient lift repression. Rather than limiting such possibilities to psychoanalytic encounters, destrangement attends to the ways that individuals make use of others (human and nonhuman) to learn about and to practice care and intimacy.

Destrangement does not categorize or compare intimacies, but embraces the unspoken nature of fleeting moments of closeness. As discussed in the introduction regarding defamiliarization and familiarization techniques, avant-garde theories offer insight regarding the effectiveness of playing with expectations and disrupting them. By pushing us out of modes of habituation, estrangement can highlight truths that had been tacit and offer a perspective to see new possibilities. Destrangement can make strangers unexpectedly familiar. This offers new understandings of intimacy—or intimation, as a process. Theorizations of the uncanny, discussed in chapter 1, have mined relationships between familiar and strange. Children, Jentsch ([1906] 2008) argues, are most susceptible to the "psychical uncertainty" of the uncanny because there are so many phenomena they do not understand. Concerns about the uncanny provoke us not only to consider an internal psychological state but also to explore the effects of contact, of unexpected meetings, calling on us to wade around in murky boundaries. However, the children at Hope House make productive use of ambiguities—developing relationships with humans who are at once familiar and strange and taking joy in objects that alternate between animate and inanimate.

Transference implies that the new relationship will somehow be modeled after the primary one, rather than allowing for distinction between these relationships. Hope House avoided substitution. Constant celebrations of motherhood, and caregivers' denial of occupying such a role, suggest anxiety over the primacy of the mother and a resultant insistency on it. As a consequence, the home simultaneously practiced destrangement within, while cultivating a longing for a mother who remained out of reach. War and famine created overcrowded orphanages all over the Soviet Union in the 1930s and 1940s, making children's lives unbearable, impossible. In 1934, there were an estimated sixty thousand orphans in Kazakhstan (Kindler 2018, 165). As orphanages struggled to manage the populations they had, Soviet propaganda appealed to mothers to not abandon their children. Motherhood became idealized both to prevent overcrowded institutions and to counter the profound demographic crisis the Soviet Union faced after World War II.[6]

In Kazakhstan, certain substitutions were possible if the child stayed within kin networks. Kazakh traditions include temporary fostering of young children by grandparents and the exchange of children between brothers. Extended kin and other social or "household" networks continue to play important social, political, and economic roles for Kazakhs.[7] Various social and material dynamics—from the smallness of Soviet apartments to norms acquired through contemporary labor migration—have contributed to an emphasis on the nuclear family without eliminating the importance of more extensive kin ties.[8]

Attachment experiments often leave a child alone with an adult stranger. However, at Hope House we could consider the children to be strangers. Georg Simmel (1950, 402) describes the stranger as "the person who comes today and stays tomorrow . . . the potential wanderer: although he has not moved on, he has not quite overcome the freedom of coming and going." The temporary nature of the home, with its attendant discourses of hope and future return, rendered the children potential wanderers (though they had little choice over this coming and going). They were like guests in a house that was never quite theirs. At the same time, they had to be constantly prepared to greet new guests—as sponsors, volunteers, and government representatives came in and out of the home.

Thinking of the children as guests and hosts fits them into a trope of hospitality in Kazakhstan, in which warm locals provide a welcoming environment despite the harsh climate and barren terrain. It was a trait that Kazakh friends often articulated to me. Semey—the new name for the city of Semipalatinsk, where Dostoevsky was so reluctant to go and eager to leave—celebrates the writer's time in the city.[9] The small house where he lived became a museum that I visited in 2010. Not having any of Dostoevsky's own belongings, the museum's small rooms were filled, instead, with objects donated by people of the city dated to the period when Dostoevsky was there. Embroidered pillowcases were donated by someone who happened to share his initials. With the museum, the people of the town conjured an imagined Dostoevsky, positioning him not as a prisoner or an exile, but as a guest.

Exhibits at ALZhIR and KarLag similarly emphasize the hospitality of Kazakhs toward the forced deportees and prisoners. ALZhIR tour guides tell this story: the women prisoners were working outside one day when they felt themselves being pelted with small, hard objects. At first, they wondered at the cruelty of the nearby villagers—throwing rocks at them! They realized that what looked like pebbles were actually *qurt*, a hard, dry ball made of a salty kind of yogurt. This anecdote made it into a film about ALZhIR, as well (dir. Raibaev 2017). In the film's main plot, a prisoner's first child dies while they are living in the camp. Her second child (fathered by a kind Kazakh guard) is temporarily placed with a generous Kazakh family before the mother is freed and resumes care of her child. The film upholds salient tropes of Kazakhstan as a cold and harsh land made bearable by local hospitality.[10]

Forced deportees, reluctant "guests," made their own contributions to Soviet Kazakhstan. The children's theater director Natalia Sats was arrested and sent to ALZhIR in 1937. Once released, she established the first children's theater in Alma-Ata (years after the puppet theater was first built), before returning to Moscow to resume her work in children's theater there (Adler 2012). Many deportees stayed in Kazakhstan. The legacy of forced deportations and other catastrophic state projects profoundly shaped the region's demographics and institutions, so Kazakhstan's history and identity are tied not only to Kazakhness but also to a complex multiethnic, multilingual coexistence. As groups were forcibly moved from German, Polish, Ukrainian, or Korean borderlands, these identities were maintained, in part, through government-funded theaters and other institutions.[11] Kazakhstan was the only nation to emerge from the Soviet Union without its titular nationality comprising the majority of the population, due in large part to the ethnic Russian population, but with a number of other significant minorities as well (Dave 2007).

Since then, demographics have shifted, with ethnic Russians and other non-Kazakhs leaving (Bandey and Rather 2013), while government efforts to repatriate *kandas* populations have increased the Kazakh population. State policies have worked to maintain a delicate balance promoting the Kazakh language without alienating minorities, encouraging citizens to become trilingual in Kazakh, Russian, and English.[12] The Soviet spirit of the "Friendship of the People" can still be found in various celebrations and ceremonies in Kazakhstan.[13] At the puppet theater and at Hope House, the Friendship of the People as ideology was sustained when children and puppets donned ethnic costumes to offer traditional folk dances and reenact scenes in which native Kazakhs played generous hosts to their guests, offering sustenance and respite.[14]

To host can be an act of kindness, but it is also a mark of power. Describing Kazakhstan as "host," rather than as colonized subject, overlooks the ways in which these "guests" arrived uninvited and often did not particularly wish to be there. This narrative stakes claims to land and to identity. Historical narratives presuppose and entail authority.[15] The independent Kazakhstani state could deny responsibility for the Soviet government's actions, promote their attention to Kazakh interests, and maintain a rhetoric of inclusivity regarding the hundreds of nationalities that comprise the population.[16] When the stranger takes in Kashtanka, it is as if the dog is his guest, but he seeks to make something else of their relationship, to establish himself as a new master. He mentions, already, that she may be of use to him someday. In the theater, there is no question that the puppet artist masters the puppet. At Hope House, the children called the women "aunt," but did it index intimacy, respect, or both?

# Unspoken Fascinations and Intimate Animations

The structure of Hope House meant that children had multiple women looking after them, none of these caregivers or aides seeking to replace the mothers to whom the children eventually would return. Nonetheless, affection and trust were inevitable and indispensable to their work. A number of rules kept this order of attachments in place. Children should not call teachers "mom." They should not sit on adults' laps. Directors did not describe the group as a family. The children were not encouraged to see one another as brothers and sisters, as they were in *detdom*, but rather as friends (*dostar*, in Kazakh) to one another.

Nonetheless, each apai had her own style for handling the children. Some caregivers had clear favorites; for others, particular children got under their skin. After the children awoke from their afternoon nap, teachers and aides often had them sit quietly and watch television until all the children awoke. Television time often went on for longer if only an aide was on duty. Children were to sit still during these times and take out no toys. They often grew restless, especially when viewing a program that didn't particularly interest them. They sometimes made up tiny games, contorting their faces at each other, manipulating a button on their shirt or a piece of string they had found on the floor. Ainura liked to tap my shoulder and then deny having done so, while I feigned confusion and exasperation. We played these games quietly, lest we annoy the aide on duty. One day, before entering the classroom, I thought I overheard the sound of a slap. When I entered, I found Tamilia, one of the twins, crying. The aide was minding the children while Zhanel Apai, the teacher on duty that day, attended a meeting. She offered me no explanation for what had happened to Tamilia. They watched a Chinese soap opera, dubbed into Kazakh, with fight scenes that the children enjoyed reenacting afterward. When Zhanel Apai returned, the aide recounted the unfolding drama of the television program. Suspecting the aide on duty of having struck Tamilia, I debated whether to go to the director or talk to someone else about her, not having witnessed anything directly. As I stalled on making a decision over the course of a few days, I gradually realized that she had already left the home. The constant rotation of helpers made it hard to keep track of who was supposed to work on which day. I did not ask what had happened to her.

Teachers' affections for the children were often difficult to perceive. A pat on the head or holding a child's hand offered a bit of extra physical comfort to a child who was having a hard day. The teachers of my group were warmer toward children in other groups, especially the younger ones. When Aigul or Saltanat took our group outside and happened to find a group of toddlers along the way, these teachers' voices got higher, their faces more expressive. They would find their favorite child, smile, and hug them in a way they must have felt unwarranted to do with the children in their charge. They needed their group to stay in line and follow commands. At the same time, teachers performed care constantly, maintaining order to ensure effective lessons, threatening to withhold treats if the children did not eat their more nutritious food, and going through the trouble of bundling the children up so that they could get fresh air on a cold winter day.

The children knew who would give them more affection, and they had their favorites. Maksat, an outgoing five-year-old when I met him, doted on Zhanel Apai. On my first day at Hope House, in the fall, Zhanel confided in me that she was pregnant. As the winter wore on and she began to show, she spoke with me, in Russian, about feeling sick and tired, or needing to pee all the time. Maksat often insisted on holding Zhanel Apai's hand when they walked from one place to another. He would hug her, whether she was sitting in one of the small chairs or standing up, so that he only reached her waist. Zhanel Apai sometimes accepted Maksat's attention. Other times, she shook him away. When she was quite obviously showing, Zhanel told me how Maksat had surprised her by pointing to her belly and asking her if there was a baby inside. Apparently assuming the children knew nothing of pregnancy, she wondered how he could have known. She had still said nothing directly to any of the children about it. I guessed it was because he was the only child who spoke Russian and Kazakh fluently. She supposed that explained it. One day, a couple of months before Zhanel was due, it was her last day at Hope House. This was when the children were told she was leaving. She planned to take two years of leave. The children being in their penultimate year, they would depart from Hope House before their teacher's return. That afternoon, she had tea with the other teachers in the bedroom while the children played in the classroom. There was not, as far as I could tell, any kind of ceremony for her to say goodbye to the children. She said she would come to visit, but I never saw or heard of her returning. She ended up taking another job.

Just as the assurance of parents' return was embedded in daily lessons, teachers cultivated affective bonds within Hope House in ways that often appeared routine and perfunctory. Each morning at the beginning of her lessons, Aigul Apai had the students emerge, single file, from the bedroom into the classroom. Before they made their way to their desks, they stood in a circle. Aigul Apai often led them in a round of blessings. One by one, they would turn to the person next to them and wish them something—"Don't get sick," "Study well." As they went through these routines, Aigul Apai's smile was restrained. The children's voices, as they announced their wishes for one another, were loud; they enunciated as if reciting a poem they had memorized. "Be good!" "Be healthy!" "Listen to the teacher!"

At larger orphanages, such as those in Soviet or post-Soviet Russia, caregivers looked after so many children that they came to see them as bodies—as mouths to feed, as bottoms to clean.[17] The teachers at Hope House saw the children as individuals: Ainura was the star pupil. Maksat was the ham, on whom teachers would call to offer a risqué interpretation of the "Gangnam Style" dance. Erlan was the "most hooligan." Olzhas was spoiled and babyish. The teachers assessed certain children differently, some more tolerant of crying, others more patient with rowdiness.[18] The mild children, the quiet ones, may have fallen between the cracks a bit, but not completely. Not everything was ideal or fair or easy, but caregivers and children, like the parents, were mostly doing their best amid a difficult situation.

The caregivers at Hope House had to learn to manage the children in order to care for them as they saw fit. I understood the challenges of this as soon as the teachers left me alone with the children. Even the best behaved began climbing on furniture and taking out forbidden toys. They laughed at my efforts to stop them. The teachers impressed me with their abilities to get the children to sit in their seats with hands folded, to memorize and recite poems or offer wishes to one another, or to help the adults sweep leaves on the playground. On the day I returned to Hope House and found Nurlan had gone home, Saltanat Apai expressed surprise that I was sad. He was supposed to go home. They were all supposed to go home, she reminded me.[19] Aigul Apai would make similar remarks. However, she kept in touch with the mothers. She would assure me, in the weeks that followed a child's departure, that she had heard from the mother, that the child was doing well in school. She would note, after Nurlan had left, how he had been quiet but intelligent. He knew how to observe, and he watched and learned before acting because he was a thoughtful child. This was as close as she would come to admitting that she missed him.

## Useful Objects and Persons

"Manipulation" implies violation, in the sense of a nonconsensual handling of another's body or emotions. However, it can take the form of care. The psychologist D. W. Winnicott posited that children needed to learn to use objects in order to use other people properly. The transitional object helps the infant distinguish self from mother. This thing—a doll, a stuffed animal, the corner of a blanket—exists somewhere between "me" and "not-me." It provides comfort rather than the uneasiness suggested by the uncanny. Simultaneously within and beyond the child's control, the child can hate the object and wish its destruction; yet because the object has a real, physical presence, this wish will go unfulfilled. The infant, able to understand that the mother, too, is beyond the child's control, will be able to move forward in the world without worrying about the destructiveness of their own thoughts (Winnicott 1971). In this way, the children learn to manipulate objects and eventually to use people in ways that are helpful rather than violent and abusive.

Both caregivers and puppet artists are defined by their work with animated bodies. In popular discourse, to call one person a puppet of another implies a clear definition of roles—of one being in control of the other. Yet puppeteers' description of the puppet as an extension of self erases the division between the two bodies.[20] The puppeteer must be responsive to the doll's affordances. Animation was described in chapter 1 as a transposal of energy from one body to another. Puppeteers employ mostly their hands and arms to make the whole body of their puppet move. As the puppeteer tilts the crossbars of a marionette down to the left, the puppet's right leg takes a step into the air. Sometimes the puppet latches onto the feet of the puppeteer as well so that their steps are in unison even if the puppet is half the size of the puppeteer standing behind it. Puppeteers might work to hide themselves from the viewers' sight, or they might try to make the work invisible by staying entirely in view of the audience, interacting with the puppet as if they are interlocutors or friends. While puppeteers play with the possibilities of being present as figures on the stage to a greater or lesser extent, regarding their own relationship with the puppet, they often speak of the puppet as a "second I" (Barker 2019b; and see chapter 3).

Both power and sentiment are part of animation, whether a master is taking in a new animal, an artist holds a puppet and manipulates it, a teacher looks after a child, or a child feeds a doll. An act of intimation suggests an incomplete narrative: "To intimate is to communicate with the sparest of signs and gestures, and at its root intimacy has the quality of eloquence and brevity. But intimacy also involves an aspiration for a narrative about something shared, a story about both oneself and others that will turn out in a particular way" (Berlant 1998, 281). The primary narrative that the caregivers and children at Hope House cultivated together was one in which the future would not be shared. They nonetheless managed to intimate to one another certain signs of their closeness, of their resonance.

Puppetry requires a complex production format of participation, in which the author, principal, and animator are usually completely separate from one another. Who deserves responsibility for an utterance might be up for debate.[21] The notion that multiple bodies make up a unified being is one Émile Durkheim ([1912] 1995, 151) proposed regarding totemism, that "all the beings classified in a single clan—men, animals, plants, inanimate objects—are only modalities of the totemic being. . . . All really are of the same flesh, in the sense that they all participate in the nature of the totemic animal." Various parties participate in animating the figure located in the puppet's body, from the puppeteer, who manipulates the object, to the viewer, who projects meaning onto it.

Puppetry is also a kind of possession, a conjuring of the figure and a placement of that figure into the body of the animated. Puppeteers of the southern Italian Pulcinella tradition apprentice with an elder master who can trace a genealogy of learning back for generations. As a result of this lineage, these puppeteers describe themselves as possessed by the spirits of the Pulcinella puppeteers who came before them. As they give life to an inorganic body, a past life occupies them. The puppeteer transposes the self into the puppet, creating a separation of body and soul. However, the puppeteer's body remains connected, physically, to the puppet's, even if kept at the distance of the strings or rods that are necessary to this manipulation. In the case of Pulcinella, the puppeteer's hand literally possesses the puppet's body, filling the puppet's otherwise empty interior. The voice of Pulcinella enters the body of the puppeteer through the mechanism of the swazzle, a reed that the puppeteer positions in the back of the throat and employs whenever voicing Pulcinella but not the other characters. Gaspare, a Pulcinella puppeteer (who appears in chapter 5), noted the danger of choking on this device. It is not only Pulcinella—subject to and perpetrator of much violence among puppets—who is made vulnerable in this relationship. This is another way of letting oneself be haunted: while the vivifying of Pulcinella projects life outside, the puppeteer offers their own body as a space to be filled by another's spirit and voice.

Animation acts as a process of proximation. Intimacy is both a necessary precondition and an outcome for acts of possession, manipulation, and imitation at Hope House and in the puppet theater. Through these acts, parties transform relationships from strangers into something else. If they are not family, they are at least familiar to one another.

## You Scold Your Own More

In examining the tensions between the familiar and the strange, whether thinking of the effect as uncanny or artful, we tend to focus on the strangeness. However, a stranger can become a new intimate, even if we find traces of someone from the past. Meyerhold, who worked mainly with humans but was intrigued by puppets, describes a director who attempts to make the puppet imitate a real human as closely as possible. He inevitably fails. In another (imagined) theater, the director realizes this impossibility and embraces it for greater effect. The director accepts the puppet as it is. Meyerhold uses the puppet as a model for the actor to adopt. Instead of imitating a real person when acting on stage, the actor should create a "mask" through gesture and movement (Meĭerkhol'd and Braun 1969). Both puppet and mask, by not resembling any particular person too closely, create distance between the performing body onstage and the viewer watching across the proscenium. Generality leaves room for the spectator's imagination. The spectator, through their own work of suspended disbelief, brings the characters closer by projecting a familiar face onto the mask of the actor onstage. Meyerhold's process is one of creating distance that projection then overcomes.[22]

There were various ways in which the staging of *Kashtanka* at the puppet theater worked to remind the spectator that what they watched was only make-believe, challenging them to do part of the work of animation through projection. The beginnings and endings of scenes made and broke points of contact between puppeteer and puppet, as they moved in and out of instances of animation. When Kashtanka slept, her puppeteer separated himself from her, so that she lay inert on the floor. With this, the spectator watched as the puppet moved from animate to inanimate. This technique of deanimation was exploited in a later scene (discussed in chapter 5), but these routine acts of taking out and putting away the puppet enabled the spectator to witness moments of contact and release between puppeteer and puppet. Privy to the artifice, the spectator can participate in its construction.

Kashtanka's initial encounters with the new home and its inhabitants are full of wonder and delight. On her first morning, Kashtanka makes her way through the door and offstage. The doorway is wheeled aside, while Maral and Koralai push large wooden boxes out with their puppets, the gander and the cat, resting on top. They awaken and begin their morning grooming routines while Kashtanka enters this new room and sniffs around. When she finally looks up and notices them on their boxes, there is a pause. The animals regard one another silently. Then a cacophony of squawking, barking, and rawrrring explodes. The master rushes in, yelling, "Quiet! Quiet! To your places!" He reprimands the goose and cat and tells Kashtanka not to be afraid, assuring her that she is in good company (*khoroshaia publika*—literally, that they are a "good public," perhaps a way of hinting at the fact that their little household is also a troupe). They rehearse this scene many times, trying to work out the master's way of dealing with each of the animals. In early rehearsals, the master works to quiet all of the animals at once.

Staging this moment led the artists to consider their own relationships to one another. One day, having rehearsed the scene a couple of times, Kuba realizes:

"In fact, with Kashtanka you need to scold her less." He explains, "Usually you scold *your own* more" (*obychno bol'she rugayesh'sia na svoikh*).

"*Da da da da*," Baqytzhan agrees.

"And for those you're used to it's already more dangerous, right? . . . If some new actors come in," Kuba elaborates, "I'm going to scold them less than you. You I know better. You're mine." Some of the actors smile at this. *Svoi* is a reflexive, possessive pronoun that indexes a relationship of belonging between the grammatical subject and object of a relationship. It is also used without an object that is possessed to refer broadly to people one thinks of as one's own—or as "our own." It signals a relationship of closeness (Yurchak 2005). Here, Kuba describes his relationship with the actors as analogous to the master-animal bond in the narrated event in a way that presupposes (and thus entails) a relationship of *svoi*—of belonging—despite his relative newness to the theater and the novelty of his directorial style. The dog is not yet *svoi*, but now the new master will bring the dog closer. He and the other animals sit to think about a name for the dog (though the director insists the master knew from the beginning). Finally, Baqytzhan waves his index finger and says, "*Vot chto*"—"That's it! You'll be '*Tëtka*.' Understand?" he asks, smiling, rising from the table and leaning down to Kashtanka. "Tëtka!" He walks offstage, calling behind him a third time, "Tëtka!"

The new master has renamed Kashtanka "Auntie," for reasons that will become apparent in the final scene, at the circus. For now, however, choosing a name that acts as a kinship term helps to draw the dog into the new home. It helps make her *svoi*. The relationship here, of master and pet or trainer and trainee, is complex, as suggested by the name *Tëtka*—a term for both family and respected women—so that the master will seem to speak up to her, while he will literally talk down to the small dog (Friedrich and Dil 1979). Kuba's comparison not only helps the actors to understand the action on the stage but also has effects on their relationship. While the act of naming the dog a kin term creates closeness, Kuba creates an iconic indexical link between himself and Baqytzhan by likening the master-animal relationship to the director-actor relationship. The actors are *svoi* to the director, while the master stands in for the director on the stage.

Kuba was, himself, a new master with new methods. The actors claimed that his approach was different from any they had known before. They called this approach "completely new," "European," and thus not "Soviet." Kuba had been working with them for approximately eight months, while many of the artists had been at the theater for decades. There were several puppeteer couples who were married to one another and had children together, including two couples within the cast of *Kashtanka*. There were levels of belonging—to one another, and to the theater—that would be impossible for Kuba to achieve over just a few months. Yet the cast worked with an intensity and enthusiasm that they had lacked in other productions. They were receptive to his new techniques. In his efforts to bring them closer—to make them *svoi* to one another—Kuba here acknowledges that there is a danger that comes with it, that he might scold them harshly.[23]

## Strange Situations

The trajectories of Kashtanka and of the children at Hope House are structured, in some ways, as prolonged versions of a "strange situation," a type of experimental condition developed by psychologists to study children's reactions to new people and environments. Mary Ainsworth's is the best known, developed as a way to classify attachment styles. Ainsworth's situation consisted of eight "episodes": (1) Mother (M), observer (O), and baby (B, forty-nine to fifty-one weeks old) entered a room, then (O) left; (2) M put B down; (3) A stranger (S) joined them, and M left; (4) B played alone if "happily engaged," if upset, S tried to distract or comfort B; (5) M returned, and S left; (6) M left B alone in room; (7) S returned; and (8) M returned.[24] Each of these phases lasted three minutes or less. The reunion moments were of undetermined length, and the phases in which the child was alone or alone with the stranger were shortened if the child was too distressed (Ainsworth and Bell 1970, 54).

The stranger's position is ambiguous. She might heighten the strangeness of the situation or she might provide comfort to the child. The child's reaction to being left alone was barely relevant to Ainsworth's concerns, however. The child's reunion with the mother was the crucial moment for her. Could the child be comforted?[25] Ainsworth had previously carried out naturalistic home observations, in England and in Uganda, but this was time-consuming. Her strange situation allowed her to study something as complex as a child's attachment to their mother in the efficient environment of a lab. The study, which established the "styles" of attachment, was widely replicated. Ainsworth believed the environment and stranger should not be particularly threatening in and of themselves. She designed her eight episodes to progress in such a way that they would introduce the least threatening situations first (Ainsworth and Bell 1970). The strange situation should be strange, but not too strange.

Other experiments around this time studied children's reactions to novel people and places.[26] One focused on the stranger rather than the mother. In this case, girls three and a half to four and a half years old were put into four groups and introduced to an unfamiliar situation designed to elicit a range of anxiety levels, depending on whether they were left alone with the stranger immediately or not, and depending on whether they were placed in the "low anxiety" room or the "high anxiety" room. A description of the latter reads like a horror film screenplay:

> The child, on entering the room, faced a slow-burning alcohol lamp standing on a stainless steel tray. Next to it was a pair of scissors, a white paper tissue, and a pencil. The pictures of the smiling faces were replaced with a group of sad faces. The soundtrack heard from the adjacent room was made up of the following sounds, a loud banging on a metal object, a child crying, and a high-pitched shriek. . . . After about 12 min, and following a loud continuous shriek, the red door opened very slowly . . . and a hand in an arm-length black glove reaching in slowly, put out the lamp and withdrew, closing the door once more. Within two or three minutes a crying sound was heard. (Rosenthal 1967, 123)

In Ainsworth's study, experimenters only left a child alone for up to three minutes. Here, the child is left in this room for twelve minutes—and then is faced with the opening of a red door and a gloved hand that extinguishes a light in an already threatening environment. The child was not totally alone; there was an adult—either the mother or a stranger—in the next room. With this experiment, what Miriam Rosenthal aimed "to induce was some kind of vague apprehension. We tried to make the child wonder 'Who knows what is going on behind that red door . . . it is obviously very strange . . . is it coming to get me?'" (123). Rosenthal then charted how each child sought attention and proximity to the stranger.

This study interests me, not merely because of its weirdness (and its usefulness in illustrating the need for research ethics oversight). Unlike Ainsworth's focus on the mother-child dyad, one of Rosenthal's main findings was that in high anxiety conditions, children will seek proximity to strangers. It focuses not on categorizing a particular child's bond with their primary caregiver. It investigates instead the conditions under which a child will seek comfort from an unknown entity. Psychologists have long cited institutions such as orphanages as offering proof that a child lacking an attachment figure will fail to develop properly in all sorts of measures. Such studies are useful in advocating for intervention, but they also contribute to a pervasive stigmatization of institutionalized children. Attachment needs to become broader and less hierarchical if it is to hold up across cultures (Gaskins 2013). In Kazakhstan, the mother-child relationship was certainly highly valued, but alternative configurations were part of Kazakh tradition, as discussed earlier. In this respect, Hope House was not so removed from local tradition, and yet the adults there needed to remind the children of the abnormality of their situation so that they would be prepared to leave the home.[27]

Despite a seeming flexibility regarding caregivers within kin networks and sometimes by the state, not just anyone could care adequately for just any child. Many I met in Kazakhstan told me that the adoption of an unrelated child was bound to fail. These individuals usually had no experience with adoption or with institutions such as Hope House. Though UNICEF officials whom I met in 2010 and in 2017 believed domestic adoption was increasing, official publications from the organization show an actual decline in the rate of adoptions from 2010 to 2015.[28] Moreover, representatives of UNICEF with whom I spoke averred that domestic adoption remained an act to be conducted secretly. Parents strove to adopt the youngest child possible, one who resembled one of the adoptive parents. The child could be strange, but not too strange. The adoptive family might move to another town, and would keep the adoption a secret—from their own child and from outsiders alike.

Rather than making a simple distinction between mothers and strangers, families I met in Kazakhstan prioritized the categorization of family over not-family in their considerations of alternative arrangements for child rearing. Each solution—whether institutional or private—required an understanding between the children and adults regarding who they were to each other. Children at Hope House exhibited, on the one hand, the ability to discriminate among the various adults coming through their lives. They also accepted that care from mothers or from others might, in the end, look quite similar in practice.

## Playing the Doll

Just as Kuba characterized the director—and the animals' master—as sometimes harsher or stricter toward his own actors, so did the teachers take responsibility for the children of their own groups in ways that sometimes looked stern. Nonetheless, they treated the children with respect, promising them a life as future leaders. Hope House offered a more intimate child-to-adult ratio than many larger orphanages, and the teachers stayed with groups fairly consistently. However, the rotation of helpers meant that children found themselves looked after by a number of different adults. They understood that they were expected to allow themselves to be picked up by strangers, whether it was a new caregiver or a representative from an organization making a one-time visit. All the same, with known caregivers, they exhibited a sophisticated understanding of what they could do in front of whom and which caregivers were most likely to show affection upon seeing them. I didn't need to exert authority over the children, so I had the luxury of allowing myself to be soft, even if it interfered with my status as observer. I have a video of the following example, in which I let myself become a pliant body of sorts.

I sit down in front of Zhamilia, who stands in front of me with play scissors. As she styles my bangs and smooths my hair behind my ears, Maksat and Maisa see what she is doing and come over. Maksat takes a stethoscope from the shelf and trades it with Zhamilia for the play scissors. He cuts my hair from behind while Zhamilia checks my heart. Maisa gives me a shot. Zhamilia announces that we will have tea. Other children, unconcerned with my grooming, begin to take toys from the play kitchen area as well.

The children's behavior changes suddenly when Altyn Apai, an aide, enters the room. As she crosses to the bedroom, carrying clean laundry, the kids casually back away from me, hiding their toys behind their backs or setting them down. They stand, rather awkwardly, in front of the television, pretending to watch it. They wait until Altyn Apai is in the bedroom before they resume playing with the toys and with me (See Illustration 9). Maisa touches my front and my back, dressing me in invisible clothes. The boys try to take blocks from the shelf, but I tell them to ask Apai. They run into the bedroom and return, having received the teacher's permission. The children leave me to dump blocks onto the floor.

When the children fixed my hair, gave me shots, or applied pretend lotion to my face, they treated me at once as an object of their care and as a kind of living doll. They knew they were not really cutting my hair or injecting anything into my bloodstream; they normally carried out these actions not on other adults or even on other children, but on inert dolls. They sometimes tested my willingness to act as an object: They sandwiched bits of my hair between interlocking blocks so that they hung around my head like curlers. They laughed and called for the teachers and helpers to see how ridiculous I was. Sometimes they pulled my hair or pushed the needle into my skin, and I told them it hurt. Occasionally, in doctoring me, they pulled at my clothes and I had to tell them to stop. They knew what was allowed and what was not. They suspended certain actions when another adult walked through, and with this they recognized that I was a different kind of adult, one whom they could feel safe treating like a toy.

Later the same day, the children play while the television shows a Soviet-era animation, *Nu, pogodi!*, on DVD. It captures their attention only when something frightening befalls the protagonist, the Wolf, but it turns out to be just a dream. The children, relieved, resume their play. Tamilia, Olzhas, and I are occupied with a baby doll with a large head. Tamilia voices the baby by making high-pitched noises. Olzhas declares himself the baby's father and calls it a beautiful

**ILLUSTRATION 9. THE CHILDREN FIX ME** With known caregivers, the children exhibited a sophisticated understanding of what they could do in front of whom. I did not need to exert authority over the children, so I had the luxury of allowing myself to be treated as a toy.

baby (*ädemı böpe*). Tamilia hits the doll's head and then brings it to me for comfort. I rub its head. Once the doll feels better, Tamilia helps the baby scoot away.

Olzhas looks up at me, I smile at him, and he laughs for a long time. I ask, "What is it?"

He says, "You're a really funny person." (*Qyzyq adam syz ğoi*) He laughs as he says it, yet this phrase—*qyzyq adam*—describes a person who is interesting, unusual, or even strange.

On this day, the children shifted between fantastic frames they watched on the television and those they created through their play. The children's recognition of primary frameworks included an ability to distinguish among different kinds of adults and their authority over them, whether they showed this by ignoring a new teacher's commands or by backing away from the toys, and me, when an adult with greater authority entered.[29] In my own relationship with them, I was a funny person. I was there to observe their "naturally occurring" play, which in theory meant directing none of their activities and having minimal participation. In reviewing the videos from their play, I see that I put myself in the midst of them so that I could understand what was happening. Even if I was not much of an authority figure, I did interfere, more than I realized at the time, subtly directing their play toward activities I found more interesting. Meanwhile, I took their play with me, their use of me, treating me as a doll or as the doll's caregiver, as an index of their own affections toward me.

## Animating Care

Upon my arrival at Hope House, I was somewhat like the stranger in Ainsworth's study. Though it was some time before teachers or aides left me alone to watch after the children, they seemed to warm up to me quickly, something I observed in other institutions. Children who have spent years in orphanages have been described by psychologists as "indiscriminately affectionate" (Tizard and Hodges 1978, 105), later diagnosed as "disinhibited attachment . . . a valid, and handicapping, clinical pattern that is strongly associated with an institutional rearing" (Rutter et al. 2007, 17). Disinhibited attachment is seen as dangerous because what is to stop such a child from wandering off with a stranger? At the same time, rather than treating such children as pathological, I saw the children at Hope House as ready to accept that a variety of adults coming through the home were there, in different ways, to care for them. That is, they were perhaps less shy than some other children, but they knew how to discriminate among different kinds of adults.

While Freud's essay on the uncanny tends to focus on the displeasure that comes from encountering something that is familiar yet strange, recognizing the qualities of someone you once knew—and loved—can aid the process of destrangement. Transference uses one relationship as a model for another, but there might not always be a straightforward starting point. At Hope House, the children encountered new masters—new apais—on a regular basis. They sometimes figured out how to get away with more when a particular apai, including me, was watching them. Saltanat and Aigul Apai would have denied seeing the children as kin, but they held themselves responsible for the children's care, even if this sometimes meant sharp words or tones. Children often animated the role of caregiver in their play. When they did, they often used kinship terms—*mama* or *papa*—to describe this role.[30] For many of the children, this could scarcely have been modeled after their own individual memories of parental care. Exemplary care came from teachers and helpers.

The useful ambiguity of relationships of care that went undefined became apparent to me when I observed a day of play between two girls who barely knew one another. On a beautiful day in May, just a few days before I am to leave Kazakhstan for the end of my fieldwork, I am filming the children playing outside. My attention turns to Toghzhan and Näziliia. Toghzhan has just joined this group from another. Barely five, she is several months younger and much smaller than Näziliia, but she has no problem stopping Näziliia from taking the fake Barbie with which she plays. Näziliia backs off and acquires a My Little Pony. Later, the two girls sit, side by side, at the bottom of the slide (See Illustration 10). Children in Kazakhstan are to cover their heads when outside, year-round, but Toghzhan and Näziliia have taken off their floppy, round spring hats and have made them into cradles for their doll and pony. They rock their babies back and forth, singing a lullaby. They stand up and set their dolls down at the foot of the slide. Toghzhan begins to walk away. Näziliia puts her foot higher up on the slide, grabbing onto it, as if to scale it. Toghzhan, in the fierce whisper one uses in the presence of a sleeping child, warns her not to. Näziliia pays no heed. Holding onto the slide, she works to shift her weight from her left foot, on the ground, to the right one, on the slide. She loses her balance and falls to the ground, knocking her hat and equine baby off the slide in the process. Näziliia and another girl laugh and take turns reenacting the fall. A more relaxed caregiver than Toghzhan, Näziliia only eventually retrieves the fallen pony and replaces it on the slide.

Their babies sleeping soundly, the girls go to another piece of the playground equipment and run their hands over it, tapping the bars. I ask them what they are doing. Näziliia says they are doing work. Toghzhan announces it is 2:30, and they run back to their dolls. The scheduling reminds me of Hope House's routine, along with the fact that they were doing work while the children were sleeping. "Are you teachers?" I ask. Näziliia explains that Toghzhan is a teacher, while she is an aide. Toghzhan corrects her. "We're both mothers!" Näziliia

**ILLUSTRATION 10. THE GIRLS CARE FOR DOLLS**  Toghzhan and Näziliia have taken off their floppy, round spring hats and have made them into cradles for their doll and pony. They rock their babies back and forth, singing a lullaby.

wastes no time in making this adjustment. She points back at Kaisar, a boy who has been trying unsuccessfully to join them, and adds, "And he's the father."

The girls "paint" their dolls, taking twigs, dipping them into a small plastic container, and tracing the lines of the dolls' faces.[31] There are different ways one can care for another, for a toy or for a child. You can be careful not to break them. You can give them medicine, fix their hair, or paint them with makeup. You can feed them. This is what the girls do now. A boy has given Toghzhan a stuffed mouse, so now she has two mouths to feed. She sets both on the slide and leans over them. She puts grass up to their mouths and then throws the blades behind her. Näziliia crouches in the grass next to the slide and offers leaves to her pony. Every so often, she disposes of the already-eaten leaves by hiding them underneath the slide.

Feeding an organism and cleaning up after their waste are two primary burdens of caring for an organic being. Humans go to great lengths to make inorganic objects that can do precisely this—consume and defecate, whether in the girls' simple game with the dolls or with elaborate automatons, such as Jacques de Vaucanson's 1739 invention of a "digestive duck" or the Tamagotchi toy pet craze of the 1990s.[32] These functions require continual care from another. Their dependence on others becomes the feature that enlivens them.

Protection, too, can be a form of care. Kaisar comes over with the bag of toys on his back and a ball in his hand. Toghzhan shoos him away from the dolls but claims his bag of toys as belonging to the babies of whom he is supposed to be the father. She hushes Kaisar, though he is quiet. When the girls go to gather more food, Toghzhan calls on a different boy, Erlan, to look after the dolls. (I do not know why she asks him rather than Kaisar. Both have taken toys from other children on this day already, so neither strikes me as particularly trustworthy.) Erlan wraps the dolls in their hats, but Kaisar soon distracts him. Erlan prepares to chase Kaisar, but first Kaisar grabs the bag of toys that were supposed to be for his babies, while Erlan tries to steal Näziliia's pony and hat. She grabs the baby from his hands, yelling "Apai!" Erlan gives up the pony without a fight and runs off.

Later, my research assistant remarked that she was impressed with the girls for knowing all the words to the lullaby, and with Toghzhan, in particular, for acting as if she really was the mother of her doll—Toghzhan who guarded her doll fiercely, warding off noises that might wake her when sleeping, and who demanded gifts of toys for the children from their papa. Näziliia, nonetheless, stepped in to save the pony before Erlan could take it away. Erlan and Kaisar engaged in play that day that alternated between collaborative and antagonistic, between generous and mischievously hurtful, taking things apart and putting them back together again. Though Toghzhan and Näziliia did not know one another well, though Näziliia tried to take Toghzhan's doll before their game started, and though the girls had been unclear about the setting and roles at the outset, their play on this day was unambiguously one of giving, an elaborate and extended game of care.

# On the Not-Mother

The strange situations measured by Western psychologists in the 1960s and 1970s used the stranger as a tool to understand the child's relationship with their mother. There is a clear distinction between the mother and the not-mother. The not-mother is alien. She will not become much more familiar before these experiments are over, though she might be able to comfort the child if the other stimulus is frightening enough. Kuba distinguishes *svoi* from not *svoi*, but the new master will work to bring the dog into a relationship of belonging, just as Kuba describes himself as already having done with the actors. Even if Kuba acts as if they have already achieved this, closeness requires maintenance.

At Hope House, there is a distinction between mothers and not-mothers, but the not-mothers who work there are far from strangers. They are, in fact, more familiar to many of the children than the mothers themselves. Lauren Berlant (1998, 285) calls on us to explore what she calls "minor intimacies," which "have been forced to develop aesthetics of the extreme to push these spaces into being by way of small and grand gestures." Teachers established minor intimacies with children through small gestures—a wink or the squeeze of a hand. There is ambiguity in the girls' play, and ambiguity in the home itself. This ambiguity is not the same as confusion or muddling, but could in fact serve as a strategy of expansiveness that helps the children. Kathryn Woolard (1998, 6; see also Urciuoli 1996) introduces simultaneity and bivalency in analyzing particular instances of bilingual talk, in which words or utterances could "belong" to one code or another, instances she describes as "unresolved copresences." The copresence of imaginary and material worlds, the seeming conflation of roles or spaces, at first presents problems for analysis as it becomes difficult to decide what exactly is going on. A semiotic strategy of ambiguity, however, keeps the world of play open to multiple truths.

In animating the figure of the caregiver, the girls permitted an unresolved copresence of parent and teacher. It was possible that before I asked them if they were teachers or mothers, Näziliia had one scenario in mind, Toghzhan another. The two stories had no problem coexisting as they played. I might have asked them to define roles that they were quite comfortable keeping vague.[33] My line of questioning assumed that they held the same understanding I did of distinctions between mother and teacher, and between Hope House and family home.

Instead—perhaps like Meyerhold's description of the space necessary for projecting onto the actor—ambiguous actions permit the girls to see themselves, expansively, as caregivers, who might be mothers or teachers.

Ambiguity and uncertainty are not always desirable in foreign encounters, as it can make a stranger, such as a migrant, illegible to locals (Nasritdinov 2016). However, when two foreigners meet, a "diasporic intimacy" can form, as "the mutual enchantment of two immigrants from different parts of the world or as the sense of the fragile coziness of a foreign home" (Boym 1998, 501). The children's home would seem less than foreign, of course, the children having spent more time within its walls by now than they had at their family homes. Nonetheless, the sense that this is not their real home is reinforced—is intimated—to them in various ways. Throughout this process, they learn to use small gestures to mark closeness to one another and to the adults around them. Simmel (1950, 402) describes the stranger as unifying nearness and remoteness, organizing human relations so that the stranger, "who is close by, is far, and strangeness means that he [the stranger], who also is far, is actually near." As the girls animated figures of care, the play also made Näziliia, Toghzhan, and even Kaisar into coparents, moving their own relationship closer, if only for a moment.

This status of stranger might be positive to Simmel, but it is not always easy. Diasporic intimacy offers a painful reminder of what has been lost: "Just as one learns to live with alienation and reconciles oneself to the uncanniness of the world around and to the strangeness of the human touch, there comes a surprise, a pang of intimate recognition, a hope that sneaks in through the back door, punctuating the habitual estrangement of everyday life abroad" (Boym 1998, 501). As an interloper myself, I had to remind myself that any closeness to the children was only temporary. Tamilia and Zhamilia, the twins, were mostly in the background on the day I observed Näziliia and Toghzhan. They swept dead leaves and occasionally called for me to look. At one point, Zhamilia called me over to ask whether they were going somewhere that day. I had been trying to arrange for the kids to see a show at the puppet theater. I told her that they should be going to the theater the following day, but without me, for I would be traveling. Zhamilia seemed more concerned with the puppet show than in my own coming and going, but I pressed on. I will go to Astana, I continued, and then I will come back, but then I'll go back to America, to my home. I added that she and her sister, Tamilia, would be going to their home. The aide stepped in, "She'll go back to her mama, and you'll go back to yours." The helper switched to Russian then to ask me some questions about myself. Zhamilia returned to her sweeping. A few days later, I returned for my last day at Hope House, to say goodbye to everyone. It was supposed to be the twins' last day, too. As it turned out, they had gone home over the weekend.

During our time together, Zhamilia and Tamilia occasionally came up to me and called me "mama." They did it, looking up to me, perhaps hugging my waist, in a baby voice. They framed it as play. Other kids played this game with one another. When addressed as "mama" by the twins, however, even if they keyed it as play, I would break the frame and remind them that they had a mother. I would promise that she would soon come to visit, and that they would someday go home with her. I could rotate my position: Sometimes I was an apai who was supposed to teach English or tell them to stop eating the grass. Sometimes I was a kind of living doll who could receive their care and grooming. Sometimes I was a silent cameraperson, trying to get them to forget I was there. I could act as a caregiver—even a mother—to their dolls, comforting them when they were crying or needed help bending their legs. But even in play, I couldn't take on the role of the children's mother. The teachers would not have liked it. And even if the children were capable of keeping these two truths in their head at the same time—even if they could play that I was a mother while remembering they had a real mother coming for them—it was difficult for me. The twins were my favorites. The aide likened me not to a substitute mother but treated me more like a child by making equivalent the twins' immanent departure and my own. We were all something like strangers or guests.

As the children moved through their world at Hope House, one of the most important things they learned to do was to recognize and get comfortable with a kind of simultaneity in play, in which the iconicity—the relationship of resemblance between their play and the "real-world" scenarios they represented—remained underdetermined. A mother could seem to be more of an imagined figure than a remembered reality, but sooner or later the real mothers or fathers showed up and the children went home. In the meantime, certain relationships of closeness might be discouraged or disavowed through teachers' and helpers' rejections of making a big thing of goodbyes. Nonetheless, children and adults, in various ways, came to belong to one another, perhaps never standing in a relationship of parent-child or even kin, but coming close—as friends, as familiars, as intimates.

# JUMPING THROUGH HOOPS

*A little while later the stranger returned, carrying an odd object resembling a gate and the letter Π. From the crosspiece of this wooden, crudely made Π hung a bell, and there was also a pistol tied to it. . . . He turned to the goose and said:*

*"Ivan Ivanitch, please!"*

*The goose approached him and stood with a pose of anticipation.*

*"All right," said the stranger, "let's begin from the very beginning. First of all, bow and curtsy! Quickly!"*

*Ivan Ivanitch stretched his neck, nodded his head in all directions, and shuffled his feet.*

*"Good work. . . . Now die!"*

In the last chapter, the stranger brought the dog one step closer to belonging. In the next scene, Kashtanka takes on the distinct role of spectator. As it turns out, the new master is a clown and an animal trainer. The scenarios he rehearses with the animals get more complicated: The house is on fire, and the gander must ring an alarm bell. The gander owns a jewelry store and finds robbers. He must shoot. In Chekhov's story, the rehearsal goes on for hours. The gander rides the cat, the cat learns to smoke, *i t.p.* ("etc."). A sow is brought in. The goose and cat balance on top of her to create an "Egyptian" pyramid (See Illustration 12). In their adaptation for the puppet theater, Kashtanka's barking topples their first attempt. The creation of the pyramid is easier for the puppeteers to pull off than its undoing, for the puppets must fall or fly off, not the way inanimate objects would but as animals. The cat hurtles through the air with the help of a human. They try again and succeed.

The last chapter examined processes by which strangers become familiar. This chapter notes the usefulness of this proximity, with socialization including routines of imitation and repetition that resemble the rehearsals of Kashtanka's new master. Performance and pedagogy are intertwined, and children participate in such projects in important ways. The transformative agenda of Soviet performance finds a continued mission in contemporary Kazakhstan, with institutions such as the puppet theater and the children's home maintaining childhood as a collective project. Here, cute figures of late Soviet children's culture find new life in animating Kazakhstani childhood. Persons and performing objects slide into one an-

**ILLUSTRATION 11. THE GANDER AND CAT REHEARSE**   *"All right," said the stranger, "let's begin from the very beginning. First of all, bow and curtsy! Quickly!"*

other, as artists learn to treat their bodies as instruments, and as children play puppets. Examining play between puppet and object reveals aesthetic and ideological tendencies surrounding childhood. Vulnerability as an aesthetic tendency helps comprise the cuteness of children, as do indices of potential. Children were asked to animate figures that moved ambiguously between categories of human and object, but childhood is a dynamic category. The violent fantasies enacted by the gander—fire, robbery, death—foreshadow threats to performing objects and children addressed in chapter 5. As the children grew, they needed to show that their institutionalization had not diminished their potential, to assure spectators that they could continue to rest their hopes on them as the faces of the future.

## Nothing to Hide

At Hope House, children performed frequently, for a range of visitors. Adults' ideologies of childhood often contrast with lived experiences of actual children, and childhood studies work to disentangle the two.[1] An analytical and methodological separation of ideology and experience, however, overlooks the ways in which children are called on to contribute actively to public culture. Beliefs, experience, and action inform one another. Children sometimes defy expectations

**ILLUSTRATION 12. THE PUPPETS MAKE A PYRAMID**    A sow is brought in. The goose and cat balance on top of her to create an "Egyptian" pyramid. Kashtanka's barking topples their first attempt.

imposed by adults, but they also learn them, identify with ideal figures of child-hood, and perform some variation of the role of the child. Teachers often complained that frequent performances disrupted their schedule, especially when guests arrived late or unannounced. However, some children loved to sing and dance. They pouted when not chosen for a particular number. Rehearsals and performances sometimes wore them out, but they also served as a source of pleasure and pride. I came to see performance not as compelling children's complicity in their own subjugation, but instead as offering the children a means for attaining the affection and attention they needed or desired. Children, in many different contexts and different cultures, are made to perform. They copy routines playfully, citing them while transforming their significance.[2]

Like animations made for them, performing children strategically slip between person and object. One morning in the spring, I had planned to take some children from Hope House to the puppet theater, but could not because the children had guests of their own to entertain. Teachers dressed the older girls, five to six years old, in traditional Uzbek costumes, while a group of three-to-four-year-olds donned tutus and curly wigs in bright green and yellow. The tod-dlers in tutus were mostly boys, as the size of the costumes and the children determined who was cast for this number. They went outside and waited for the adults to arrive so that the ceremony could begin. First, Hope House directors welcomed the guests, and the visiting representatives praised the work of Hope House. The children watched, clapped, and chanted "thank you" when prompted. The visitors presented their gifts to the children—new tricycles, scooters, and balls—followed by a struggle among the children to get a first ride. Before any could pedal far, however, the adults had the children set the new vehicles aside so that they could each take a balloon and release them into the sky at the same time for a photo op. The younger children, watching the balloons float away and realizing they were not coming back, began to cry.

It was time for the children to perform. The teachers arranged the toddlers in their tutus on the carpet that was to serve as a stage (See Illustration 13). The song was about dancing dolls. Toghzhan—the girl who confidently cared for her doll in chapter 2—wore a green wig and stood in the front as the group's leader. The other children followed her actions only when the lyrics of the song reminded them when to squat and when to stand. One child shook his head furiously, as if trying to fling his wig from his head. When they finished, the older girls did their Uzbek dance. The guests clapped politely. Then a performance for the children began, while the business group, who had hired professional entertainers, slipped away.[3]

The children's performance was a way of thanking the sponsors for their do-nations. On other occasions, representatives came from the Department of Education that oversaw the home. Parents visited on special holidays. Volunteers came from the pedagogical institutes to entertain the children. Hope House usu-ally greeted them with a performance of some sort. On my first visit to the home, the children donned costumes of a hen and her chicks and of Kazakh war-riors. They sang and danced for me, then offered a puppet show, having heard of my interest in the medium. Visits usually involved more than a simple dona-tion from a sponsor, but instead set off an exchange of performances, or of gifts and performances, between the children and their guests. Some shows sought to edify the children, such as when a group of vegetarians used stuffed animals to put on a puppet show about healthy eating. It was completely in Russian, so few understood what was happening, and the children had no choice over their diets. They seemed, nonetheless, to enjoy the puppets.

The home's habit of receiving a constant influx of visitors likely helped make them open to my research. While I had come to see orphanages as wary of out-siders, when I approached the director of Hope House about my research, she offered an unexpected reply: "We would be happy to have you here. We have nothing to hide." When I asked, months later, if it was all right for me to begin

**ILLUSTRATION 13. THE CHILDREN DANCE IN TUTUS**  It was time for the children to perform a song was about dancing dolls. Toghzhan wore a green wig and stood in the front as the group's leader. The other children followed her actions only when the lyrics of the song reminded them when to squat and when to stand.

filming the children, she showed me her computer monitor. She could see all of the classrooms at once, thanks to security cameras. She repeated, "We have nothing to hide."

The children's shows for outsiders initially seemed beside the point of my ethnography of the children's home. These were the songs and dances they did for everyone. My goal as an ethnographer was to discover—and eventually, to uncover for readers—the everyday lives of children about whom so many assumptions have been made by other outsiders. For this, I wanted to look at their play. Performances, I thought, offered little evidence of the children as persons, as creative individuals, or as agents. In this way, I fell into a trap that ethnographers often set for ourselves, of seeing the goal of our work as pulling back a curtain, to move beyond the images readily available to outsiders and to expose hidden realities. A more productive approach can be to examine the construction of publicly available images. Indeed, it is a common trope of Western scholarship and popular media to portray socialist and postsocialist Eastern Europe as a land of fakery and theatricality, an artifact of Cold War stereotypes.[4] Soviet scholars have nonetheless mined the notion of theatricality to explore the complexity of relations between the theatrical and the real, whether in looking at early Soviet mass performances designed to erase boundaries between performer and spectator or at show trials and their counterparts on stage and screen.[5] Scholars have underlined the continuity in form of Soviet performance genres into twenty-first century central Asia, with state support of the arts persistently providing a way to use the stage for political ends.[6]

Teachers at first insisted the children's rehearsals would not interest me. Bored in the classroom by myself, I began to wonder if the performances were more interesting than I had first thought. These displays, and the work of preparing them, acted as nodal points for adults to animate childhood, through acts of modeling, manipulating, and projecting onto the children. They comprised a significant part of the children's everyday lives and of the world they were coming to understand. Visitors appeared far more often than the children left the grounds of the home. Performance framed the majority of the children's interactions with the outside.

Of course, performance was the chief endeavor of the puppet theater, but staging *Kashtanka* raised new issues of hiding and showing. In an early interview with Kuba, when he and the actors were only reading through the script, Kuba stated that his main goal for the production was one of getting the puppeteers to "stop hiding behind their puppets." This surprised me. The Almaty puppeteers hardly struck me as timid.[7] Actors showed and hid themselves in various ways, depending on the spectacle.[8] The artists had explained to me that if they did their jobs properly, all eyes would be on the puppets, so there was no need to hide.[9] In observing the rehearsals leading up to the premiere of *Kashtanka*, nonetheless, there was something different about the ways the actors held themselves onstage, whether animating puppets or not. Kuba's production of *Kashtanka* cast artists in roles that shifted from actor to puppeteer frequently and suddenly, moving from narrated event into narrating one for a moment, then returning to the narrated. One moment, Bolat voiced Kashtanka's bark as the puppeteer; the next, he regarded her with concern. Another actor, Altai, shifted between acting as a kind of onstage assistant—bringing food for the animals—and occasionally stepped in as the second puppeteer to the gander, controlling his wings while

Maral manipulated his head.[10] If the puppeteers' previous goal was to transpose themselves so completely into the puppets that audiences would forget about them whether they hid or not, Kuba encouraged them to call attention to themselves. He offered a way for the artists to show spectators the unexpected.

The puppet as metaphor for pure passivity does injustice to the form, as it assumes a consistency in relations between puppets and masters that real artists constantly trouble. The work of puppetry can instead call our attention to slippage between persons and objects. The puppet artists-turned-stage characters move between puppeteers and performing objects, much like children do in moving from their play with dolls and toys to rehearsals and performances for adults. Objectification can be an experience of profound violence, particularly when power differences due to racialization, gender, or other inequalities prevent any movement from object to subject.[11] While children and actors might shift from using their own bodies as instruments to manipulating inanimate objects, hierarchies ensure that they cannot suddenly treat their teacher or director like puppets, and that authority figures determine when a person remains a person or becomes a performing object.

## Living a Public Childhood

While Kuba worked to surprise spectators, child performances at Hope House seemed designed to meet visitors' expectations of what childhood should look like and, less explicitly, to dispel doubts that these children might be less than exemplary, given their situation. Childhood was prominent in the public landscape of Almaty. Since May 2012, Almaty has held the UNICEF designation as a "Child Friendly City," a program designed to encourage local governments to ensure universal rights for children.[12] Children's upbringing (*vospitannye*) under state socialism was treated as a public affair—as the responsibility of all rather than just a kin unit. These commitments persisted in the region.[13] Parks and courtyards of socialist apartment blocks invited children to gather, as did the multiple children's theaters around the city. The public nature of childhood in Kazakhstan did not always mean free of charge and government funded. Almaty was certainly friendlier to children and families of certain means and abilities than others. While public playgrounds (in the courtyards of apartment blocks) sometimes languished, new shopping centers offered indoor play areas with bright equipment and ball pits, along with art centers and petting zoos, to attract parents with children on cold winter days. Trendy restaurants offered free classes—in English or art—on weekend afternoons, the expectation being that parents would consume food and drink while leaving their children under the watchful eye of these teachers. Commercial or not, an array of spaces encouraged children to participate in public life when they were not at home or school.

Government discourses—and press coverage of them—celebrate efforts to ensure a better future for all children. A 2016 article in the *News of Kazakhstan* titled "Children—Future of the World" (*Deti—eto budushchee mira*) covers an international conference in the capital on "Kazakhstan, Friendly to Children," in which several prominent government figures spoke of the efforts the government had made in recent years to ensure the rights of all children. Portrayals of children as the nation's hope nonetheless intersect with mentions of children's weaknesses—thus justifying the need of state care. For example, Strategy Kazakhstan-2050 is cited by one representative: "Children are the most vulnerable and least protected sector of our society" (Parkhomenko 2016). Amid such warnings, the main point of the article—and, apparently, of the conference—was to celebrate the great strides the government had already made in protecting children and in offering equal opportunities for all.

Children have long served as potent political symbols of state paternalism and of the future of the nation in the region. Propaganda posters of Stalin regularly featured children—particularly prepubescent ones of non-Russian nationality (Kelly 2005). In Kazakhstan, I encountered billboards featuring photographs of President Nazarbayev, surrounded by children, promising a bright future for the nation-state. City billboards featured blown-up photographs of children's own drawings. Pictures of children in public restrooms in the city reminded adults to clean up after themselves because children might be using these facilities. Helpless faces appealed to citizens and to the state to take responsibility. These children help define adult citizenship and leadership as a readiness to ensure proper conditions for an imagined child.

Adults also celebrated children's performance in Kazakhstan. At kindergartens around the city, parents periodically gathered to watch their children's *utrenniki* (Russian for "morning programs"), similar to those that visitors viewed at Hope House, but less frequent. For public holidays, parks, squares, and malls erected stages where children sang and danced. Before performances began at puppet or children's theaters, animators (*animatory*, in Russian) not only engaged the children in games but also solicited young volunteers to sing or recite poems. At the new luxury shopping center that opened during my fieldwork, a "Baby Model" competition featured children, five to fourteen years old, parading down a leopard-print staircase, singing and dancing for a panel of judges to win cash prizes.

None of this meant that the children who performed well were ideal children, but that they took on roles as figures of cute children.[14] With bright costumes and cheery songs, they offered aesthetic displays of childhood, which included tropes of helplessness (baby chicks chirping for their mother hen), unclear divisions between objects and persons (dancing dolls, puppets come to life), or innocent nationalisms (skits dramatizing friendship between Kazakhs and other ethnicities alongside patriotic songs). The temporality of childhood itself influences the way a performance is evaluated. Unlike a gendered category such as "woman," children's performances of childhood—or their animations of ideal figures of childhood—required them to show that they followed proper trajectories toward increased competence. Performance promised to index and aid this transformation. More fully autonomous, children's proper internalization of instruction makes them, at once, more adept at following directions and in need of less constant direction. Rather than characterizing children as moving from dependence to independence, children's performances become increasingly animated by internal forces.[15] Yet the children are not little robots. Mastering routines offers novel techniques for familiarization.

## Cute Objects and Promising Children

The children's cuteness indexed vulnerability and potential, resulting from a combination of biological and historical forces.[16] Cuteness, as an aesthetic of vulnerability, makes young children's helplessness attractive. It elicits interaction. Human infants are peculiar animals: they are primed for social interaction yet utterly unprepared to fend for themselves.[17] Because human mothers can bear a second child before the first one has become fully independent, they need help from others, such as grandparents.[18] Babies need to recruit nonparents to care for them. Konrad Lorenz, an ethologist, proposed "baby schema" as a set of characteristics that define the cute face of human and other animal babies.[19] The argument underlying baby schema studies holds that babies evolved to be cute. Adults (and even children) are hardwired to respond to these characteristics— large eyes, round heads, large foreheads, small noses, and small mouths.[20] Sarah Blaffer Hrdy (2009, 212) describes baby faces as "sensory traps." The large eyes of cute faces emphasize the baby as taking in stimulation, while also suggesting interiority, inviting intersubjectivity. With their eyes, babies recruit adult investment. This becomes crucial when children find themselves in precarious situations, and parents and other adults must make difficult decisions about who is a worthy investment and who is not.

The kids at Hope House effortlessly checked the boxes of the baby schema. So why did teachers work so hard to cultivate the children's cuteness, dressing them in costumes that turned them into animals and dolls? People have learned to make use of cuteness in various ways. Large eyes and small mouths become ideals of particular femininities.[21] Adorable commodities ask consumers to express some kind of affinity with them. Everyday objects, like a vacuum cleaner named Henry, endowed with upturned eyes and a smiling mouth, make themselves companions in domestic life. Cultural celebrations of cute children, women, baby animals, and things serve to inform one another.[22] Children are cute, but children dressed as stuffed baby animals are really cute. Cuteness invites consumers to see resemblances between cute objects and persons. We should be wary of creating a false dichotomy of person/object, but cuteness in commodity and entertainment culture can nurture affection for cute objects while encouraging viewers and consumers to see connections between diminutive objects, people, and animals.

Cuteness and the commoditization of childhood developed in the US and elsewhere in tandem with specific trajectories of capitalism and branding in the twentieth century. Aesthetics of cuteness in childhood often overlap with ideologies of innocence in the American context, regularly excluding particular categories of children.[23] In contemporary Kazakhstan, consumer and media products resembled those of the US, in general. Stores offered dolls and toy trucks. Television channels featured globally branded characters such as Masha and the Bear, Peppa Pig, and Spider-Man but the historical trajectory differed and remains relevant.[24] The late Soviet period gave birth to animations—and characters from them—that clearly exhibited baby schema.[25]

While broad stylistic commitments have shifted, popular culture in the region has nonetheless consistently treated the performing object of the puppet as rife with pedagogical potential. Puppet animations (on screen) played an important role in early Soviet animation, while Bolshevik puppeteers used Petrushka, the Russian carnival puppet of the nineteenth century, to spread revolutionary messages to the masses. During the 1930s, cel animation (making use of layered drawings rather than three-dimensional objects) arrived in the Soviet Union, yet it was during this time that many of the government puppet theaters were founded in capital cities, so puppetry continued to flourish.[26] Through the mid-to late-twentieth century, Soviet puppet theaters such as the Moscow Puppet Theater, led by Sergei Obraztsov, traveled the world, popularizing puppetry and promoting the Soviet Union as a center of puppet culture.[27] In the 1960s and 1970s, the early puppet animations were rediscovered and celebrated by a new generation of Soviet puppet animators (MacFadyen 2005). Kazakhstanis continued to celebrate late Soviet animations during my fieldwork, as they popped up on screens and in classrooms.[28]

The figure of Cheburashka has served as a particularly enduring icon of late Soviet cuteness. With his distinctive furry, brown, round ears on either side of his smooth face and large eyes, I found him in classrooms and at toy shops during my fieldwork. The hero of this stop-motion (puppet) animation easily slips between thing, child, and animal. In Eduard Uspensky's original book, *Krokodil Gena y ego druz'ya* (Crocodile Gena and his friends), the narrator introduces the characters as having been his favorite childhood toys, similar to the way the English author A. A. Milne transformed his son's toys into the characters of *Winnie the Pooh*.[29] Cheburashka, we learn, "was made in a toy factory, but they made him so badly, that it was impossible to say who he was, a rabbit, a bear, a cat, or even an Australian kangaroo?" He is composed of a strange combination of features, each of which is typical of other cute animals—large, yellow eyes, "like a feline's, his head round, rabbit-like, and his tail short and puffy, like you usually find on a teddy bear."[30] In the animated adaptation of Uspensky's story, Cheburashka is described as looking like a "defective toy" (Kachanov 1969). Despite aspersions cast at the creature's appearance, in the animated version he is unquestionably cute.

Nonetheless, this unusual mishmash of familiar features renders him beyond classification. The narrator's parents told him Cheburashka was a "beast unknown to science" (*neizvestnyĭ nauke zver'*).[31] His status as animate or inanimate is fuzzy as well. His friends, Crocodile Gena and Galia, a plastic doll, become unquestionably animate in the book-to-screen adaptation, but Cheburashka continues to operate somewhere between the status of person and thing. He is found in a box of oranges—as if he has been confused with products from an exotic, warmer climate, and is, like the oranges, destined for sale. Rejected by the zoo (because they don't know what he is), he is placed in a storefront in order to attract customers.

The inability to classify Cheburashka into any species means that he has no clear parentage, no known kin—like Kashtanka, frequently described as a "mongrel." Yet the defects also render him unique and thus distinct from mass-produced commodities. Once he sets out on his own, Cheburashka is intent on establishing and aiding social relations. He seeks friends, finding other solitary individuals, beginning with Crocodile Gena who has placed fliers around town in search of companionship, followed by Galia. They work together to build a House of Friendship, a title reminiscent of other Houses designed to construct Soviet society—such as the House of Culture—though we might also think of the children's home and baby house (*detskiĭ dom, dom rebënka*), a collective solution to a problem of people needing other people.[32] By the time the House of Friendship is complete, Cheburashka and the others realize that such an institution is unnecessary, because their shared labor has made them into friends. Productive labor without capitalist goals has successfully fostered sociality rather than alienating individuals from one another. They opt to extend their efforts into socialization, repurposing the new space into a kindergarten. Cheburashka offers to serve as a toy for the children. After all his organizing and socializing efforts, he voluntarily reverts to object status.

Not a simple commodity nor an inanimate object come to life, Cheburashka alternates between cute object and active citizen.[33] Cheburashka wants friendship, education, and to become a good Soviet citizen. He wants to serve as a Pioneer (the Soviet alternative to scouting).[34] But he is also willing to offer himself up, to stand in a shop window or sit on a shelf, waiting to be played with by children. Being a good citizen, Cheburashka suggests to children, sometimes requires a movement from the position of agent to that of patient. Cheburashka's name means "topple"; in the opening scenes of the series, a sleepy Cheburashka topples over and must be propped back up. "Topple," like "toddle," suggests fragility, inviting us to guard these bodies from their own limited abilities to balance.[35]

As people make and reinforce connections between objects and people—between Cheburashka and children, for example—they encourage the anthropomorphism of objects and attachments to them. Chapter 4 explores the ambivalence regarding children's relationships with inanimate objects and the general role of materiality as part of, or substitute for, adult care. Here, the prominence of objects in cultures of cuteness naturalizes objectification of cute persons, particularly those who are detached from others and those who are small and malleable, likely to fall over. These small bodies are easy to pick up. The vulnerability of the cute increases their risk of damage and enables their movement in the hands of others. The features of cuteness—softness, large eyes enabling a mutuality of regard—invite interactions, while the diminutive nature of their bodies suggest they can do little to prevent it, anyway.

## Spectacular Traps

Adults projected their hopes onto the bodies of performing children, yet the children learned to master various skills through their imitations, repetitions, and rehearsals—for actual performances and for new responsibilities as they progressed in school and took on new roles. Performances should transform performers and audiences alike, according to Soviet models of mass spectacle. "Mass actions" of the early Soviet period blurred distinctions between spectator and audience by incorporating thousands of participants, such as Nikolai Evreinov's reenactment of the Storming of the Winter Palace on the third anniversary of the October Revolution. Children participated in these as well as adults.[36] Artists explained to me that puppetry offered a pure form to show children absolute truths of good and evil, and that child audiences readily accepted the puppet's liveliness—both because it resembled their own play, their own manipulation of objects, and because the puppets were at a scale closer to the children, so that the puppets resembled children in a way that they, the adult actors, did not.

The mutual metamorphosis promised by performance requires shared understandings of one another—of performer and viewer. Centuries apart, Denis Diderot and Alfred Gell saw acting and art (respectively) as traps, emphasizing the work of the artist in imagining and anticipating the viewer, so art is intersubjective at the moment of conception (and not just an expression of an inward state that later meets an audience).[37] The trap sounds insidious if we assume the goal of the trapper is to consume its prey, yet it requires—and reveals—an understanding of another point of view, an imagining of another's perspective. If sympathy is the result of imagination (Smith [1759] 2011), then cultivating an understanding of others must simultaneously enhance imaginative capacities. The sixteenth-century occultist Giordano Bruno (Bruno 1998, 146) uses "bonding" to describe a universal force or agency that "vivifies, soothes, caresses and activates all things." It is an animating agent. Bruno insists on profound variation regarding the types of bonding agents and their powers, just as the children and adults at Hope House revealed a readiness to form a range of bonds.[38] Kuba's goal with *Kashtanka* was to reach an audience of older children. This required a different kind of trap, a different bonding agent. The children at Hope House adjusted their performance not according to the audience but according to their own age, so that they could index their development.

On the puppet stage, inanimate objects brought to life act as bonding agents between the producers of the spectacle and the viewers. When preparing their shows, puppeteers consider how things look from the other side of the puppet. Their view of the puppet is usually opposite to that of the audience. Parts of the stage are hidden to them entirely if they control a rod puppet from below, for example, and are blocked by a screen that also serves as a set. Some of these sets contain multiple layers to create the impression that two puppets are great distances away from each other. Much of the work of the director or assistant director in rehearsals consists of checking on details of visibility, such as whether a puppeteer's hand is popping above the screen that is to create the ground for the puppet controlled from below. In rehearsals I watched, the substance of the play itself only occasionally arose amid otherwise detailed work on execution. If the animation looked sloppy, the play's theme mattered little, for it was unlikely to hold the children's attention.

In rehearsals, directors played the child, anticipating lively spectators. Puppet plays often addressed audiences directly, asking where another character was hiding. They sometimes invited the children, at the end, to sing or dance with them. Directors nonetheless reminded artists not to wait for the premiere to find the energy necessary to bring their role to life. They should imagine their dynamic audience already during rehearsals. Thus, a puppet performance is not only an exercise in artists and children collectively imagining that these objects really are alive, but it is also a constant endeavor in adults cultivating their own imagining of what it is to be a child.[39]

Through intersubjective encounters between performing bodies and spectators, performance often works to transform and even elevate audiences. Kashtanka, who begins as a spectator at the clown's house, will eventually learn to perform. Chekhov's story anticipated Soviet celebration of entertainment's powers to civilize lower orders. He reportedly wrote "Kashtanka" based on an anecdote recounted to him by Vladimir Durov. Durov and his brother performed as famous animal trainers and clown-satirists. After the Bolshevik Revolution, the Durovs ascribed revolutionary import to their own dancing animals, claiming that their satire had helped destroy the old regime and promising that their acts could help build socialism by enlightening the masses.[40] The animals—able to be tamed and taught—served as models for the mass publics watching them. In order for this to work, circus spectators of the Durov brothers' shows would have needed to recognize themselves in the goose playing dead or as the smoking cat and think, "I, too, can change."

Bolshevik celebration of puppetry rested on a similar logic of co-opting a form of popular entertainment to draw in mass publics and then to transform these captivated audiences. The carnival puppet, Petrushka, was lauded for having opposed authority under Imperial Russia. He was remediated by the puppet theater and in other forms of children's culture. Soviet planners ascribed to puppets, and to Petrushka in particular, a unique power in socializing children and the masses alike to understand new socialist ways of life.[41] Puppetry was one of many ways that early Soviet performance committed itself to goals of transformation, beyond mere entertainment. In theater for children—especially puppetry—the principle of incorporating audiences as coparticipants remained a key tenet in the planning of shows. Puppeteers in Kazakhstan often defined themselves and their profession according to the audience—of children—rather than the medium, when I asked them how they chose to study puppetry. Many puppeteers, especially women, explained that what they loved about their job was that they brought joy to children, even though neither traditional Kazakh puppetry—orteke—nor the Russian carnival puppet of Petrushka were historically geared exclusively at children.

Engaging child audiences required a special understanding of their abilities and limits regarding attention and enchantment. Even in the 1930s, the first years of the theater in Almaty, artists preceded their puppet shows with a series of warm-up games before asking the children to take their seats and watch the show. Audience reviews in the archives praised these activities, encouraging them to do more. The puppet theaters in Almaty often greeted children outside or in the foyer with the help of animators, who were either dressed in playful costumes or donned full-body puppet gear, the kind of costume one would wear as a sports mascot in the US. The goal of such animators was to enliven the children rather than puppets, and the same term was used for entertainers at children's parties. Theater animators (who were also puppet artists) greeted the children, initiated dances or games, and then led them into the theater. Once the show began, emcees or characters directly addressed the audience, framing the narrating event by reminding them of basic rules of the theater—that they were to be quiet, sit in their seats, and that if they liked something, the appropriate response was to clap.[42]

Just as children worked to distinguish themselves with increasing competence in their performances at Hope House, the puppeteers treated child audiences of different ages as requiring a tailored approach, decreasing direct engagement as the children got older. This corresponded with a view, articulated by puppeteers, that young children believed the puppet was really alive. Older child viewers, they said, had a harder time regarding the puppet as living, yet these kids would be increasingly capable of sitting still. Though the puppet theater shared with avant-garde theater a commitment to active participation, this participation seemed to be an intermediary step in socializing children to become obedient spectators. Though we should not assume spectators believed and internalized the content they were shown, we might think about other effects of such routines of performance and spectatorship. These embodied practices become part of what it means to be a good citizen.

## Pedagogies of Performance

Elements of performance appear throughout learning processes. School and socialization routines often resemble rehearsals for performances, insofar as they rely on imitation and repetition.[43] Teachers at Hope House valued performance's pedagogical potential. They exhorted the children to sit quietly if they were watching television together, but if a certain song came on, they might suddenly command the children to get up and dance for the duration of the song and then sit back down again. Besides the programs they prepared for guests, the teachers planned and staged programs just for the children to mark holidays or other special occasions. The teachers themselves dressed in costumes and memorized lines for special skits for the children. Because there were no male teachers at Hope House, women donned fake beards to play men's roles. Teachers undertook these elaborate projects even though the children attended multiple similar programs outside the home during the holiday season and welcomed visiting groups who put on shows for them.

The children's daily lessons had elements of performativity and of theatricality too.[44] Every few months, three teachers offered an open lesson in which directors and other teachers observed a lesson, each lasting around twenty minutes.[45] Afterward, the children would wait in their bedroom with a helper while the teachers and directors discussed the lessons they had just observed, evaluating the teacher's pedagogical abilities. Critiques were sometimes harsh. In one, a director advised a teacher to use the summer to look for another job, perhaps teaching history at a high school, because she had no special rapport with young children. Teachers prepared for open lessons by creating elaborate visual aids, sometimes recruiting me to help create drawings or props. They prepared extensively with the children. Such thorough planning seemed to diminish the creativity that they were supposed to be encouraging. One day, I could only feel pity as I watched a teacher coach Zhamilia on how to paint a watercolor landscape, making her try, again and again, to paint a boat the correct size in the middle of the page. As the teacher demonstrated, repeatedly, the correct proportions of the boat to the size of paper, she urged Zhamilia to work faster, before the water dried. Other children gathered around to watch, ultimately declaring each of her attempts as "bad," shaking their heads. Finally, the teacher gave up on Zhamilia and let another child try.[46]

Teachers employed repetition to the point of correct execution in part to ensure that some child in the group, if not all of them, would be able to complete a task when asked by a director. Because emphasis was placed on result over process, children less adept or slower in achieving mastery often suffered from the shaming of teachers and peers. However, whether the children were painting a landscape on command, dancing to a song they had practiced for weeks, or simply sitting in their seats with their arms properly folded like schoolchildren, they took pride in their abilities to carry themselves with increasing maturity and self-control. By the time they were in their last year at the children's home, teachers regularly asked them at the beginning of classes, "How do we sit?" and reminded them that these were the rules they would be expected to follow next year, when they were back in their family homes and attending school.

Certain lessons explicitly encouraged children to take on the role of schoolchildren while also imagining them as leaders and as citizens. Aigul Apai modeled one open lesson after a popular television quiz show for Kazakhstani schoolchildren, *Leaders of the Twenty-First Century*. She made a game board with categories of questions, directed me to prerecord videos of other teachers asking questions to be replayed to the children on their television during the quiz, and incorporated natural materials to "test" the children's abilities to distinguish different smells. She rehearsed with the children ahead of time to ensure that they would answer questions correctly. When it was time for the group to give their open lesson, Aigul dressed the children in outfits modeled after the traditional school uniforms worn around Almaty—white shirts and navy pants or skirts, the girls with white pom-poms in their hair. Onto their shirts we stapled paper badges that said "Leader of the Twenty-First Century" in Kazakh. The directors and other teachers sat on one side of the room, and Aigul played the role of quiz show host. After the children filed in, Aigul asked them to say what they wanted to be when they grew up. She emphasized to them, at the beginning and at the end of the lesson, that they were the leaders of the twenty-first century. She rewarded them with gold medals (with chocolate inside). The teachers and directors spoke effusively of Aigul Apai as an inspirational teacher, praising her own creativity in devising lessons.

While performances for sponsors often mentioned the children's precariously "hopeful" state of separation from the parents to whom they would return, these lessons emphasized another level of belonging that was also future oriented. They were citizens of Kazakhstan, its future leaders. Watching the less successful open lessons was a painful reminder that, while teachers placed great pressure on children to perform as model pupils, it was the teachers who risked a damaged reputation, and even a threatened position, from these lessons. To borrow from Goffman's participant framework, the teachers were seen as principals of the children's acts, attributed responsibility for their successes and failures, whereas the children were, to a certain extent, animators of the teachers' pedagogical efforts. This did not mean that the children were expected to be puppets or parrots of whatever responses had been given to them. Directors highly praised lessons in which it was evident that the lesson had made the children really think about a problem or issue. Moreover, it was the children who would presumably suffer if they ultimately left Hope House unable to perform expected routines, at school or in other settings.

## Looking into the Future, Onstage and Off

Hope House taught children to show how they were cute yet competent. They should promise spectators that they were the future. Kuba pushed the puppet actors to plan ahead in other ways. This required an internal split in which they would learn to treat their own bodies as instruments of manipulation. In *Kashtanka*, puppets interacted with human actors—most frequently when the actor Baqytzhan, playing the master, worked with the animals. Directors used theorizations of theater along with puppetry in their work with the artists. Puppeteers described the process of animation as one of transposing the self into the puppet body, referring to their own bodies as the *first I* (*pervyĭ ia*), while the puppet became a *second I* (*vtoroĭ ia*). This created a division between their own bodies and the bodies of the puppet, even as they described the puppet as an extension of self. Kuba, however, instructed them to treat their own bodies onstage as the *second I*. At times, this unfolded in explicit ways as actors approached or detached from the puppets they animated. When they did this, their human bodies became characters interacting with the puppets or with each other. At other times, the two *I*s were to be thinking about different things and to possess different understandings of the scenes unfolding.

Kuba explained his theory of the two *I*s when discussing the relationship of time and contrast between scenes. The first was Kashtanka's first meeting with the animals (described in chapter 2 and at the beginning of this chapter), followed by the scene of boredom a month later (at the beginning of chapter 4). The *first I* knows, in the earlier scene, that Kashtanka will soon be bored, and thus the *second I* acts with that much more delight when these impressions are still new. The concept of the *second I* that the puppeteers had described extends their own subjectivity outward, whereas Kuba's new conceptualization of it makes an internal division. Upon hearing Kuba direct this shift in the placement of the *second I*, I asked him if this meant the puppet was a *third I*, but he said no, the puppet was an extension of the *second I*. The body and the puppet, like a violin to a violinist, were all instruments. In this way, his shift rendered the body a performing object, not unlike the puppet, subject to the same precision of performance onstage as the animated object. Rather than a movement of perspective, self, or soul from the body of the puppeteer into the puppet, the *first I/second I* required puppeteers to see themselves from the outside.[47]

Following Kuba's redrawing of the boundary between *first I* and *second I*, the human bodies onstage become equivalent to the puppet bodies, not only for the actors animating characters specified in the original Chekhov text, such as the animals' master played by Baqytzhan, but also for the puppeteers.[48] Puppeteers were coached to enter and exit the stage with more dramatic flourish, and to interact with their puppets when waking them. Animation was, in this way, an agreement between puppet and puppeteer. By treating the human body onstage as an instrument—as a *second I* also directed, in some sense, by the *first I*—the puppeteer became a character and a dicent sign, a sign whose meaning requires some understanding of causal processes to be understood.[49] It takes work from the spectator to see the puppeteers onstage as characters and not as mere puppeteers. If the show were to impress new audiences, Kuba and the artists needed to transform the work of the puppets and of the humans onstage. At the same time, Kuba pushed for a production in which the audience would see humans and puppets as equals.

If the performances of Hope House were to produce commitments of adults to care for the children, the children needed to set the right kind of trap, to offer the bonding agent that would work best to secure continued support. This required an understanding of the adult audiences and of those audiences' expectations of the children. Despite the diversity of visitors, Hope House treated them as rather homogeneous. Children and teachers referred to the various groups who passed through simply as "sponsors" (*sponzory*, in Russian) or as "guests" (*qonaqtar*, in Kazakh). When I asked for more information about the visitors, teachers themselves rarely knew. Some I took as businesspeople, for they wore suits and gave gifts of new toys or clothes. Volunteer groups and university students were younger and offered educational entertainment, as well as offering smaller gifts. The Department of Education representatives evidently held the most weight, because teachers simply referred to them as "the Department," and were the most nervous when they were due.[50]

The figures whom the children animated, in contrast, changed constantly. Aesthetics of childhood in Kazakhstan required children to show helplessness and innocence accompanied by potential. As they got bigger, children outgrew costumes they had worn for certain numbers. They became capable of more complex tasks. The smallest children wore perhaps the most ridiculous outfits, such as their tutus and wigs for the "dancing dolls" number. This was not because the discomfort of such getups annoyed them less, but because their resemblance to playthings and animals—dolls and baby chicks—and the over-the-top nature of their outfits helped make up for limitations in their dance abilities. As they got older, the children performed emulations of adults, sporting little suits or evening dresses, dancing as Kazakh warriors or urban youths with NYC baseball caps. They moved away from disarming spectators by showcasing their vulnerability, instead displaying increased skill and precision in memorizing movements, in comporting themselves uniformly, and in taking themselves seriously. If they did this well, there could still be an element of cuteness in their attempt at precocity. In preparing for performances, they had to figure themselves as ideal children, yet this was a heterogeneous category. Ideologies of childhood rest on figuring them as dynamic creatures.

The peculiar state of total institutions for children creates both a burden of showing that the children have nothing to hide (discussed more in chapter 5) and an opportunity for adults to cultivate the children's abilities to perform, as they faced fewer barriers to consistent rehearsal. Every year in the spring, the Palace of Schoolchildren hosted the *Meiirim* Festival of Children's Creativity

(*Meiırım festival' detskogo tvorchestva*), a showcase of song, dance, poetry recital, and musical ensembles. The festival consisted entirely of children from the various special institutions around the city, which included orphanages, boarding schools, and schools for the blind and the hard of hearing, along with institutions for children with a range of developmental and intellectual disabilities. *Meiırım* means "kindness" or "pity" in Kazakh, so it was, in effect, a festival of pity and of creativity.[51]

A jury decided who would perform alongside professional artists at the opera theater a few weeks later. A certain ambivalence surrounded the festival regarding how the children should be celebrated for abilities while taking into account their (diagnosed or presumed) disabilities. Jury members evaluated the children based on ability, but the festival was structured to include only children growing up in special institutions. Journalists reporting on the 2015 festival wrote: "Looking at these kids, you forget that the majority of them have developmental issues. They simply want to prove to themselves and others that they too can do what their peers can do." By "peers," we must assume that the authors are referring to able-bodied, typically developing, never-institutionalized children. Bakhit Ospanov, president of the sponsoring fund, is quoted in the same article as admitting that the children's issues do, in fact, complicate the task of judging them: "Some of the children don't see, others don't hear. . . . There are children with impaired memory, and there are simply orphans from children's homes. . . . Bringing them together and evaluating them according to a single criterion of creativity is difficult" (Umarekova and Kudykbaev 2015). The article underscores the ambivalence surrounding institutionalization, ability, and performance in Kazakhstan. This suggests that a good performance requires reference to bad performance, real or imagined. Potentially criticizing the performance of children with special needs or circumstances makes the judges uncomfortable. At the same time, the journalists' quote suggests that for these children, a "good" performance is one that makes them seem average.

The feats of Kashtanka's animal companions in their rehearsal at the beginning of this chapter made them exceptional. The children of Hope House, and those growing up in the other institutions showcased in this festival of pity, merely needed to evince mainstream normativity in order to achieve applause from outsiders. In addition to proving ability, these performances were sentimental spectacles that distributed agency and responsibility by building emotional ties.[52] "Responsibility" can be used to talk about who has caused a situation or about who should take charge of changing that condition.[53] These need not point to the same actors. Corporate sponsors and teachers might not see themselves as the cause of the children's plight but as nonetheless taking on a duty to the children, assuming at once agency and responsibility for the children's well-being. They might accept none of the blame for the children's placement in these institutions, but nonetheless call upon themselves to take on some of the burden of caring for them, in hopes of a future Kazakhstan populated with more capable (or fewer needy) adults.

In my second year of research, the children and their music teacher prepared intensely for the festival, rehearsing a series of acts totaling about twenty minutes. Of the several numbers the children performed—which included songs, dances, and poems, in groups and solo—the jury chose two acts for Hope House to offer at the final concert at the opera theater. In both of these, the children animated inanimate objects: the middle group (mostly around five years old) performed a dance from *Buratino*, while the younger children danced behind them in their doll tutus. The children of Hope House were among the youngest represented at the competition. Perhaps because of this, they were called upon to embody the more vulnerable aspects of cuteness for the adults. They showed how convincingly they had learned to play the puppet, and to play increasingly skilled puppets, pliant and reliable.

Buratino is another late Soviet cultural phenomenon of ambiguous animation who still finds popularity in contemporary Kazakhstan. A loose adaptation of *Pinocchio* (Collodi [1883] 2020), Aleksei Tolstoy's *The Golden Key, or the Adventures of Buratino* was first published in 1935, with multiple adaptations for stage and screen following its release. The 1976 live-action version appeared most often on television in Kazakhstan, and this was the version the children of Hope House reanimated.[54] Buratino is a puppet who has come to life and can move on his own. Unlike Pinocchio, Buratino makes no attempt to become a real boy, to move into a clearer position of personhood. Rather, he goes on adventures, loses and becomes reunited with Papa Carlo. He helps to free other puppets from their own evil master. Afterward, though free from the obligation to perform, the marionettes agree to continue their occupation as performers, with kind Papa Carlo as their new master. Like Kashtanka, the marionettes' liberation leads not to independence but to dependence on a different master. In addition to fortifying connections or blurring boundaries between cute objects and children, Buratino and Kashtanka make use of the trope of the orphan as especially vulnerable, calling out to be taken up by a kind adult or at risk of being taken in by a villain. Other people are objectified and commoditized in acts of utter violence, often permanently, offering no chance of return.[55] In many fictional accounts of orphaned children, however, the lack of kin ties creates the possibility for adventure (and for a more direct form of citizenship). This allows the orphan, as figure, to play a central role in the structure of the folk tale.[56]

Real children, such as those at Hope House, should get bigger, smarter, and more able to care for themselves. In addition to vulnerability, the children needed to show signs of growth—to become more competent and, in fact, to become better adults than the existing order. Cheburashka need not worry about this. In fact, viewers would likely be disturbed if Cheburashka grew taller, if he lost the whispering dreaminess in his voice. Children make a promise that objects and animated characters do not, that even domestic animals cannot: that they—children—need us now, but they will not always. You will not always have to feed them. You will not always have to take care of them. In fact, someday they will take care of you.

When the children performed their Buratino song at the opera theater, the emcee for the evening introduced them by informing adults in the audience that they should get ready to experience nostalgia. Nostalgia is not just a project of regretting a loss in the past. It mourns a lost future as well (Boym 2001).[57] Issues of memory, loss, and childhood scale up to national longing. A Kazakh legend of the *mankurt*—an enslaved person who suffers memory loss—became an icon of Soviet forgetting of past atrocities during *glasnost* in the 1980s, as people struggled to recover the past.[58] Forgetting creates an opportunity to create a new memory, one perhaps more fantastic than what came before. Nostalgia helped sustain the popularity of late Soviet figures of childhood, such as Buratino and Cheburashka, into twenty-first century Kazakhstan, making them potent characters to be reanimated by new generations. Childhood is not merely a site of hope—of looking ahead and anticipating narratives of personal and cultural progress. Adults infuse childhood with nostalgia, whether for a childhood that really was or for one that might have been. An imagining of the Soviet past can shape responses to the present and planning for the future. At the Almaty State Puppet Theater, the administrative director often cited Leo Tolstoy as having said that one only lives for the first seven years of one's life; then you spend the rest of your life trying to get it back.[59] He envisioned the puppet theater as a site for adults to recuperate that lost childhood. Such projects inevitably contain elements of fantasy. The children of Hope House worked to show a particular figure of the vulnerable child—one in need of care from others but still capable of being recovered, of realizing the optimistic narrative.

The teachers at Hope House did not ask children to perform with some internal split between *first* and *second I*. It was enough, for the littlest ones, to keep their wigs on and to squat when the song told them to. Yet the ideology of childhood as a delicate site makes each performance a fragment of a potential narrative of growth and of hope. The children animated figures that they resembled, but which they were not: animals, adults, objects. At the same time, the disjuncture between the child and the puppet, the leader, or the warrior meant that if their childlike nature leaked through appropriately, it would assure viewers of a certain authenticity. If Hope House's commitment to performance seems unremarkable, this suggests that the call on children to animate ideal figures of childhood extends beyond the borders of the Kazakhstani institution. Adults pin hopes on toddlers in tutus and tiaras; we dress them in clothes that amuse us and look for the correct combination of vulnerability and potential that will secure our investment in them. I point this out not to condemn anyone who does this. Taking care of a child is hard work. The danger lies in a readiness to turn away when we find elements of cuteness or potential lacking (See chapter 5).

The proper way to facilitate the realization of potential, nonetheless, was not always clear. As the next chapter demonstrates, there is a tension between materiality and sentiment in ideologies of the proper care for the child.

# GETTING COMFORTABLE

*A month passed. Kashtanka was already used to the fact that every night she was fed a delicious dinner and was called Auntie. She got used to the stranger and to her new companions. Life passed smoothly. Every day began the same way. . . . The lesson and lunch made the day interesting, but the evenings were tedious. Usually in the evening the master went off somewhere and took the goose and cat with him. Left alone, Auntie lay on the mattress and began to feel sad.*

On Kashtanka's first day at the second home, everything was exciting and new. Just a month later, it has grown habitual, expected, and dull. The narrator shifts from "the stranger" and "Kashtanka" to "the master" and "Auntie." Destrangement has taken place, but this familiarity leads to tedium and melancholy. In the puppet production, the audience sees Auntie's apathy toward everything around her. Instead of delighting at the gander's singing, Auntie curls up, using her tail to cover her ears. Whereas before, the gander had gotten annoyed with the dog for trying to eat from his bowl, now Ivan Ivanitch calls Auntie over, but the dog declines. On the first night, the dog ate rapaciously (*zhadno*, as Kuba had directed). Now she has lost her appetite.

Interpretations of this moment regard material comfort as the enemy.[1] The last chapter noted children's slippage into roles as objects in performance. This chapter notes the ways in which material provisions—and other aspects of materiality, in the sense of things given to children—become loaded with moral weight. "Materiality," as used in this chapter, is intentionally vague. Discourses surrounding the provisioning for another—through food, clothing, or toys—are articulated in opposition or in competition with immaterial qualities such as independence and love. At the same time, when people engage with specific objects—especially those with the power to become animated—the qualities of these objects matter. It is necessary to choose the right objects, made of good stuff and well-constructed, and to care for them properly. In this way, things sometimes threaten social relations and sometimes act as recipients for ideal care.

**ILLUSTRATION 14. KASHTANKA LIES ON HER MATTRESS**   *Usually in the evening the master went off somewhere and took the goose and cat with him. Left alone, Auntie lay on the mattress and began to feel sad.*

The child's "material satisfaction" evoked ambivalent stances in Kazakhstan. Institutions such as Hope House needed to evince nutritional, sensory, intellectual, and emotional variety and abundance, as they emerged from a double legacy of deprivation. These institutions came into being as a result of past crises of scarcity and have been described by psychological literature as sites of emotional deprivation. At the same time, the caregivers at Hope House needed to position themselves as never offering enough. This upheld the stance that the child's proper place was the first home, where they would find fulfillment beyond the mere security provided by state institutions. The puppet theater inherits a socialist celebration of puppets as ideal objects for socializing children. A similar object—the doll—has long been treated with profound ambivalence in the West as threatening to steer girls toward improper femininity and excessive consumption. While adults seem undecided on the morality of materiality for children, they also teach children to care for objects as extensions of their care for others. In this way, dolls and similar toys offer children a means to develop their capacities for animation, as instruments for practicing familiarization techniques.

## Free but Hungry

On the day before the premiere, Kuba told me the main theme of *Kashtanka* was the choice between freedom or stability:

Either he lives in stable society, but without freedom, but he eats well. There's work. In the morning he gets up for work. Things go. His life passes, scheduled to the very end of death. Everything is good, everything satisfied, but there is no freedom. Yet there is something else: when you feel free, sometimes hungry, sometimes you don't know how tomorrow will finish. You don't know what's waiting for me. That's the life that I am for. That I don't know what waits for me ahead or that every time I do everything like it's the last time. I simply don't know. Tomorrow I will die. (Interview, November 29, 2013)

The two homes represent these two options. Freedom is uncertain but exciting. This is what the first master represents to Kuba. In the original story, the master's son, Fedyushka, ties a piece of meat to a string. He lets Kashtanka swallow the meat and then pulls it out again. Kuba does not include this in the adaptation, nor does he note the carpenter's roughness onstage when he grabs the dog by the throat and she yelps in pain. Kuba sees the unpredictability of the first home as a kind of liberty in and of itself, even if the dog doesn't exactly choose what she will eat or where she will sleep. The free Kashtanka (or Kuba) lives every day as if it were the last. The second master and the second house, meanwhile, represent security that becomes monotonous to the point that life becomes indistinguishable from its opposite. There is no change, with everything "scheduled to the very end of death."

Chekhov names the lessons and dinner as the bright spots in an otherwise bland existence, yet Kuba emphasizes that Kashtanka must reject both in favor of a less predictable life. Hunger drives one forward. This differs from Kafka's hunger artist, for whom asceticism becomes a performance of self-discipline.[2] For Kashtanka, hunger is not a feat but a side effect of independence. However, like Kafka's artist, she will liberate herself from this bodily need. She will not allow hunger to master her. The dog's eventual refusal of the safe second home will also act as a rejection of performance. The circus routine relies on the predictability of interactions between the animals and the clown. Other analyses of Chekhov's story argue that Kashtanka's return to her first master signals a favoring of sentimental attachments over material satisfaction.[3] Freedom and sentimentality are not the same thing, but both interpretations signal a prioritizing of an intangible quality of life over the comforts of the second home. The description of the play on the puppet theater's website offered a similar captioning of the main idea as a universal truth—that Kashtanka goes through a journey in which she realizes that freedom and happiness are more important than fortune and fame.

Puppet artists argue that the form of the puppet—simpler, and thus purer than the human actor—lends itself to universalization because of its more general character.[4] Kuba previously aligned himself with the second master, the clown. In this interview, he gradually transposes himself into the perspective of Kashtanka. He first casts Kashtanka's choice as everyone's, using the third-person masculine to refer to a universal subject ("he lives . . . he eats . . ."). He then shifts from third to second ("you feel free"), and finally moves to first person ("That's the life that I am for. . . . I simply don't know, tomorrow I will die"). He invites me (as "you") to identify with her and finally aligns himself with her position.

Kashtanka becomes a universal protagonist with whom we are all invited to identify, in these readings, but the story also draws political interpretations. The artistic director articulated the play as a metaphor for happenings in Ukraine. This was early in the winter of 2013–2014—before the Russian occupation of Crimea—when citizens filled the streets to protest then President Yanukovich's rejection of an agreement with the European Union. Kuba later also described the protest movement of Ukraine as acting as inspiration for his wishes for Kazakhstan, articulated through the story of Kashtanka. Kazakhstani citizens needed to reject the stability that the current administration offered in order to be free. However, most were afraid to lose the safety they perceived they had under Nazarbayev. The spirit of demanding freedom over comfort lay in the protest movement itself. This metaphor troubled me because Kashtanka does not merely escape; she returns to a first master, as if this is something she cannot live without. Neither director identified a master to whom Ukraine or Kazakhstan should turn. As Russia occupied Crimea in 2014, and as conversations in Kazakhstan turned to comparisons between Crimea and areas of northern Kazakhstan with Russian-majority populations, I could not help but warp the metaphor to account for this new development. The directors took inspiration from protesters who were pro-Europe (but neither Europe nor Russia was part of their interpretation), yet I kept imagining Russia as the carpenter, returning to reclaim its status as master, and rather aggressively.[5] This equation of freedom and a return to an origin point—of the first home, of early attachments—rests on an assumption that the first home was a place of liberty, and that the unpredictability of it endowed the hero with greater agency and happiness.

## We Give Them Everything

Material comforts can act as a useful contrast to loftier priorities. A glass case in the ALZhIR museum features a letter, from 1938, to a woman's relatives. The letter, written in faint pencil in Russian on yellowing paper, had been retyped for the display:

My dear relatives! I write from the road, they sent me warm things here. . . . My relatives, beloved! Don't worry about me, it's possible to live anywhere. I hope that I will still be able to see you and my born children. Where are they? I think that you will take pity on me and Yashutka and take my little ones. I don't think about [my] things, they say that they have distributed them, other than what they sent me. . . . Did they send Yashutka money? He is without a kopek. . . . *I beg you to take the children in*. I hope that I will be able to take them later. *Get the children*. I live with the sole hope, that my relatives will not leave the children, and that I will not perish. . . . Your Mania (On display at ALZhIR, emphasis in original)

This letter does not say where the author, Mania, is writing to, or where she has come from. She mentions the redistribution of her things, but this is not worth worrying about. The needs of her family are more urgent. Did they send money to Yashutka (presumably her husband)? She negates any need for concern about herself by insisting that she can live "anywhere"—even the Kazakh steppe! The children, however, should not live with just anyone. Things can get scattered; the children should not. In other contexts, the presence of things can give a sense of belonging, but in a time of utter displacement, when the entire household has been dissolved, the woman must make clear her priorities. She underlines them.

At Hope House, teachers and directors prided themselves on the material comforts they offered the children. "We give them everything here," the teachers would tell me. They said this when complaining that a parent was ungrateful for all they had done for their child. They said this when showing me around, impressing me with the advanced technologies they offered the children—a computer room, an interactive board, a flat-screen television in every room. The director bragged that the children's classrooms were better equipped than most public schools. Enough sponsors donated new clothes to them that they no longer needed to rely on donations of used clothing. On the days of sponsors' visits, teachers dressed the children in bright new play clothes reserved especially for such occasions. Sometimes guests wished to observe the children playing outside. Teachers watched the children uneasily on such days, quietly warning the children not to dirty their pristine jeans or white tights as they jumped from a piece of playground equipment onto the muddy ground. However, at Hope House, adults worked not merely to provide a bright picture for outsiders. On days when no one came, the children wore clothes that were slightly faded, but they enjoyed a variety of experiences. The sensory room offered light shows and soft furniture. Lessons included tactile activities and tests of smell. Medical staff gave the children oxygen cocktails—juice with oxygen bubbles—to provide mental stimulation. Teachers and aides kept the classrooms and yard bright and busy. Children performed ablutions at the end of each day, pouring a bucket of cold water over their heads outside in their swimsuits—even during the winter— then running back in to dry off and warm up.

This sensory richness contrasts with popular accounts of socialist-era orphan- ages, which have commonly been cast as spaces of deprivation and sterility. In Chekhov's original text, Kashtanka finds the new home to be sensorially sparse, other than delicious meals, lacking the rich smells and textures she knew be- fore. The children's home in the twenty-first century finds itself inheriting mul- tiple legacies of scarcity: These institutions proliferated in response to large-scale conditions of lack, such as the Kazakhstani famine of the 1930s, as discussed in chapter 1. The stigmatization of orphanages in the US and UK appeared around the same time, as discussed in chapter 2, with studies describing such institu- tions as sites of emotional deprivation where children "insatiably" demanded af- fection (Goldfarb 1955, 108). In the twenty-first century, studies of institutional damage consistently use the language of "deprivation" to describe the conditions, whether researchers tested the children's psychosocial, scholastic, linguistic, or cognitive development.[6] Many studies were conducted on children who had been adopted internationally, so the exact nature or extent of the children's early years in institutions remained unknown and unstudied. These previous conditions are consistently described as "profound deprivation," without specifying what was lacking, and rather than focusing on the fact that many of the children studied also experienced various traumas.

Such studies, like journalistic portrayals, depict the postsocialist orphanage not only as a place of displacement, but moreover as a site of poverty on a number of sensory and emotional levels. Eastern European orphanages are often treated as the epitome of deprivational environments and as a metonym for a more dif- fuse grayness that was emblematic of state socialism.[7] Western and local critics alike take sparse surroundings as pointing to a lack of sentimental ties between teachers and children, even though the presence of vivid colors or soft textures carries no guarantee that outsiders will imagine greater affection. Images of "waiting children" prompted international celebrities to swoop in and save them from these conditions of emotional deprivation.[8] Anthropological accounts of post-Soviet Russian orphanages have emphasized these institutions as materially impoverished, with toys bleached until they lost their color, and with the bright, new toys kept on a top shelf for the admiration of visitors.[9] Kazakhstanis also criticized reliance on orphanage care and stigmatized the children who grew up in them, but these discourses were less inflected with this language of deprivation and instead focused on the children's dependence on the state.[10]

Children, especially orphans, are useful icons of socialist sterility and deprivation, since they have already been deprived of something seen as essential—their
parents.[11] The last time I visited Hope House, in 2017, a teacher articulated the familiar sentiment, "We give them everything here." Then she added, "But there's no
replacement for a mother's love." The teacher said this with resignation, as if no
matter how hard they tried to give the children what they needed, they were bound
to fail in this aspect. A friend of mine, a single mother, expressed a similar sentiment when she said she had considered placing her children at Hope House but
decided against it. Here, she painted a contrast between the material "everything"
that Hope House offered and the "mother's love" that she gave her children. She
said this to explain her own choice of keeping her sons despite her struggles to afford their care.[12] Such statements mark the attachment to the mother as original,
irreplaceable, and primary (even though it is possible that many children spent
time before Hope House being cared for by grandparents, a father, or others). Pit-
ting material comfort against the mother's love suggests that the things Hope
House provided must be at least pretending to replace something that has been
lost through the child's displacement.

Hope House had to show that it was not depriving the children of anything—
except the mother's love. Teachers and directors were careful not to describe
themselves as replacing mothers, but the "everything" they offered was open to
include emotional work and affective bonds. Sometimes they went further in list-
ing what they gave: food, clothes, lessons, excursions. The provisions they offered figured prominently, but so did the work they put into educating the
children, providing experiences and opportunities to thrive. Some of their lessons and rehearsals pained me with their focus on imitation and repetition, but
the teachers also impressed me with the scope of stimuli incorporated into their
curriculum. For the teachers, material comforts were not a replacement for the
mother's love as much as an extension of their pedagogical care. The sharing of
food and other substances can play an important role in the constitution of kin
bonds (Carsten 2004; Parkes 2004). Kazakhs draw on discourses of blood to
mark connections, but these are mediated through other substances, human and
nonhuman. Shrines and other sacred sites anchor Kazakh relations to ancestors,
their reanimation enabled by poets and caretakers.[13] Things need not only stand
in the way of social relations but can aid them as well.

One day, the group was outside when Aigul Apai used a piece of playground
equipment with a bar and colorful rings as an abacus for an impromptu math
lesson. She created story problems for the children. For example, a tree has five
leaves, and three fall off. How many are left? After a number of these, she introduced stories of her mother coming to visit and bringing gifts. After giving the
children these problems, Aigul Apai invited the children to try telling a story

problem while others managed the rings. Though their teacher had offered a range of topics they could employ in telling their stories about objects, the children imagined stories of gifts, almost always from mothers. They also brought the teachers and other children into their story problems. One boy, Maksat, in a cheeky move, narrated that his mother brought him cake, but then Aigul Apai and another teacher ate it. Aigul Apai announced that Maksat's turn was over, but she also smiled at my camera. Maksat hugged her from behind.

The objects featured in the stories—gifts brought to the children by their mothers—indexed children's relationships to absent parents, along with ties among the children and adults present at Hope House. Maksat at once expressed affection for his teacher, but also treated her as a threat to the relationship with his mother. She had consumed—and thus deprived him of—an imagined gift. The narratives were designed to make the abstraction of numbers more concrete by offering "real world" examples, but the constraints of the formula forced the children to think about relationships and transactions in simplified terms. Experiences with objects and people are more complex—more relational and emergent—than can be expressed on an abacus. Objects, real and imagined, from playground equipment to birthday cakes, work in different ways to make and maintain ties between children, teachers, and absent family members.[14]

# You Are a Doll

The children at Hope House used objects to draw and maintain a variety of affective bonds—between one another, between themselves and their parents, and between themselves and the teachers. At times, children stood in for the caregivers, and dolls stood in for the children as objects of care. However, the children were adept at navigating the ambiguities between iconic objects and the persons they indexed. They acknowledged that objects could serve affective relationships without replacing them. Just as the children slip between persons and things, so do they shift objects between the two, between animate and inanimate.

A video I recorded during my first winter at Hope House illustrates this. The children have been quarantined because of a chicken pox outbreak, and the winter is even colder than usual. Out the window of their ground floor classroom/playroom, through the gauzy, Hello Kitty-patterned curtains, snow covers the ground and fills the trees. There are eight children in the group on this day, all around five years old. Backlit by the snow and without overhead lights, the children's play looks rather dark, the colors blue, gray, and brown. They dump a bucket of blocks on the floor. Offscreen, Olzhas is crying, Maksat demands blocks, and Maisa whines. In front of the camera, farther back and more difficult to hear, Tamilia and Zhamilia, the twins, play with dolls. Zhamilia's doll is thinner, and consequently looks older. Zhamilia herself is slightly bigger and more serious than her sister. She uses the blocks to make a box with an open top and fills it with small, loose pieces. She buries her doll's feet at the bottom of the box, in this way helping the doll to stand up. While she works at this, Tamilia alternately drops her doll, props it up against the kitchen set, and dangles it off the ground by a strand of hair, like a marionette. She looks at her doll and says, *Sen quyrşaqsyn*. "You are a doll."

In this scene, the twins vacillate between treating their dolls as things and as persons. When Zhamilia creates a box to help the doll stand up, it is as if she recognizes the doll's iconic resemblance to a type that likes to stand up—humans—but also notes the object's limitations in being able to balance on its own two feet. Zhamilia constructs a means to support this endeavor. She creates physical scaffolding, the structures used to elevate children according to certain pedagogical theories.[15] When Tamilia tells her doll, "You are a doll," she interpellates the object as a doll, as a toy, which is not the same as a person, and yet she treats it as an interlocutor by addressing it. The dolls become a special kind of social object for the twins, one whose ambiguity is productive. The children at Hope House often played with pretend food, putting plastic fruit into a little plastic coffee maker and stirring it around, pouring it for me into a plastic cup, and telling me that it was tea. Because it was hot, I should blow on it. Other times, they shaped their hands as if holding something and handed it to me, telling me it was *bauyrsaq*. In the children's play, there are different ways that the physical and imaginary interact, whether the remembered, real *bauyrsaq* influences the ways children cup their hands or whether I hold an actual plastic cup in my hand and blow on it as if it had liquid inside.

The toys' materiality sometimes shaped and sometimes got in the way of imaginary activities. When Tamilia saw a doll that looked especially baby-like, she often voiced the baby's crying. She might bring it over to me to comfort it. One day Maisa could not get a doll's legs to bend so that it could sit, and she started crying, out of frustration of the object's limits. Zhamilia offered her a different doll, but Maisa was too distraught to play anymore. When children play together, the pretend actions of one child can so upset their playmate that they must move outside of the play frames to negotiate the terms of their game.[16] The frames of play or not-play also get blurred or are allowed to coexist, such as when Tamilia talks to her doll as a doll. I treat questions of framing in more depth in chapter 6, but here the doll creates an opportunity for a double framing. Tamilia treats it as a fantastic creature with material affordances and limitations.

With her act of speaking to the doll as a doll, Tamilia highlights the paradoxes that dolls present: As objects that establish a play frame, interactions with them are both real and not real. They can act as a pivot point between the concrete and the abstract. And they mediate between me and not-me.[17] Objects and substances—toys, food, clothing—mediated relations at Hope House in various ways. Dolls were not in this way special. However, dolls bring human and nonhuman closer together in particular ways. The children at Hope House played with a range of things, including "open-ended" toys such as blocks, which resembled nothing in particular and left children to create and point to similarities, and iconic toys such as play food, toy cars, and a few toy guns (which were usually kept in a special cabinet and only taken out by the children in the absence of authoritative adults). Toy cars and toy guns are miniaturized versions of instruments used by humans—the toy versions not working in the same way as the real ones.

Dolls, as toy humans, have the potential to represent the children themselves or to represent others with whom the children have social relations. Children might talk to a doll, they might speak through the doll, or they might use a doll as an instrument to hit another child. Alfred Gell (1998, 18) describes dolls as "truly remarkable objects" because of the importance granted them by girls. He naturalizes and universalizes generalizations about girls and dolls, without empirical evidence, but he also treats children's play with dolls as equivalent to adults' engagement with art objects. He notes particular features that, when added to objects, make them more likely to be treated as social beings. Namely, with the addition of orifices, especially eyes, "there is no definitive 'inside,' but only a ceaseless passage in and out. . . . It is here, in this traffic to and fro, that the mystery of animation is solved" (148). Dolls interest Gell for their ability to come to life, to be treated as social beings, inviting intersubjectivity.[18]

Objects can anchor social relations with other humans as well. One day I asked Maisa what her doll's name was. It was a fake Barbie her mother had given her, so it was uniquely hers. She answered that it was named "Meghanne." It was only Meghanne, as far as I saw, for that day, or for that moment, and probably only became Meghanne as soon as I asked.[19] However, Maisa's answer made me wonder what it might mean in regard to my relationship with her. One way that objects mediate social relations is in considering them transitional objects, which children use to distinguish between themselves and their mothers. The goal in the effective use of a transitional object, as discussed in chapter 2, is not for the object to replace the mother. It will instead help the child understand their own separation from their mother so they will not imagine that their own destructive thoughts led to the mother's disappearance (Winnicott 1971). Hope House presents a complicated context for considering the significance of objects and of mothers. Children had few belongings of their own there. Their parents were mostly not only beyond their control—that is, they were not simply dealing with an undesirable separation from their mothers at bedtime—but existed completely outside their direct experience for weeks to months at a time. There were objects that parents left with their children and to which the children attached special importance, but not all of them had such things. While D. W. Winnicott's theory of object destruction seems to assume children will hate the object but not actually destroy it, many of the children's objects did get destroyed, discarded, or lost.

Children living in institutions such as Hope House may have had no problem imagining themselves as separate from their mothers, but they used fantasy to imagine life outside the home and their connections to absent others. Social relations between humans sometimes resembled human-doll interactions. One day, Zhanel Apai took Nurlan's hair and fixed it into little ponytails, smiling as she did this. Nurlan frowned to show he didn't like it, but he didn't swat her hand away. She was a figure of authority—one whose affection the children frequently sought. As someone who had no need to manage the children, I made myself pliant to them. Nevertheless, I did this from a privileged position. I could object, push them away, or go home when I pleased. The toys could not do this; neither could the children.

# The Overpowering Agency of Objects

The iconicity of the doll—its resemblance to humans—shapes children's play and adults' expectations surrounding interactions with these toys, but children's play is full of surprises. On the shelves behind the play kitchen area were dolls kept in packages, left untouched. Other dolls—those used for play—were lined up along the ledge behind the play kitchen, taken out with the teachers' permission. One day, Maksat held up a leg that had fallen off a doll and said to Zhanel Apai, "Apai, a leg!" She told him that dolls were for girls. Her assertion surprised me— not only because Maksat's point was that the leg had fallen off a doll and needed to be fixed—but also because Olzhas often played with the girls and the dolls. He was sometimes the father and sometimes the baby. Other toys—such as toy guns—likewise garner adult worries regarding how children's play with them might impact their real behavior. Dolls are unique, however, because they have the possibility to act as a friend and interlocutor or as a *second I*, as an extension or representation of the child.[20]

Dolls' abilities to represent the children playing with them have made them the object of a great deal of attention. Adults fret about how dolls should look, what they should (or should not) be able to do, and who should be allowed to play with them. Pedagogues, parents, and social scientists have worried about whether "fashion dolls"—French dolls of the nineteenth century or Barbie in the twentieth and twenty-first—encourage feminine consumption and obsession with physical appearance, sometimes insisting that girls should be given baby dolls so that they will learn to be good mothers (Peers 2004). These debates assume a number of things: that dolls are for girls, that girls and women must primarily choose between two roles of fancying clothes or loving children, and that vanity and consumption are bad. They also presume, however, that dolls have the power to dictate to children how they will take them up.

The agency of objects emerged as a multidisciplinary concern toward the end of the twentieth century and the beginning of the twenty-first.[21] The anthropologist Daniel Miller (2010, 52) has described the "humility of things" in the ways they get taken for granted. However, for a long time, adults have not only recognized but panicked over the agency of objects in children's worlds. Perhaps because of beliefs regarding the vulnerability of children—especially girls—adults expect them to fall victim more easily to material determinism rather than perceiving objects' features as affordances that simply invite or suggest particular uses.[22] People assume that if a girl plays with a doll that looks like a teenager, her pretend play will largely follow "typical" teenager pastimes such as shopping, flirting with boys, and talking about how "math class is tough" (as an early talking Barbie complained).[23] These hyperfeminine objects threaten to render the girls (or—worse—boys) playing with them hyperfeminine teenage subjects.

Debates surrounding dolls often focus on the visual—assuming that girls will want to look the way that Barbie looks, for example. Manipulation and animation are sensory experiences, however. At puppet shows for very young children (one-to-two-year-olds), you can see the toddlers' hands reaching out from their seats, attempting to climb onto the stage to touch the puppets, which are often seductively soft. Sight and touch work in tandem.[24] Philosophers have mused over hierarchies of senses and their ordering as species-specific (Condillac and Carr 1930), though certain media theories have argued that the dominance of a new form, such as television, can significantly reorder the senses (McLuhan 2001). When the narrator describes Kashtanka's arrival, the stranger's surroundings are characterized as "poor and ugly" because, other than the furniture, it has "nothing," and it smells of "nothing." The carpenter's space, on the other hand, had been stuffed full of things. The air a thick fog, the whole place smelled of glue, varnish, and shavings. The food may have been scarce or even a trick at the carpenter's house, but smell reigned supreme. Chekhov's prioritizing smell indexes certain assumptions regarding the sensory ordering of Kashtanka, as a dog.

In nineteenth-century America, women advocated for dolls that were soft and thus easy for children to pick up and carry. Male-dominated doll industries used new technologies to create walking, talking dolls. Thomas Edison spent an enormous amount of money and effort to create talking dolls that never succeeded because their hard bodies were cold to the touch and too heavy for little children to pick up. The problem was not what the dolls could or could not do, but what children could or could not do with them.[25] Disputes about the types of dolls that are best for children—and for which children—dominated discussions about dolls among parent groups, pedagogues, and academics alike throughout the twentieth century.[26] In the twenty-first century, new advances in interactive dolls, which link to smartphone apps and store children's responses in the cloud, raised new worries about privacy along with reviving old objections to the ways the toy's voice impinges on the imagination of the child.[27] These arguments often remain oblivious to how children play with dolls and to the various ways dolls become part of a wider net of relationships. Books and other media offer culturally constructed scripts which children prove adept at elaborating upon for their play (R. Bernstein 2011). Nonetheless, children often defy expected engagements with dolls.[28] Children at Hope House articulated opinions about who should do what with certain objects, yet they were also ready to ignore such rules.

Despite stereotypes of socialism as a world sparse and gray, scholars have described a complex consumer environment of state socialist Eastern Europe, in Stalin's time and later, with consumer goods becoming increasingly important to youth culture in the late Soviet era.[29] Children's consumption of material and screen culture worried parents, pedagogues, and puppet artists in Kazakhstan during my fieldwork. Accounts of the rise of children's consumer culture often focus on the insidious influence of advertising as inciting an insatiable appetite for toys, especially those of particular brands.[30] However, toys are ephemeral not just because of market-driven campaigns. Branded toys still sometimes carry a promise of quality.[31] Though I had owned knockoff Barbies as a child, I was unprepared when shopping for toys in Kazakhstan for the remarkable decline in the quality of off-brand toys, along with the range of quality one could find. For my first New Year's in Kazakhstan, I wanted to give each child a present. Toys from stores were outside my budget, so I went to the bazaar, where I could afford seven toys along with gifts for the teachers, helpers, and directors. I ended up with four fake Barbies and three toy cars.[32] Sometimes the toys from the bazaar came in boxes imitating those of the authentic branded toys. Others had English words printed all over the package that made little sense or contained spelling errors, but gave a sense of brandedness to the product.[33] The toys I bought came in the most modest packaging of clear plastic bags.

On the last day I visited before the holiday, I handed out the toys without paying attention to who received which toy. I thought that all the cars were the same, but one of them was a police car, which Maksat received. Olzhas, upset with his civilian automobile, tried to return the car I had given to him, demanding a police car. I told him I had no more cars and no more money. He took the gray car and tried to play with it, but the bearings on the rear wheels were loose. It would not wind up and lurch forward like the others. Nurlan did not complain about being given a plain car, even though the rear wheels kept falling off. The first time this happened, I fixed it for him. The second time, he insisted on doing it himself.

The dolls were even worse. It turned out everyone but Zhamilia had received a small hairbrush with her doll. She watched me as I looked through the empty bags until she was satisfied that hers had not somehow fallen out. She went to play with her doll, borrowing others' brushes enough that she didn't seem to mind not having her own. Ainura demanded that I return her doll for another because she disliked the doll's hair. I took the rubber bands out so that the doll's hair was loose instead of braided. Ainura was satisfied, but I was horrified. I realized the dolls' hair was not threaded all over their plastic scalps—as they were for a real Barbie—but had hair just around the crown, so that removing the rubber bands revealed a large bald spot in the middle of each doll's head.

The leg of Zhamilia's doll kept falling off. I reattached it, but while the Barbies (and fake Barbies) of my childhood had legs of solid plastic that could bend at the knees, these doll bodies were all made of a thin, hollow plastic. Their joints were fragile. The more I worked to put the leg back into place, the more the doll's butt got misshapen, and the more easily the leg fell out again. The dolls talked to one another for a minute, but then Tamilia's went to sleep. Zhamilia's could not do much, for risk of losing its leg. Soon, all the dolls were lying on little shelves in front of a mirror. Maisa played with hers the longest. She sat in front of the vanity, brushing the doll's hair and talking to her about how pretty she was. I wished I had given them nicer toys. On the other hand, the teachers could not afford gifts for the children. It would have been awkward to give better gifts, even if the children already recognized differences between the teachers, the helpers, and me.

Unlike debates about which things are good for children because of what adults see them as representing, those toys simply failed to do what they were supposed to. The following year for a New Years present, I sewed the children capes of shiny polyester satin, each with the first letter of their name on the back. I assumed they would all become superheroes, and was curious what their special powers would be. For the first few minutes, the children donned their capes and pretended to fly around the bedroom. Then one of the girls pulled the cape over her head, using it to frame her face, and said, "I'm a grandma" (*men äzhemyn*). The other girls all began to do this as well, speaking in creaky voices and bending over when they walked. They still used the gift to remark on their gendered categorizations, but in a way that utterly surprised me.

# Instructions for Care

Adults foster children's relationships to toys in different ways, sometimes worrying that toys threaten social relations, other times articulating a moral obligation to give the right kinds of toys. They also urge children to care for toys by suggesting that toys can feel. In encouraging them to treat toys as sentient, adults invite children to imagine toys' secret relationships—friendly or antagonistic—with one another. Media created by adults and for children also does this—from Soviet texts such as *Buratino* and *Cheburashka* to international sensations like *Toy Story* and *The Velveteen Rabbit*.[34] During a lesson one day, taught by Saltanat Apai, I started the morning distracted by the realization that Nurlan had gone home and was not coming back (as described in chapter 1). Saltanat Apai must have found the children's thoughts to be elsewhere as well. During the first part of their lesson, on letters, she kept stressing to them that they needed to think faster.

Then Saltanat puts up a new picture and asks what the children see.

"Toys," they answer. She has their attention now, as well as mine.

"Who plays with toys?" she asks.

"Children," they answer.

"What kind of toys do you know?" she asks.

They have no problem now coming up with answers quickly, especially as Saltanat Apai takes toys from the table behind her and places them on the table in front of her. "Ball," they offer. "Bear, doll, car, computer."

These are objects they have probably been able to identify correctly for several years already, but they participate with enthusiasm, as if calling the toys' names brings them closer to playing with them. Saltanat Apai discusses different properties and materials of toys, then continues the lesson with the question: "Now, children, look. What do all children do with toys?"

"They love toys," the children answer.

Rather than affirm or deny this, she adds, "All children break toys."

"They get taken outside," the children add. (Broken toys became outdoor toys, kept in the shelves of their playhouse.)

"Now," she continues, "these toys, among themselves, at night when you're sleeping in the bedroom, they talk to one another. When you go off to sleep, they talk to each other. For example, this toy got broken." She walks over to a shelf and brings back a car with a broken window. "Let's say this car. . . . You go to sleep in the bedroom, it's quiet there, and then they start to talk. You've seen toys like this in cartoons. You know, right? They all, when the kids come, sit still, they lie like that, but when you go off to sleep, they shake off their lifelessness, they turn to one another—"

"They talk," the children offer.

"So this car is talking to this one, mocking it." On the table, the yellow car and the red car face one another. She pokes the red car, the one with the broken window. "'Ey, red car, look at your window. It's broken. That Bekzhan doesn't like you. That's why your window is broken.' That's what the yellow car says to the red car, making fun of it."

Her voice gets louder, as if pulled from this imaginary world back to a more public one of the lesson. "For example, if your nose is running, you make fun of one another about your appearance, right?"

"Yes," the class confirms.

"Toys are like that, too," Saltanat Apai explains.

"It's bad," Ainura observes.

"Toys are like that! Like, you dress badly, in those clothes, you make fun of each other, right? That's what toys do, too! So then, what does every child need to do correctly to every toy? It's necessary to love it."

According to Saltanat's lesson, the toys—who are peers to one another—cannot be relied on to love one another. Weakness leaves them vulnerable to attack. She naturalizes the tendencies of peers to pick on one another for their faults, rather than condemning such practices as Ainura does. Because toys are vulnerable to one another's criticism, it is up to the children—their owners and caretakers—to love the toys by not damaging them. Saltanat draws parallels between the children and the toys as susceptible to being made fun of for their faults—implying that the children, like the toys, require a certain amount of care. However, she does not specify who might be responsible for ensuring that the children remain intact. Children, moreover, often care for and break toys; these are not mutually exclusive.

Saltanat Apai opens the book she has been holding in her hand and begins reading aloud the story that has motivated this discussion of toy care. In this story, toys do not make fun of one another, but fight over whom their owner, Sania, loves most. A dove intervenes and asks each one, "Who among you really loves Sania?" All of the toys assure the dove that they love the girl who owns them. Saltanat Apai breaks from the narrated event to assure the children that if she asked the classroom toys which of them loved the children, they would all answer, "Me! Me! Me!" as well. She resumes reading the story. The dove warns the toys that they need to help Sania or they risk getting discarded or given away. The dove reminds the toys that Sania cannot possibly play with all the toys at the same time. The toys stop fighting, and this is the end of the story.

Saltanat Apai does not dwell on the dove's threat that useless toys will be thrown out or given away. At Hope House, it was the children who left—moving from one group to another, and eventually from Hope House entirely, back into their family homes. The toys stayed behind, to be played with by the next children, taken outside, and eventually tossed into the dumpster. The book's story places the responsibility on the toys to make themselves useful—and therefore lovable— or to risk obsolescence. Saltanat Apai again reminds the children of their responsibility to love the toys properly. She asks the students if they have a lot of time to play with toys. They answer, "A lot."

"You don't have a lot of time," she corrects them, then reminds them of all the other obligations they have during the day—lessons, music, mealtime. "What do you need to do to toys?" she asks. "This one, should you break the window, should you throw it out?"

"We shouldn't," the children answer.

She takes a baby doll, one with a huge head who wears a hat that the children sometimes like to put on their own heads as a joke. Removing the hat, she asks, "This hat, should we throw it around?"

The children agree that they should not.

"Wearing this cap, it's pretty," she shows them, then removes it again.

"But how is it now, with the hat gone?"

"Bad," say the children.

"It doesn't have hair. But wearing the hat it looks nice, right?"

In discussing the toys in the classroom and those in Sania's playroom, there is no mention of the toys' origins and thus no indexical tie between these objects and other persons. The social relation is purely between the children and the objects. In Saltanat Apai's story about the classroom toys, the children need to love these toys by not damaging them. In the story she reads, the toys must love Sania by being useful to her. In both, the time constraint on toys is an everyday time. Sania cannot play with all of her toys at once; they must wait their turn. The children cannot play with their toys all the time. When they do, Saltanat Apai stresses, they should treat them with care. This differs from other narratives about the lifespan of toys in relation to the general development of the child, including Winnicott's expectation that transitional objects will gradually lose their importance and get forgotten. In such time scales, the relationship between child and toy is finite, and childhood itself is fragile because of its temporary nature.

The only toys the children personally possessed were those given to them by visiting family members. Often, gifts were simple. Once, the twins' mother gave them coupons. They brought them back into the classroom and shared them with the other children, including with Maisa, who declared the little papers were "money." The aide on duty overheard them and asked to see the coupons more closely. She smiled and explained to the children, "That's not money." She showed them real money and then gathered the coupons and put them in the trash. Maisa began to cry. For a long time, I remembered it wrong. Until I revisited my notes from that day, I assumed it was the twins who had cried, over losing objects their mother had given them. Perhaps the twins could cope more easily with the loss of the coupons because they had just seen their mother. But why was the fantasy so important to Maisa? The social value of objects of exchange gives them meaning.[35] When the coupons became fake money, they enabled social relations of exchange among the children, which the aide abruptly curtailed. The twins did not need objects passing between them to ensure the continuity of their relationship. For Maisa, who badly missed her mother and who had arrived the most recently in the group, social relations were fleeting, at best.

Gifts from visitors became communal property. Gifts from parents got broken more quickly. They could play with them at times when other toys were to stay on the shelves. Other children sometimes got jealous and treated them roughly. When Maksat received a remote-controlled car, Olzhas threw it on the floor out of frustration that he had no right to play with it. When he received a couple of action figures from his mother for his birthday, their special features—buttons on the back that illuminated their chests—were quickly broken, but he also cared for them. I have a video of him tucking a Spider-Man carefully into his own bed, making a pillow from a small rectangular block and pulling up the covers to the doll's neck (See Illustration 15).

**ILLUSTRATION 15. OLZHAS TUCKS SPIDERMAN INTO BED**  Olzhas tucks a Spider-Man carefully into his own bed, making a pillow from a small rectangular block and pulling up the covers to the doll's neck.

# The Humility of Things' Creators

At the puppet theater, things—performing objects—played a central role in the theater's mission and in most of their activities. However, when I asked puppeteers at the theater how they got into puppetry, they laughed off my suggestion that they must feel a special affinity with the objects they brought to life. "My parents didn't let me play with dolls as a child!" one puppeteer joked when I asked how she decided to study puppetry. Many said that they had wanted to be performers of some sort. Art schools in Almaty only accept stage actors, voice actors, and puppet artists on a rotating basis each year. Their decision to study puppetry had been largely accidental. Others cited a wish to work with children. Puppeteers I met from Western Europe who made and animated their puppets, such as Pulcinella puppeteers, did express an affinity with the puppets as objects, since they were constantly repairing them. Perhaps the division of labor surrounding the creation, care, and animation of puppets at the Almaty theater foreclosed close connections between particular puppets and artists.

While Kuba wanted to unhide the puppet artists, it always seemed that the puppet makers were the truly shy artists.[36] The costume designers had special training, but the women in the props department (*butafor*) who made the puppets described their paths to the puppet theater as even more random than the puppeteers'. One of the puppet makers who had been there the longest, Liuba, had first worked as a cook, she said. Then she heard the puppet theater was hiring and that the hours were better. Having worked at the theater for more than forty years when I met her, she was described by her colleagues as a true artist, shaping foam rubber into animals' faces with a pair of scissors (See Illustration 16). A small woman with short red hair, Liuba was humble and reserved, never wanting me to interview her, and insisting that I keep the audio off if I wanted to film them working so that their conversations would remain private. Perhaps because they had mostly trained on the job themselves, they allowed me to join them in backstage participant observation. They gave me the easiest jobs, checked my work, and fixed it as necessary. It was during the production of *Kashtanka* that I began this part of the research. After so much time simply watching the puppet artists at work, I hoped at last to be useful.

On the day before the premiere of *Kashtanka*, Kuba became irate about the movement of Kashtanka's leg, which stuck in the air when she was supposed to be lying down. He called Liuba into the rehearsal space and berated her. He called the leg "pornographic." When Liuba said that she had not made the dog's leg, I shrank in my chair—for I had made it. However, Kuba insisted that she, as an artist, needed to take responsibility for these creations. He then berated her for not

**ILLUSTRATION 16. LIUBA CUTS OUT THE CAT HEAD**   Having worked at the theater for more than forty years when I met her, she was described by her colleagues as a true artist, shaping foam rubber into animals' faces with a pair of scissors.

attending earlier rehearsals to see how the puppets were faring once animated. Liuba insisted that she had not been invited to the rehearsals. Kuba found it preposterous that she thought she should await an invitation; she should have taken the initiative, as an artist, to show up at rehearsals to inspect the work in action.

However, her seeming passivity struck me less as a sign of a disregard for her creation. I saw it instead as born out of the rather delicate intermediate position in which she and the props department found themselves. They often had to wait, idly—for the carpenters to make the structural and mechanical bases of the puppets that they would cover with soft materials, for budgetary issues to be resolved so that they could go to the bazaar to buy the materials they needed, for the designer of the puppets to instruct them—and then had to hurry to complete their work as quickly as possible. As the premiere for *Kashtanka* neared in November, the theater was also preparing for their New Year's spectacle (*ëlka*). We were making a dragon's head covered with sequined cloth that was big enough for a man to walk through. The women were working without rest—through the weekends—until all of the props, costumes, and puppets were completed.[37]

As an artist who had little control over the temporal dynamics of creation, Liuba had learned to practice patience. She waited for Kuba to finish reprimanding her. He left to fetch the administrative director about another issue (See chapter 6). Then Liuba asked the puppeteers to specify the problems each puppet was showing. The pig's tail was also broken (which was in no way my fault). She took the puppets away, and she and the others set about fixing them before the rehearsals resumed. I remained in the rehearsal space.

# On Not Getting Broken

There are important differences between children and toys or puppets. The toy, like the puppet, does not change, or should not. In the month that passes for Kashtanka in her new home, all of the animals, it seems, are adults, past any point of growth. Their daily meals—and the lessons of the already-trained animals—are acts of maintenance. The child, in contrast, should grow, and should show no signs of damage until long after this life phase has ended. Any violation of this is viewed as tragic and even dangerous, as chapter 5 explores. The toy cannot grow; it can only decay. In some stories, the toy's decay, as a product of its use, becomes proof that it was loved.[38] The stable iconicity of the toy in the face of a shift in its use can make it a potent symbol of nostalgia for lost childhood. The administrative director of the puppet theater expressed this sentiment when he articulated his dream of making the puppet theater into a site for adults to recuperate that childhood. Childhood is supposed to be ephemeral, whereas toys' decay is a kind of tragic abuse. According to Saltanat Apai, to love toys is to protect them. She appeals to the children to show kindness to the toys out of pity for their vulnerability.

When food and objects get in the way of feelings and social relations, they must be rejected, yet sensorial austerity can be taken as an index of emotional deprivation. It is insufficient, however, to have just any things, especially when dealing with objects that should come to life. Improper objects can be dangerous to the children playing with them. They can be harmful to child viewers, such as when a puppet leg is pornographic. Or children themselves can endanger objects, breaking them and then making them vulnerable to peer abuse. In talk about objects, we find the children entangled.

The puppet makers and other workers at the theater maintained, repaired, or replaced the puppets as necessary. It is not so easy for the children. Saltanat opens the door to comparing the children to their toys when mentioning the children's mocking of one another, but she does not extend the simile of toys-are-like-children to consider her own role as caretaker. Kuba, at different points, compares himself both to the new master and to Kashtanka herself. Saltanat keeps herself out of this narrative, though she leaves me to wonder: If the children are like the toys—susceptible to verbal abuse if discovered in a state of disorder or even, in some way, broken—does she consider it her responsibility to keep the children from falling apart? The dove warns the toys that if they fail to make themselves useful to their owner, she will discard them. Do the children face similar threats? They may not get thrown out, but neither are they given any choice regarding when they will leave or what will happen afterward. The caregivers at Hope House never imagine that they can replace the mother's love here at this second home, but we can ask to what extent their acts of provision help prevent the children from suffering damage. Perhaps it is better for Kashtanka, or an adult, to be hungry and free, but isn't it better for a child to be kept safe and satisfied, at least for a little while?

# LOSING A FRIEND

*Auntie dreamed a dog dream that a street cleaner chased her with a broom, and fear woke her.*

*The room was quiet, dark, and suffocating. The fleas were biting. The dark had never scared Auntie before, but now for some reason it felt eerie and made her want to bark. . . . Thinking about food lightens one's soul, so Auntie began to think about how she had today stolen from Fyodr Timofeyitch a chicken leg. . . . But suddenly, not far from her, a strange cry rang out, which made her flinch and jump to her feet.*

The dog and cat have already begun to rest. Their puppeteers crouch behind them and rest their own heads on the wooden boxes. Puppets and masters are all startled awake when Ivan Ivanitch, the gander, emits a low moan. Maral—the gander's puppeteer—looks at him with concern. Eventually the master wakes up as well and emerges onstage in his robe to see what's wrong. He scolds Ivan Ivanitch for waking them all and goes back to bed.

Maral tries again to settle the goose, but now the puppet falls out of her hands as if by accident. The beak bangs against the front of the wooden box. Maral regards the puppet with surprise, as do the dog and cat (See Illustration 18). As she studies Ivan Ivanitch, Maral touches his head and helps him slowly raise it to let out another cry. The head slips from her fingers and knocks back down again. Maral, here, moves from animator of the puppet to the gander's caretaker. Bolat has done this in subtler ways in his animation of Kashtanka, but the scene with the gander is striking in Maral's apparent loss of control and her bewilderment at the gander's state.

Maral strokes the goose's wing. She helps him raise the other and groan again. She looks shocked by the cry she has just voiced, and she rushes offstage. The master returns onstage and asks sarcastically, "What, are you dying?" He touches the goose's wing and rubs his fingers together to indicate there is blood on them. Recalling an accident with a horse earlier that day, the master realizes the gander is, in fact, dying. Maral returns with a small metal bowl and puts it up to the puppet's beak. The master commands Ivan Ivanitch to drink, but it is no use. The master laments that he had planned to take the goose to the country to run

**ILLUSTRATION 17. KASHTANKA RUNS FROM A BROOM** *Auntie dreamed a dog dream, that a street cleaner chased her with a broom.*

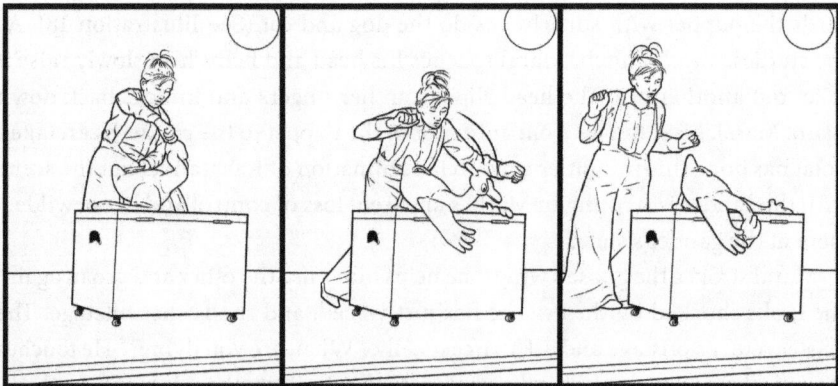

**ILLUSTRATION 18. MARAL LOSES THE GANDER PUPPET** Maral tries again to settle the goose, but now the puppet falls out of her hands as if by accident. The beak bangs against the front of the wooden box. Maral regards the puppet with surprise.

in the grass. The piano plays sad music throughout this scene, and Baqytzhan hams up his distress before cutting it off abruptly. He blows out his candle and returns to bed.

Just before the scene of the gander's death, the master had begun to train Kashtanka, declaring her to be a real talent. Now, Kashtanka has just witnessed the threat that this seemingly secure home carries with it, as she sees how quickly one can pass from star performer to a useless object, easily discarded. For puppets, moments of animation and deanimation are temporary. Kuba worked with the puppet artists so that they could move back and forth internally. With these shifts—between first and second home, between *first* and *second I*, between persons and objects—something is lost, but something else is gained, and the loss is emphasized as temporary.[1]

However, when the gander dies there is no chance for recovery. Kuba, in the last chapter, worried that routine creates monotony, anticipating death before it arrives because everything has already been planned. He suggested that we should work to reject such a fate while we can. The scene of the gander's death reminds us that some losses are final, and that some deanimations cannot be undone. If movements between animate and inanimate were always fluid, the uncanny would not trouble us. If the uncanny is the return of the repressed, it relies on an expectation of time and life trajectories moving forward in a linear manner, in order that the disturbance should be noted at all.

In this chapter, I return to questions of the uncanny to address more permanent losses that threaten the protagonists of this book. Puppets and dolls, as objects that can be animated and deanimated, enable children to confront death. Children are not as far removed from death as we might want to think, and adults' insistent figuration of children as the future elides the knowledge that many children will not see such futures. At Hope House, children risked being placed in an orphanage and lost to the fate of the institutionalized child. I look at a particular case of a child at Hope House who teachers saw as being in danger of becoming a "bad subject"—the child who becomes a cautionary tale, a warning.[2] Such children are at risk of losing the potential that makes their vulnerability and dependence cute and thus desirable. As they grow up, if they are not more competent (or if they mature too early), children become creatures to be feared rather than pitied. Such children are frequently figured as broken beyond repair, as wasted potential that could not be recuperated, as improperly socialized to the extent that they might no longer be considered human.

Uncanny feelings arise surrounding children when they are seen or portrayed as marginally human, as more wild than tame, as more animal than human. Such cases reveal anxiety about the fragility of the child as well as the porous boundaries of humanity. Transnational portrayals of wild and evil children stick to real postsocialist Eastern European institutions. Fascination with the elusive "feral child" and fear of the dangerous orphan reveal and contribute to otherwise unspoken anxieties surrounding the products of incorrect socialization. This calls on us to consider not only what is at stake within institutions working to save children from such fates, but also how representations reflect and propagate stereotype. When we make children into tropes—or cautionary tales— what do we accomplish? And who are the casualties in our quest for the children we desire and hold up as proper and worthy of love, care, and hope?

The gander's death scene transforms Maral as well as the puppet. The gander— once her puppet to animate, briefly a wretched creature under her care—is now a mere object that cannot perform. Whereas a moment earlier she knelt before it with a dish of water, begging it to drink, she now picks it up by its tail, flings it into its wooden box, and closes the lid with a thud. She wheels the black box offstage. Kashtanka and Fyodr Timofeyitch, the cat, snuggle up to one another to go back to sleep.

# The Uncanny Valley of the Dolls (and Puppets)

I have been describing the animation of intimacy as a familiarization technique— bringing two or more bodies closer together—yet movement between animate and inanimate can stir uneasy emotions. This was key to understanding the stranger in chapter 2, a danger that could be overcome through destrangement. This discomfort is also important for understanding permanent, insurmountable difference. In an essay designed to help roboticists create machines that would not scare consuming publics, Masahiro Mori ([1970] 2012) charts the increased affinity that humans supposedly feel as a nonhuman object more closely approximates human likeness—but only to a point. When a robot or other humanlike object resembles humans too closely, he argues, there is a sudden drop in humans' feelings of affection toward it. This "uncanny valley" is where we find objects that make humans uncomfortable because they cause us to question the boundaries between human and nonhuman, animate and inanimate. Mori acknowledges the possibility of an entity moving up or down the valley, depending on its state of animation. When a person suddenly dies, they tumble down the slope into the uncanny. On the right bank of the valley, climbing up out of the uncanny, he charts only two beings: an ill person and a Bunraku puppet. The latter, a traditional form of Japanese puppetry, requires three puppeteers to work together to manipulate one puppet.[3] Mori writes of this distinct form of puppetry:

> I don't think that, on close inspection, a *bunraku* puppet appears very similar to a human being. Its realism in terms of size, skin texture, and so on, does not even reach that of a realistic prosthetic hand. But when we enjoy a puppet show in the theater, we are seated at a certain distance from the stage. The puppet's absolute size is ignored, and its total appearance, including hand and eye movements, is close to that of a human being. (Mori [1970] 2012, page NA)

This affinity results from a combined closeness to and distance from human likeness. It differs from the identification enabled by the projection that Meyerhold lauded of puppetry, which rested on the discrepancy between the two forms. Yet even here, Mori describes a productive combination of similarity and difference, for the form does not match ours (in size or skin texture). It is the movement that matters. Moreover, the physical distance between spectator and puppet, as Mori points out, enables us to focus on relevant similarities.[4] Separation helps produce familiarity. Kleist's essay on the marionette theater, discussed in chapter 1, also finds beauty in what the puppet lacks. He concludes that the most graceful bodily form emerges either from infinite consciousness (such as that of God) or from no consciousness at all (i.e., the puppet).[5] Between the extremes of puppet and God, humans are unfortunately full of affectation, graceless, so that it is to puppets or God that we should aspire.

The deanimation of a human through sudden death, which Mori mentions as a slip down the slope into the uncanny, is no doubt a ghastly, but rare—and, for now, irreversible—event.[6] Puppets, on the other hand, might be manipulated to sing and dance one minute and placed to the side in the next. In fictional stories and films, we can find ample exploitation of the liminal (in)animacy of puppets and dolls as uncanny objects.[7] When hearing of my research, plenty of friends, colleagues, and students admitted that they found puppets and dolls creepy. Exploitation of the uncanny is not a purely "Western" technique. As early as 1912–1913 in Russia, Ladislaw Starewicz pioneered techniques in stop motion animation by making dead bugs into puppets (Tsivian 1995). When I teach the "uncanny," I rely on clips of the Czech animator Jan Švankmajer's (1988) *Alice* to produce audible reactions of discomfort from my students.

In Kazakhstan, no one expressed to me a phobia of puppets. Child audiences only feared particular puppets when the characters were themselves aggressive—such as the wolf (who, along with the fox and sometimes the bear, often appears as the villain in puppet plays). Even these, puppeteers argued, were less scary to a child in their puppet form than if a human actor had played them. The fact that puppets are far from always creepy meant that the puppet theater needed to cultivate uncanny effects for their audiences. In the staging of the night of the gander's death in *Kashtanka*, after the master has gone back to bed, Kashtanka dreams of the goose and the cat. Ivan Ivanitch flies up into the sky, is shot down by a gun sticking out from the right wing of the stage, but then suddenly rises back up, cackling. The cat and dog fly off with him. Here, the reanimation of the gander is hardly comforting.

# Keeping Death from Children

The insistent cheerfulness of childhood aesthetics often accompanies an ideology that places birth at the opposite end from death, particularly when we envision linear movement through a long life. Yet we often find children and death in close quarters, especially when families are poor, marginalized, or otherwise lacking resources for care. Pedagogical and medical staff at Hope House attended closely to the children's health, with a doctor on staff. Historically, however, institutionalization of a very young child significantly raised the likelihood of their death. American institutions saw astronomical mortality rates at the beginning of the twentieth century. At one institution, children under a year old who were placed in foundling homes only survived to their second birthdays if they were removed to foster care that year. Those who stayed all died. In response to reports on these effects of institutionalization, the mid-twentieth century saw the rise of paid foster care and permanent adoption replace American reliance on orphanages.[8]

In Kazakhstan, the famine of the 1930s had particularly devastating effects on children (as discussed in chapter 1). Existing orphanages teemed with children. Funds for those institutions were often embezzled, and food rations disappeared. Makeshift solutions—crowding orphans into abandoned houses or shipping them off to remote villages—resulted in "death camps" of starvation and disease. Children often ran away from such homes and traveled in packs to protect themselves, hunting for whatever provisions they could find (Kindler 2018, 166–167). Children who lived in Soviet orphanages in the 1940s recalled, as adults, a hunger so powerful it made them feel like animals (Green 2006, 99–101).

Children do not necessarily understand the copious dangers they face, though they often comprehend more than the adults around them realize, despite efforts to shield them.[9] Not all adults try to protect children from confronting grim realities, nonetheless. At a puppet festival in Almaty in 2013, I accompanied Gaspare, a Pulcinella puppeteer visiting from Italy, to translate as he performed at a children's hospital. Gaspare set up his puppet booth in the lounge of one ward. One by one, with help from their nurses, children emerged from their rooms and gathered to watch Gaspare's Pulcinella. The children wore masks over their faces to protect themselves from our germs. Perhaps it was just the masks muting their reactions that made the performance seem more subdued than Gaspare's show at the puppet theater two days prior had been. The hospital visit was also more intimate. For a Pulcinella show, one puppeteer, inside his small booth, animates a team of hand puppets. The mobility of his booth has made him ideal for traveling. Emerging from the eponymous character of the commedia dell'arte tradition in southern Italy, Pulcinella traveled through Europe, was adopted and given new names such as Punch, Petrushka, Don Cristobol, and Dom Roberto.[10] For these children, who could not make it out to the theater downtown, the show could come to them.

The star puppet, Pulcinella, is a masked trickster with a voice that traditionally comes from a swazzle. The swazzle helps exaggerate the distinction between the voice of the puppeteer and that of Pulcinella, though it also impedes intelligibility (Proschan 1981). Other troupes often feature a second human, outside the booth, translating Pulcinella's speech for the audience through conversations of repetition, but Gaspare traveled alone. He had learned a few words of Russian, but most of the drama was communicated with the tones of the characters' voices indexing emotional states. Pulcinella's high-pitched laughter contrasted with the anger of the landlord and the ferocity of the dog that attacked him. Gaspare's shows are masterful in the rhythm he produces as the puppets chase one another. The puppet heads are made of wood, so as they hit against the frame of the puppet booth or collide with one another they make a clack that produces a music of its own, whether from the dog's wooden jaws attempting to clamp down on Pulcinella's body, or Pulcinella trying to get a coffin to stay open so that he can place the body of his landlord inside.

The children's masks hid their mouths and muffled their laughter. I tried to read their eyes for the trace of a smile. At the end of the show, Gaspare stepped out of the booth, with Pulcinella still perched on his hand, so that the puppet could offer the children a kiss. At the end of Pulcinella's performance at the theater earlier that week, children had clamored to greet the puppet. At the hospital, the children were shy. Unlike the children, Pulcinella masks the top of his face, the eyes and nose, with the mouth and chin left bare. Gaspare often wears jeans and a black shirt when performing. Cool, but approachable, he lacked the extra-expressive affect that one might expect from a children's entertainer (and which was the general approach of the Almaty theater). He waited patiently. The first to let Pulcinella approach was a baby, perhaps a year old, held in the arms of an adult. Others gained courage. One boy, perhaps seven years old, made as if to shake Pulcinella's hand, but then pulled back at the last moment and bopped the puppet on the head.

A girl, probably around three—who, like many others, looked younger because of her lack of hair—had been especially vocal throughout Pulcinella's show, responding loudly to his greetings to the audience. After the other children had shaken Pulcinella's hand or given him a kiss, Gaspare and the puppet slowly approached her. She was silent as Pulcinella drew near, her eyes growing larger. Just before the puppet could give her a kiss, she shouted out, "*Poka!*"—"Goodbye!" The adults laughed, while Pulcinella and Gaspare backed off.

My job, at the end, was to hand out balloons. I let them get too close to the florescent lights, and some popped. The sound irritated me, and I apologized to the children. Unlike bubbles, whose ephemerality is benign because of the easy abundance with which they arrive and the gentle silence of their departure, balloons are cruel in their ability to enchant and then suddenly and loudly burst.[11] The bal-

**ILLUSTRATION 19. A GIRL GETS ALL THE BALLOONS**   As she walked down the corridor back to her room, someone joked that she looked like she was about to float away.

loons were plenty, however, and the girl who was afraid of Pulcinella happily accepted the leftovers. As she walked down the corridor back to her room, someone joked that she looked like she was about to float away (See Illustration 19).

The children gone, Gaspare dismantled the puppet booth. I offered to help, but he had a precise method, he explained, a place for everything. He had been quiet during the bus ride from the puppet theater to the hospital. As he packed things away, he told me it had been difficult to perform that morning. He had learned of the death of a friend the night before, a director from Eastern Europe with whom he had planned to work in the coming months. I asked if it was sudden—an accident. He said no, it was like with these kids.

In Gaspare's Pulcinella, as with most versions, Pulcinella must fight Death, a puppet usually clad in black with a skull for a face. In another version I had seen the year before at the puppet festival, performed by Philippe, a French puppeteer, Polichinelle beats his landlord to death but then cannot bear for his adversary to stay dead, so he (Polichinelle the puppet) takes the hand of the puppeteer and forces it back inside the limp body of the dead puppet, bringing his enemy back to life. The puppet manipulates the puppeteer to reanimate the puppet. Kleist puts God and puppet at two extremes, but here Philippe brings them together. The puppeteer's hand becomes the hand of God, and yet a puppet controls it.

On the day of the show at the hospital, I wanted to ask Gaspare if he had considered taking Death out of the show for that day. His repertoire included different storylines, and he had performed for children in hospitals before, so he could have developed a deathless version. When he told me about his friend, however, I couldn't bring myself to ask. I wrote to him later instead. He responded:

> Death is not a bad thing. . . . Death is key to discovering that we are eternal. Children are not conscious of death while adults hide away to live in a false world. . . . Children have the gift that we do not have, the children laugh at our misery . . . adults are too bourgeois and censored to take the laughter of sick children and convert it into a gift for making a world of justice and peace. . . . Children are part of the society that is reborn every time. Death and children are the face of the same coin. (Personal correspondence, 9/23/2013, trans. from Spanish by author)

Gaspare draws from ideologies of childhood that align birth and death. He characterizes children's joy as innocent and honest, in opposition to adult artifice and self-censorship. Children have the role of renewing society. Our futurity lies in them. He doesn't reflect on the fact that the futurity of the children at the hospital lay in doubt, that they might be more conscious of death than most, or that they might be eager to see Death as a comedic character.

If childhood (or birth) and death are faces of the same coin, we presume they are on different sides, though that is not always the case. Vulnerability is more than a trope of childhood, as children are more likely to experience poverty and to suffer pervasive adverse effects from various threats—war, malnutrition, abuse.[12] Puppet bodies such as Pulcinella's bring these sides—life and death—together, the wonder of the puppet occurring through the ability of an inert object to come to life thanks to the work and imagination of puppeteer and viewer. Puppets and dolls provide a medium for children to encounter Death as an object external to themselves—one that can be mocked and even manipulated or outwitted.

Animation moves in and out of the puppet, just as it can in children's play with dolls, giving children the opportunity to confront death as a thing of play. Children polled at the end of the nineteenth century revealed a variety of practices related to doll deaths and beliefs about their dolls' abilities to die. For some, their dolls could come back to life as new characters. Others held funerals for dolls or for their individual body parts when they fell off. In nineteenth-century America and Europe, children frequently played at burying dolls, their customs becoming more elaborate in keeping with Victorian fashions. Parents encouraged this play, providing French dolls with mourning clothes and building them coffins.[13]

At Hope House, the only death I encountered was that of a parakeet, and I worked to keep the children from confronting it. One winter morning, after a few days' absence for visa issues, I returned to my group in Hope House to find Galina, the helper for that day, cleaning the bathroom. I noticed the birdcage was empty. I looked closer and found the bird lying on the cage floor. I asked Galina, and she said it had died the night before. Galina, in her mid-thirties, was not much older than I was, but she struggled with family and health problems. On this day, she told me her mother had died recently. She had missed a few days of work and would have to make them up by working doubles—forty-eight-hour shifts—including this day and the following one. She seemed already tired. I said I could help her now, but she said it was OK, she would manage to finish everything in time.

She asked me to help her dispose of the bird, however, because she was afraid. She brought the trash can into the cubby room, and I opened the door of the cage. I assumed we would tilt the cage or find something with which to grab it so that we wouldn't have to touch the corpse with our hands. While I was strategizing the easiest disposal, Galina's fear suddenly subsided. She grabbed the bird by its tail and dropped it into the bucket that served as the bathroom trashcan. She went to return the bucket to the children's bathroom, but I offered to take it out right away. I put on my boots and coat and grabbed my umbrella because it was raining.

I walked out the back door and into the courtyard area. It was cordoned off as unsafe because of icicles hanging from the roof. I stepped over red and white tape and walked around to the dumpster, which sat at the outer edge of the walled-in yard that surrounded Hope House. I dumped the parakeet into the container, where two dolls, broken and discarded, also reposed. I walked back inside. The cellular structure of Hope House is such that each group has its own exit to the outside, and I mistook another entrance for our own. I walked into another group's cubby area, disoriented to find unfamiliar shoes and coats. A few minutes after I returned to the correct classroom, the children came back from music. They were excited to see me and said that they had been dancing a lot. Olzhas showed me how his forehead was damp with sweat. No one asked about the bird.

## Being Seen and Heard

Galina disposed of the bird in much the same manner that Maral got rid of the gander, but that was a play. The bird was real, and I did not want the children to see it. Perhaps I merited Gaspare's accusation of harboring a bourgeois desire to hide away and live in a false world where pets do not die, they simply disappear. Yet I also felt that the children at Hope House faced enough reality. While Hope House worked hard to assure the children that they would go home, that they were the future leaders of Kazakhstan, uncertainty seemed to lie just under the surface, creating a sense of urgency for the work of the home. There was a general tenuousness to the hope of the home, for some children more than others.

My tracing of correspondences between puppetry and childhood has been, in part, an effort to move away from an emphasis on individuals as neatly bounded units. Individuality implies both a focus on division and an emphasis on difference. Puppets and children help to trouble the former—our seeming independence and separability from others.[14] Is every child unique, however? People often consider their own child to be unlike any other. Yet many I spoke with at the puppet theater in Kazakhstan stressed the universality of childhood, insisting that all children are the same, sometimes describing children as understanding a universal language, which then made speech during puppet shows superfluous. Approaches from developmental psychology and medicine that chart normative child development assume that most children have a good deal in common.[15] On the other hand, writing on institutionalization underscores and condemns the uniformity of children's treatment at orphanages, treating this lack of acknowledging individual needs as dehumanizing. The daily regime of feeding, bathroom breaks, and other activities renders them mere bodies rather than persons (Rockhill 2010).

Children at Hope House showed resilience and sensitivity to their situation, and those who struggled found different ways to cope. Cuteness can be a useful resource. Researchers' attempts to list the qualities of cuteness, as described in chapter 2, focus on physical attributes of baby faces. However, children make use of a range of strategies to achieve recognition as cute. Erlan was a boy at Hope House who vacillated between doing cuteness badly and doing badness in a way that rendered him cute. He joined the group, with his brother, during my second year. Five years old, they were fraternal twins, soon separated because they were considered too much to handle together. His antics were sometimes funny, such as a day when a substitute teacher was unable to keep him from climbing on top of the chairs in the middle of a lesson. I captured on camera as he ascends then disappears suddenly behind a bookshelf, having toppled over like Cheburashka. On other days, he offered signs that he was not coping with the daily loss to which all of the other children seemed to have become habituated. I worried that his misbehavior would bring him more suffering from the stricter teachers. I saw treats delayed or denied to him as punishment, yet he also elicited extra affection, as teachers kept him in the front row, holding his hand or petting his forehead, apparently in an effort to hold his attention.

The recordings of certain days are hard for me to watch, even years later, such as this one: During the first lesson, Erlan is given the incorrect textbook (they do not have enough of the correct one). It is impossible for him to follow along, but no one seems to mind. For their last lesson, the children are given an art project: an origami dog head. It requires a couple of folds and cuts in order to make a hexagonal face with floppy triangular ears. Finally, they are to draw the eyes, nose, and mouth to give it a face. Some children finish quickly and then go around instructing their peers. Erlan gets his paper folded more or less the way it should be, but when he takes out a pencil to draw, he gets distracted trying to jam it into the sheath for his scissors. Many children are hesitant to draw the face, insisting to their teacher and to me that they cannot do it. I assure them from behind the camera that they can, while Saltanat Apai goes around and draws the face for them. She appears to draw a face for Erlan as well. But while the others are still working, he unfolds his paper and refolds it in a different direction, without even realizing it. The face gets lost.

Saltanat Apai begins to display the dog faces on the white board. When she arrives at Erlan's, she hangs the blank face and jokes that the dog is blind. Erlan begins to cry, clutching his pencil so tightly that his arm shakes. "*Soqyr emes!*" he insists. "It's not blind!" Saltanat Apai usually manages to quiet the children simply by raising her eyebrows and enlarging her eyes in their direction. Now, however, she coolly rescinds the words that unmoored Erlan. "OK, it's not blind. It's beautiful."

Saltanat Apai and the other kids clean up the scraps of paper strewn across the desks. She returns to the board. She asks each child their dog's name. One girl, Aruzhan, has drawn the face upside down, and Saltanat Apai comments that the eyes are below the mouth. As the other kids laugh, Aruzhan covers her own face in embarrassment but says nothing. Saltanat Apai moves on to Erlan's, saying, "But Erlan's doesn't have eyes at all." As she begins this, Erlan calls out for her to stop, but she continues. "No eyes, no nose, no mouth." Erlan sputters "no" again, but she continues, smiling. "It can't eat, because it doesn't have a mouth." The kids giggle.

Erlan roars. Saltanat Apai pauses, looking at him as if surprised that he is upset. She mutters "don't cry" under her breath, and then asks him why he is crying. She watches him. Then she takes a pencil from Aruzhan and says she will give Erlan's dog a face. She draws the face onto the dog head herself. She says that now that it has a mouth, it can eat. The other children get up from their desks to watch her draw the face, reminding her to give it not only eyes but also a mouth and a nose. Erlan stays at his seat, still crying. Saltanat says that Erlan's dog says "thank you" for giving it a face. Aruzhan goes up to the board, now able to laugh at her own upside-down dog. Erlan still finds none of this funny.

From a certain perspective, Erlan was hardly a puzzling case. According to the teachers, his mother preferred his brother over him. Whether this was true, he was in a new group of children, separated from his brother. A few children had joined the group at the same time, but Erlan seemed particularly unsettled. His teacher jokingly animates the paper dog to complain about what it lacks. Erlan voices his own protest against a teacher who mocks his failure. In response, the teacher works to appease him. His outburst was unique for a child in this home, at this age. The year before, when the children cried, they were simply told not to. I saw other children become emotional during their free play time, in conflicts with each other, but lessons were a time to maintain composure in the way they sat, their arms folded, awaiting their turn to speak.

Conflict makes compelling drama, but the ideal narrative of childhood, especially where pedagogues are involved, is one of smooth progress.[16] Written into understandings of childhood and ideologies of futurity that surround them is an expectation of constant improvement. Erlan sometimes got stuck on an activity in the children's everyday lessons. The teachers' usual response to slow students was to push them along or to forge ahead without them, in the interest of the group. But occasionally there were tasks Erlan insisted on mastering. He would not let the dog go without a face, and he would not let his teacher laugh at his shortcomings and then move on.

## The Danger of the Feral Child

Erlan's outburst seems mild, but given the general management of emotions at Hope House, he stuck out, and teachers expressed genuine concern—that he showed potential but was at risk. They worried too of the possibility that his mother could ultimately reject him, and that he would end up in a long-term children's home (*detdom*). The permanent homes that I visited in Almaty and Semey struck me as a far cry from the cruel and overcrowded postsocialist orphanages that became the subjects of television exposés and Western psychologists' studies in the 1990s and early 2000s. Still, within Kazakhstan, children living in institutional care faced stigma. Sometimes they were cast as simply incompetent to face the outside world. People in Kazakhstan complained that when young adults aged out of children's homes, they could not even make tea. Others, including representatives of organizations leading efforts to help orphanage "graduates" (*vypustniki*), described the youths as fearful of the world. People worried that these young adults, not knowing how to survive on the outside, were eternally dependent and would only survive in other state institutions—in the military, in asylums, or in prison. Others considered the children untrustworthy. At one *detdom* where I volunteered, the children attended a local school, mixed with the other children. A director admitted that the parents of the schoolchildren complained, not wanting their own children to associate with those of the *detdom*. Stigma surrounding institutionalization was perhaps influenced and bolstered by popular media accounts of *detdom* kids. News outlets in Kazakhstan were far more likely to discuss scandals or problems with institutions than anything else on the topic.[17] These articles focused largely on particular incidents and blamed the institutional leadership rather than casting accusations at the national level for structural problems. Scandals included accounts of abuse within the homes, children running away from the homes, human trafficking attempts, and descriptions of orphanage graduates as pathological, criminal, or reduced to a life of begging.

The marginalization that institutionalized children in Kazakhstan face is particular, without being unique. Adult humans place children precariously on the margins of humanity in a variety of ways.[18] David Lancy (2008; Barker 2019a) offers three primary categorizations of ideologies of children across cultures— as pure and innocent, as commodities, and as liminal or dangerous. Rupert Stasch (2009, 6) notes the ambivalence of adults toward newborn babies among the Korowai people he has studied in West Papua, who "begin life categorized as repulsively demonic, not human." Korowai parents form intense attachments to their children, but do so with an understanding of children as utterly separate. The figure of the demonic child apparently clashes with the pure and innocent one which we might associate with a contemporary, Western ideology. Nonetheless, this innocence is not freely given to all children. We find frequent mention of otherworldly children—as witches, demons, or snakes—not only in ethnographies of non-Western infanticide but also in portrayals of those excluded from the image of the innocent child.[19] Besides, both demons and cherubs are supernatural. At once more and less than human, they are capable of acting as our doubles.

The ritual of sponsors' visits to Hope House left their uptake of the children's performances somewhat opaque. That is, the sponsors arrived, made speeches, watched the performances, and politely clapped at the end, whether a number went flawlessly or if one of the children was crying audibly throughout. A rare instance in which I was made privy to the negative evaluation of a visiting outsider occurred at a traditional *detdom* where I briefly volunteered. Two groups were visiting one day—a group of Korean youths and a group of local volunteers. The Korean group first performed a dance routine to English-language Christian rock. Next, the children at the orphanage, dressed in costumes, sang and danced for their visitors. After the kids performed, we went inside for lunch. We toured the children's rooms, where they somewhat solemnly held up their favorite toys for us to see. In the cafeteria, I was seated with the local volunteers at one table; the children sat at a smaller table next to us. One volunteer, a young man keen on practicing his English, sat next to me. I was glad he was not speaking Russian when he pointed to the children and said, "You know, these kids here, they're wolves." When I insisted that they seemed very nice, he assured me that they appeared well behaved here, but once they were able to play on the playground, they would become fiercely competitive. It was an uncommon and extreme assertion, yet it marked a convergence between the children's performance and stereotypes that children of institutionalized (or otherwise nonnormative) backgrounds could not be trusted. They were not what they seemed, institutionalization having made them fundamentally different from other children, and of questionable humanity.

Stories of feral children have been popping up, developing, resurfacing, and influencing new stories for centuries, as have accounts of the consequences of nonsocialization. For example, the "forbidden experiment" promises to discover truths about the innateness of language. It goes back at least as far as Herodotus, who reported that an Egyptian pharaoh in the seventh century BC isolated two infants in a mountain hut. The servant who cared for them was not to talk to his charges, in order that the Egyptians might discover the language that humans naturally speak.[20] Cases of feral children, considered a more "natural" version of this experiment, became the subject of intense scientific and popular scrutiny at certain moments, whether in regard to raising questions concerning the limits of humanity for Enlightenment-era philosophers or incorporated into projects of racializing differences of colonial hierarchy.[21] They have been fodder for works of philosophy, medicine, and fiction. In a rare mention of feral children in anthropological journals of the twentieth century, Ashley Montagu reviews the account of Singh, a reverend who reported finding and caring for two girls who had been living with a pack of wolves in India.[22] Montagu pronounces the report unbelievable, though he admits the story is attractive because a verifiable account of feral children would corroborate a theory of development that argues that to be human is not, in fact, given, but must be earned. The story of the wild child offers evidence for the argument that human development is a process not only of becoming, but more precisely of becoming human.

As late as the 1970s, scientists attempted to use a case of nonsocialization to study the innateness of language—specifically, the critical period hypothesis.[23] Found in a home in California, "Genie" became the subject of intense scientific study at UCLA when it was discovered that the girl had spent years locked in a room, with little social stimulus. The psychologists studying her received funding from the National Institute of Mental Health (NIMH) to study her recovery, with linguistics graduate student Susan Curtiss taking on the study of Genie's ability to learn language at the late age of thirteen-and-a-half years old. Unlike the eighteenth-century reports of children who had apparently spent significant amounts of time surviving in the wild, Genie had no special affinity with animals. She was, in fact, quite fearful of dogs, her father having barked at her rather than speaking to her during her period of confinement. In Curtiss's (1977) study of Genie's limited language development, she nonetheless refers to the adolescent as a "wild child" in her title, as does a 1994 TV documentary (Garmon). To be deemed "wild," then, one need not exhibit superior tree climbing ability. It apparently suffices to possess particular inabilities—to communicate and to conform.

# Mowgli Children of Postsocialism

Eighteenth-century cases attracted attention from royalty and leading intellectuals of the day.[24] By the twenty-first century, new cases get reported as small blurbs in newspapers or in sensational print and television programs. A series on Animal Planet features an anthropologist who travels the world to investigate reports of a "monkey boy," a "dog girl," and a "chicken boy."[25] A 2007 episode of *Is It Real?* (Matthews and Christenson) explores reported cases of "feral" children, asking various experts whether they believe such reported cases are authentic or not. As with reports of "untouched" societies, the mere possibility of such cases has come to be questioned. These cases surface in various parts of the world but include a number of cases in the former Soviet Union, with Russophone press revealing a fascination with such accounts as well. The case of Oxana Malaya—often known in the press as "dog girl"—has received the most attention internationally. She is one of a series of cases of children with "Mowgli syndrome" in the former

Soviet Union that became the subject of Russian-language documentaries and television shows.[26] A clip of Oxana Malaya on all fours and barking features prominently in the English-language and Russian-language programming, often with ominous music or distorted color to highlight the eeriness of her behavior. The same clip appears repeatedly, presumably because they have little footage of such behavior. What they have is not a clip from when she was first discovered, but rather her demonstration for cameras of how she acted when she was younger. The "after" footage—after she was taken into custody and spent years at a children's home, where she continued to live into her 20s—shows a less sensational Oxana. She speaks Russian and walks upright. In many of the programs, she expresses her desire to make peace with her family, whose drinking and neglect led to her living outside and taking shelter with dogs in the first place.

Television and news reports nonetheless highlight details about Oxana that emphasize animal characteristics that she cannot shake. An Australian reporter describes her reaction to Oxana, based on a TV documentary she has watched: "In the film, Miss Malaya looks uncoordinated and tomboyish. When she walks, you notice her strange stomping gait and swinging shoulders, the intermittent squint and misshapen teeth. Like a dog with a bone, her first instinct is to hide anything she is given. . . . The oddest thing is how little attention she pays to her pet mongrel" (Grice 2006). The journalist signals Oxana's deviance in a number of ways. "Tomboyish," she fails to conform to gendered norms. Her teeth are not merely crooked as a result of poverty or lack of dental care, but "misshapen," as if from a peculiar diet. Her pet is not simply a dog but a "mongrel," a way of marking its own dubious origins. The article calls Oxana's bark "creepy," yet seems almost disappointed when a psychologist notes that the young woman was more interested in people than in animals. Oxana is cast as looking and behaving similarly to the rest of us, yet being somehow fundamentally different. One Russian-language television program describes such cases as evidence for "backward evolution" (Neob"iasnimo, no fakt, 2008). Lack of socialization threatens to revert humans as a species back into a beast-like state. The program's announcer warns that although our evolution to our current state took millions of years, backward evolution, such as that evinced by Oxana Malaya, happens much faster. These programs and articles sensationalize and exploit histories of abuse, neglect, and misfortune. They—like the scientists studying Genie, Victor of Aveyron, and others—look for signs of beastlike behavior in children and young adults who have experienced years and unknown depths of trauma. Researchers are also often uncertain if these children had preexisting developmental disabilities that perhaps factored into their families' abuse or abandonment.

Studies and reports of these sorts can tell us little about the children themselves, but they presuppose and entail pervasive ideologies of children as not yet human. They push us to ask what conditions would be necessary for them to achieve fully human status, and to what extent children's access to such status becomes more easily limited according to disparities in class, race, or geopolitical tensions. Representations of feral children can both distill and distract from the more pervasive structural violence that citizens—particularly mothers and children—experience with increased economic disparity and loss of social services.[27] English-language reports of feral children focus mainly on the strange behaviors displayed by the children. Russian-language shows place more emphasis on the conditions that led to a child's abandonment—the alcoholism, neglect, or even death of designated caregivers. They, moreover, question how neighbors, police, or other members of the community did not seem to notice a child living outside or in captivity in an apartment for extended periods of time.[28]

Stories of "Mowgli children" emerged in the former Soviet Union during the decades following the fall of communism, amid a transition into a market economy. Insiders and outsiders alike described the system that developed during this time as "wild capitalism" (*dikiĭ kapitalizm*), in which a "semi-criminal oligarchy" ruled the market instead of the "open and competitive" one found under "normal" capitalism.[29] Wildness serves as a trope for economy and for childhood done wrong, yet it is more complicated than a coincidence of metaphor; there are both iconic and indexical elements of this convergence. Children are often disproportionately affected by economic downturns and breakdowns in institutions such as educational facilities, and yet they are portrayed ambiguously in these accounts. Survivors of abuse and neglect, they are cast as creepy, even frightening, subhuman animals.

Transnational ambivalence surrounding postsocialist children occurs not despite but because of ideologies across Cold War divides that insist that children are precious, beautiful, and promising. This ideology is only sustainable if we find ways to discard those who fail, for various reasons, to fit our visions of them. Just as marking new capitalist systems as "wild" suggests that "our own" capitalism is somehow civilized, demonizing other children helps justify protecting our own. Racialization serves to exclude particular children from ideologies of childhood innocence (R. Bernstein 2011). In the case of children from institutions, the differences between children (between those from family homes and those from children's homes) are not apparent. Differences can be subtle or hidden and must be discovered. As exemplified by the volunteer in Kazakhstan who insisted the children only pretended to be nice, tropes of deception surround orphanages and the children who have inhabited them.[30]

Fact and fiction move freely in reinforcing figurations of the institutionalized child from Eastern Europe as dangerous. In the 2009 horror film, *Orphan* (Collet-Serra), an American couple adopts a girl, Esther, from a Russian institution. She turns out to be evil. The critic Roger Ebert (2009) called the film "shamelessly ef-fective" for its exploitation of "the most diabolical of movie malefactors, a child." The film's ability to play on this fear—particularly the suspicion of children adopted at a late age—drew the ire of adoption advocates (Crary 2009). Warner Brothers defended *Orphan* by pointing out that the twist at the end absolves them from the charge of perpetuating negative stereotypes regarding adoption. It will turn out—spoiler alert—that Esther is not a little girl at all. She is an adult woman with dwarfism who has escaped from a mental institution in Eastern Europe. She tries to seduce the father and kill the family. All kinds of marginalized figures are embodied in this dangerous character: the orphan, the person with dwarfism and mental illness, and the sexually promiscuous Eastern European woman.

This twist made use of Americans' anxieties that Eastern European orphan-ages were deceptive regarding children eligible for adoption. A few months after *Orphan*'s premiere, in April 2010, an American woman, Torry Hansen, put her seven-year-old adopted son Artem on a plane back to Russia. He carried a back-pack of clothes and a letter from Hansen notifying the Russian Federation Min-istry of Education that she was canceling the adoption because the Russian government had concealed information about the boy's psychological issues, and she feared he posed a threat to her and her family (George and Pan 2010). Fol-lowing the event, Russian officials threatened to halt adoptions to the US, though this only finally occurred two years later.[31] In 2019, a news story circulated that people were quick to compare to *Orphan*: an American couple was charged with abandoning the child they had adopted from Ukraine in 2010. Several doctors determined her age to have been eight to ten years old at that time, but she was diagnosed with a bone growth disorder that manifested in dwarfism. The adop-tive mother claimed the daughter only pretended to be a child and was actually a twenty-two-year-old woman. In 2013, the mother rented an apartment for the girl in Indiana and moved to Canada, claiming the child was a sociopath.[32]

While Americans rushed to adopt children with physical disabilities from Eastern Europe in the 1990s, underlying mental and emotional disorders became perhaps a greater source of concern for parents when adopted children were later diagnosed with Reactive Attachment Disorder or Fetal Alcohol Syndrome, or showed signs of complexly interlinked mental and emotional issues. These re-vealed themselves less immediately and were more difficult to diagnose and to treat. Parents felt that they had somehow been deceived during the adoption process, as the emotional bond with the child was more difficult to achieve than anticipated (Cartwright 2005; Stryker 2010). Adoption also appears as a happy ending in Hollywood films and in Soviet animations. The same year that *Kashtanka* premiered, the puppet theater also staged a musical, almost entirely devoid of puppets, about a wolf who adopts a baby chick. Most family stories, including those of adoption, are more complicated than the horror film or the fairy tale.[33]

## Institutional Ambivalence On-Screen

Just as cute children become the vehicles for adults' projections of a hopeful future, nonnormative children on screens and in real life can be exploited to foster uneasiness about the definitions of humanity. Media portrayals do little to represent accurate perspectives of children who have faced abandonment or institutionalization, yet they act as a lens into broader stereotypes that shape attitudes about real children. In narratives about "feral" or other inadequately socialized children, institutions such as state-run children's homes play a prominent but ambiguous role. Can they rehabilitate and socialize, do they simply cordon off lost causes, or are they complicit in making children wild or dangerous? Stories of feral children often end with these children living in institutions. Eighteenth-century "wild girl" Marie-Angélique Leblanc was put in a convent to be educated by nuns (Dothwaite 2002). Reverend Singh, who claimed that he found two sisters living with wolves in early twentieth-century India, was running a missionary orphanage in the area. According to his account, he rescued the girls from the wolves and cared for them in his orphanage, but both girls died before Singh's (Singh, Zingg, and Feuerbach 1960) report gained a wide audience. Genie and Oxana Malaya continued to live in care institutions as adults. Cases of "feral" children in the former Soviet Union in the early 2000s mostly reported that the children are taken to live in children's homes upon their discovery, with adoption occurring more rarely.

Fiction films in the twenty-first century from Eastern Europe show postsocialist institutions as breeding grounds for savage masculinity, with cruelty within state institutions turning boys into killers. *The Tribe* (*Plemya*; Slaboshpytskiy 2014) brings together persistent associations between disability, institutionalization, and a subhuman status. Set within a boarding school in Ukraine for the hearing impaired, the film's director Myroslav Slaboshpytskiy made the aesthetic decision to deny the viewer subtitles, so the often-aggressive action unfolds on-screen without acknowledging the characters' signs as language.[34] In an interview, the director recalls a school for the deaf adjacent to his own school. The latter was "like a prison . . . and it produced a lot of people who I'm sure are now in prison" (Seymour 2015). Slaboshpytskiy tracks children from one bad institution to another. The Serbian director Vuk Ršumović's (2014) *No One's Child* (*Ničije dete*) offers a contrast: Its protagonist, Haris, is first found in the Bosnian mountains with a wolf. The Belgrade orphanage where he is placed eventually acts as a site of civilization, education, and protection. He learns to walk and talk, finds a friend and a mentor, and becomes a Pioneer. The violent collapse of the order that the home offered—with the dissolution of Yugoslavia—forces Haris out of the children's home and into the Bosnian war. Male protagonists give these films a *Lord of the Flies* (Golding 1962) feeling, suggesting that it is not only individual deviant cases, but human civility itself that constantly teeters on the edge of a boundary it has made for itself.

When conducting my fieldwork in Kazakhstan, *Harmony Lessons* (*Uroki garmonii*; Baigazin 2013) was often mentioned in the local press for garnering attention at international festivals, such as the Berlinale in 2013. The protagonist is an orphan who lives not in an institution but with his grandmother. Nonetheless, like *The Tribe* and *Amok* (from Northern Macedonia; Toziya 2016), cruel boys at a bad institution (in this case, a school) turn the boy into a psychopathic killer. Moreover, much ado in Kazakhstani press was made over the fact that the lead actor playing the boy was discovered when living in a *detdom*. Years later, readers were reminded of this background when in 2019 the actor was arrested and convicted of fraud. A journalist describing the boy's trajectory from *detdom* to international film festival fame and eventually into crime, remembers meeting the boy at the national premiere. Their interaction was brief, yet the journalist claims she thought at the time, "Good boy, but like a wolf cub" (*khoroshiĭ mal'chik, no kak volchonok*, in Russian) as she wished him success (Tikhonova 2019).

Depictions of feral or evil children have been analyzed as a lens into or metaphor for a host of issues—race, post-Cold War tensions, and the definition of humanity. However, these images get projected onto real children. In writing this, the contrast between a boy like Erlan (the boy who got angry about his origami dog face at the beginning of this chapter) and the children portrayed as feral seemed stark. Even though his teachers called him the "most hooligan" boy at Hope House, he hardly seemed wild or dangerous. He was only five years old, after all. However, rereading articles about Artem—the boy sent back to Russia from the US—I realized he was only seven, the same age that the children at Hope House went back to their first homes. Artem was considered by the press covering his story as a "late adoption." According to Torry Hansen, he was incapable of loving, too far gone. In many parts of the world, state-run group care for children continues to be treated as a necessary evil.[35] It is a challenge to avoid casting the children themselves as evil, so badly reared that they are dangerous and should be shunned or discarded.

Erlan's insistence on giving the dog a face—once it had been given a voice—suggests a responsibility toward an object once it has been animated. The abruptness with which Maral disposes of the goose onstage once it has passed into a state of inanimacy marks a rupture in their relationship. We might enjoy troubling the borders between animate and inanimate, or human and animal, cute child and cute object. However, fuzzy classifications can lead to ambivalent treatment, which can then become more absolute. Liminal figures become sources of greater anxiety once they have moved beyond a certain threshold—once the puppet has become a corpse, or once the child has lost that precious potential. The teachers at Hope House pushed children along expected paths of progress, even when it meant rushing them on to the next lesson or carrying on lengthy rehearsals so that they could show off their increasing competence to outsiders. But breaking the momentum of imitation could disturb the power dynamics of teacher-student or trainer-performer, as Erlan sometimes demanded when he slowed down lessons so that he could achieve a goal.

In the spring, Erlan's twin brother went home before he did. After that, Erlan sometimes told me he didn't like me, that he didn't like anyone. For an important performance that year (discussed in chapter 3), the teachers chose Erlan to emcee Hope House's portion of the program. He wore a tiny tuxedo, recited a poem with utter seriousness, and received a stuffed lamb (See Illustration 20). He astonished us a little bit. He was still far from obedient afterward, yet the performance gave the teachers renewed hope for him. Erlan was young enough, small enough, and cute enough that he could draw attention to his vulnerability, to his lack of control, and not worry—yet—about being permanently classified as beyond repair, as frightfully wild. He found ways to be seen without being cast as a spectacle, to be treated as a kid who was having a hard time and needed a bit of help. He showed promise.

The uncanny evoked at the moment of death or by a marginally human child seem quite different: the dead object has been deanimated, whereas the wild child is lively to the point of being unpredictable and dangerous. Moreover, death is not merely "creepy," it is also sad. A dead child is a tragedy. Geopolitical and economic decisions often lead, quite knowingly, to the deaths of infants and children. The trope of the wild child shores up convictions that children are precious, but some are more than others. In many stories, true and fictional, of wild or evil children, parents justify abandoning one child by pointing to another more innocent one (often "biological" rather than adopted) who requires protection. Those other children, no longer cute or captivating, are lost to dangerous worlds. They have malformed teeth and strange gaits, a bestial hunger in their eyes. It is preferable to turn away.

Each case recalls past myths, blurring truth and fiction. Every story presents an abyss of the unknown regarding the child's past. Because we know nothing about the past of the feral child, they are at once a blank slate and a black box, inviting speculation regarding the past and justifying experiments regarding the potential that remains. Achieving and maintaining belief in the feral child re-

**ILLUSTRATION 20. ERLAN GETS A STUFFED LAMB** Erlan wore a tiny tuxedo, recited a poem with utter seriousness, and received a stuffed lamb.

quires a great deal of framing, fantasy, and performance. Even in the case of supposedly "true" stories, a relationship of spectacle and spectator tends to shape the child's interaction with adults, as in the footage of Oxana Malaya barking for cameras. Meanwhile, dynamics of performer and spectator lead viewers to question the authenticity of the performance, such as the volunteer I met who insisted that the orphanage children were merely skilled at seeming nice, but were actually wolves. The privileged position of the viewer as judge of authenticity places the burden of proof on the children. It becomes impossible to perform normality convincingly.[36]

Rather than asserting that these children are indeed within the bounds of normativity, we might instead imagine the possibilities of childhood and family as happily nonnormative. Mohira Suyarkulova underlines the specific conception of "women's happiness" (*zhenskoe schastie*, in Russian) in post-Soviet central Asia as normatively requiring a husband and children in order to be realized. Structural and political factors render this supposedly private form of happiness impossible for some, however. Focusing on citizens with disabilities or who reject the heteronormativity of this vision, Suyarkulova (2020, 198) recasts happiness as a public matter: "Therefore, our vision for a perfect society should not strive toward a fascist fantasy of fully self-sufficient, able-bodied, atomised individuals, but rather recognise and celebrate that we all depend on each other in a deep and profound way." It is not only nonmothers who find themselves excluded from such visions of normative happiness, but also those children who do not find themselves in the happy families that will ensure normative development. Acknowledging the possibility of various configurations of codependence outside conventional family structures enables us to envision new solutions. We might discover novel forms of happiness.

In staging a scene of performance within *Kashtanka*, discussed in the next chapter, an audience of human actors appears onstage, standing on bleachers and facing the actual audience. At first, these artists animating the roles of audience act as if they are entranced. Rather than looking at the clown, they stare straight ahead. They clap and laugh at the clown's jokes in unison. This scene of spectatorship uncannily mirrors the real viewers, as they seem hypnotized by the circus master. Suddenly, the carpenter and his son appear among them, boisterous in their enjoyment of the clown's antics. When they notice Kashtanka and call out to her, they break the spell for the others, and the audience onstage suddenly becomes lively. They cheer as the dog jumps from the arms of one of them to another (though it is they who are making her jump and are catching her), as she makes her way through the crowd to her old masters. This is the final movement of the last chapter—the careful choreography of returning the children and Kashtanka to the original masters.

# GOING HOME AGAIN

*One lovely evening the master walked into the room with the dirty wallpaper and, rubbing his hands together, said:*
  *"Well . . ."*
  *He wanted to say something more, but did not say it and left. Auntie, having made a close study during their lessons of his face and intonation, guessed that he was agitated, anxious, and, it seemed, angry. A little later he came back and said:*
  *"Today I'll take Auntie and Fyodor Timofeyitch with me. In the Egyptian Pyramid, you, Auntie, replace the late Ivan Ivanitch today. Devil knows what will come of it! Nothing's ready, nothing's been learned, we haven't rehearsed enough! We'll disgrace ourselves, we'll flop!"*

The gander's death prompts the master to debut Kashtanka, as "Auntie," earlier than planned. Though he has gone out with the other animals to perform countless nights before this, the clown fears failure tonight as much as ever. Performances can be rehearsed ahead of time to try to reduce surprises, even for supposedly spontaneous acts (such as children answering questions during a lesson). The frame of performance—the circus ring, the platform, or the carpet placed outdoors to serve as a stage—makes the performer into the object of another's gaze.[1] Stepping onto the stage together, performers assume responsibility for one another. The dog's disgrace will be the master's as well.

In the puppet production, Baqytzhan carries the dog and cat on his shoulders as he declares, "We'll be a disgrace, we'll flop!"[2] He storms out the door frame that has served as the main backdrop for the set. Bolat, Kashtanka's puppeteer, watches them leave, wishes them well through the door frame, then turns back to the artists who have been playing puppeteers and assistants. They sigh as Bolat declares, "He'll be a disgrace, he'll flop!"[3] Disconnected from the puppet, Bolat refuses responsibility for what will happen next, though he will reappear to puppeteer Kashtanka's debut.

This abrupt departure from the little room that has become Kashtanka's second home will turn out to be final. When the trainer emerges in the circus ring, he is dressed as a clown—curly wig, round nose, oversized pants held up by suspenders, and big shoes. He holds a large bag, which he announces to the audience he has just inherited. Inside is the secret to the dog's name, for when he looks

**ILLUSTRATION 21. KASHTANKA MAKES HER DEBUT** Auntie, finding the
music unsupportable, moved uneasily on her chair and howled. From all around
her, she heard roars and applause.

inside, he finds his beloved Uncle, Fyodr Timofeyitch, and his long-lost "Auntie." He first pulls the cat from the bag, and Fyodr does a dance on his own. Then it is the dog's turn. Auntie is set in front of Bolat, who animates her singing.

The second master has taken a chance by renaming the dog "Auntie." He has staked a claim not only as owner and trainer, but also as kin to this dog. By doing it within the frame of performance, he asks the audience to suspend disbelief and to accept that a man could be related to a dog and a cat. Instead of achieving this agreement with the spectators, however, an audience member—the drunken carpenter—calls out with a different name and a different claim, as Kashtanka's rightful master. The two masters and two names compete for the dog's loyalty and recognition. She chooses the first.

Kashtanka returns to the first master and his son. As they make their way home, the carpenter resumes cursing the dog just as he had done at the beginning of the story. In both, he offers a misquotation of a line from a psalm, "In sin my mother bore me," but uses the phrase "in my womb" (*vo utrobe moei*).[4] The carpenter conflates his own body with his mother's, in the same breath that he curses Kashtanka, suggesting a corporeal connection between the two. This bodily connection marks the dog as *svoi*, as belonging to him, and the chiding as permissible. Kashtanka brings disgrace upon her second master, as he had feared, but not in the manner expected. At first, the dog performs on command, showing her competence, but at the sound of "Kashtanka!" she rejects the trainer's claim to their connection altogether. In the puppet theater's staging of this moment, the dog breaks ties not only with the clown, but also with the puppeteer. Once she has made her way back to the carpenter and his son, it is they who control her throughout her final scene with them. Her movement out of the structure of the room, into the frame of the circus ring, and back out again, has profound effects on the dog's identity and social relations.

Framing is a dynamic process involving related, but not always simultaneous or identical, processes: it holds in, it keeps out, it enables reproduction and circulation, and it defines its contents in relation to others. Frames of performance, pedagogical exercises, and even the children's free play—each endures and yet is transformed by cameras. Framing is a powerful act—or set of acts—involving a regimentation of internal components so that it can be seen as whole, aided or reinforced when the frame becomes a sign itself. The stakes of setting off certain phenomena from the sensuous streams of everyday life include an ability to share such phenomena with others. The media objects produced had effects that reached beyond my own research. While everyday objects such as small gifts of toys or food often anchored the absence of parents for the children, as discussed in chapter 4, photographs and videos of the children offered adults documentation of the children's activities and development. These recordings mitigate the children's absence for parents and help caregivers deal with the loss they face when children go home. Missing serves as a powerful motif in literature on migration, which describes "how the absence of labor migrants affects the existence of their parents, spouses, and, especially, their children. It brings forth the tragedy of family evenings and celebrations that did not occur, of child-rearing and knowledge-sharing that never took place" (Nasritdinov and Schenkkan 2012, 4). Imaginative acts of processing distance involve not just anticipation, then. Separation conjures images of all the events that could and should have occurred if the missing person had been present.

Leaving the frame of the second home to return to the first creates a reunion along with a permanent loss as Hope House says goodbye to each child. Other frames—images, texts—help lessen the blow of the new loss. Visitors brought cameras into Hope House, and the home had their own, but my own camcorder was the most consistent presence during my fieldwork, shaping interactions and events. In the spring of my first year of fieldwork, Aigul Apai asked me to film a series of lessons for her group of five-year-olds. At this point in my research, I had been focusing on the children's free play, but Aigul Apai wanted to have a visual record of her teaching. I set up my tripod in the classroom according to her instructions, while she arranged the children, materials, and furniture. She told me when to begin filming and when to cut. With shots ranging from a minute and a half to five minutes, they were less like lessons and more like demonstrations of the children's knowledge of things she had already taught them. She began with phonology, the children distinguishing vowels from consonants. Then they stood in a circle, Aigul held up a number, and the children formed groups of that number as quickly as possible. Next, they identified shapes—again, as quickly as possible. Aigul directed the children and me regarding how to set up each lesson and shot. My camera and I became her instruments. While she spoke exclusively Kazakh to the children, she would abruptly end each scene by announcing "That's all!" in Russian—*Vsë!*—so that the camera would cut away.

While Aigul Apai directs the action within the frame of the camera, she also works to include extraneous noise. During a lesson on botany, Tamila, wearing an apron and sleeves, narrates as she wipes the leaves of a violet with a damp cloth. Offscreen, from the back of the room, a voice asks for Aigul Apai. A director of Hope House accompanies Marlin's father, who has come bearing cake and gifts. It is the time in the afternoon when parents normally visit, but Aigul tells him we are in the middle of something. She asks him to leave the things and assures him we will eat the cake later. Marlin's father gives the goods to the aide, says goodbye, and leaves. We resume filming. For the last scene, the children stand in a semicircle. As I film, Aigul Apai announces that it is Marlin's birthday. The children come forward, one by one, to plant a kiss on his cheek and make a wish for him. "Don't get sick," they tell him. "Study well." They are learning a speech genre that will transform into toasts as they get older. They sit down and eat the cake Marlin's father has left, accompanied by a banana, their regular afternoon snack.

I went home feeling badly—that the filming had prevented Marlin from spending time with his father, that his father's visit had been treated as an interruption—as if the filming had been more important than him seeing his son on his sixth birthday. This, along with other issues that sprang up around my camera, prompted me to consider the camera as an instrument that framed social relations in my field site. Rather than trying to diminish the effects of its presence or my own, I worked to trace its effects in shaping encounters. Other frames did similar work. Social and media frameworks get laminated on top of each other, but with different priorities. The dynamics of framing with my camera at Hope House often depended on whether I was choosing what I filmed or receiving direction from others. Architectural frames—stages, circus rings, and institutional walls—help to track relations moving in and out of them. Just as displacement and defamiliarization can give way to new intimacies, framing devices can reorganize ways of seeing oneself in relation to others.

## Making a Frame

Framing can act as a device that brings order, yet as a concept, it can quickly prove unwieldy. Perhaps it is best to begin with the literal, physical frames that go around pictures and other two-dimensional objects, and to begin with Simmel's ([1902] 1994, 11) statement regarding them, "The character of things depends ultimately upon whether they are wholes or parts." Anything can be, at once, a whole and a part, yet the picture frame separates art from nature, according to Simmel, helping to give a sense of some matter or experience as possessing a self-contained wholeness, offering a defense against all that surrounds it. This kind of distancing, rather than alienating or estranging in a way that jars us, acts as "the preparatory stepping back," giving a work of art its aesthetic quality (12). The pulling together and setting apart work in tandem. This is what makes art pleasing: "The feeling of an undeserved gift with which it delights us originates from the pride of this self-sufficient closure, with which it now nevertheless becomes our own" (12). The wholeness created through distancing makes the work of art capable of possession. It lets you take it in, as a viewer. In this process of familiarization, you permit the object to take you in and at the same time to have some effect over you.

The picture frame creates sensorial boundaries. In many cases, it also holds the picture. It often contains, behind it or above it, mechanisms enabling it to be hung on a wall or placed on a table. If it is the kind of frame in which we might place a picture—in our home, for example—it can come with a clear piece of glass or plastic that protects the image, separating it from the viewer by making it accessible as a thing to be seen, but not touched. Framing technologies include not only severing the work of art from the natural flows of life, but also a kind of fixing or freezing, of pulling a moment out and preventing it from changing or disappearing. This is true of moving pictures as well as still ones.[5] In this sense, we can think of the technologies related to framing as including considerations of what is to be included and excluded, spatially and temporally. The person wielding the camera, and the constraints of the camera itself, partially determine the maximum fields of each. Unplanned sights and sounds can enter the recording, such as the voices of guests interrupting Aigul Apai's lesson. Later, as an editor, I can zoom in and cut away, but I cannot zoom out to see what was off-screen. I cannot find Marlin's father standing at the door with a birthday cake for his son. I cannot roll beyond the clips that I have made for myself.[6] Filming makes sensory experience into an extractable object which can then be moved into new spaces and, inevitably, take on new meaning.

The picture frame is nonetheless a physical thing. It is visible. Other frames are less apparent, such as when Gregory Bateson ([1955] 1987, 187) describes the psychological frame, which "is (or delimits) a class or set of messages (or meaningful actions)." Again, the frame serves to set apart and to unify. Bateson is particularly intrigued by the paradox surrounding the frame of play and fantasy, as playful actions "do and do not denote what those actions *for which they stand* would denote" (187, emphasis in original). Having developed his theory while watching young monkeys, Bateson notes that in order for the playful nip to communicate successfully, the recipient must interpret its connection to the real bite. We must also understand that there is no real bite because the biter and its recipient are both working within the frame of play. Here, it is the qualities of the bite itself that create its playfulness, that typify the action and those that will follow.

Bateson characterizes these frames as "psychological," but they are also social. Goffman's (1974, 22) work picks up these questions in distinguishing natural versus social frameworks, the latter providing "background understanding" that guides expectations and behavior. We work to accommodate new phenomena into our already existing repertoire of frameworks but are ready to make adjustments, as necessary. While Simmel warns against the interruption of any frame as ruining the effect of wholeness produced by the work of art, both Bateson and Goffman admit that the effects do run out, bleeding beyond the borders of the frame, or leaking in. Roles get "muffed." Emotions, meant to go unacknowledged, seep out. Frames break. Play, in all its messiness, enables movement between the represented and the real.[7]

Kashtanka breaks the "fourth wall" (though she is, of course, in a ring) by throwing herself into the audience. The circus ring of *Kashtanka* creates a performance space within that of the stage—a double framing. This does not necessarily compound the regimentation. The theater creates the frame of performance, demarcating where spectators should sit. The stage, its recesses, backdrop, and wings create a space on which the actors emerge to be seen and retreat again. After the puppet theater was renovated, a team of young female ushers could be seen at the doors and corners of the hall. Dressed in blue suits trimmed with Kazakh ornament, they took their jobs seriously, ready to tell children to be quiet and sit still. The children were placed in a space of nonplay, only allowed to enter the play frame if the actors onstage invited them to participate. Kashtanka's violation of these boundaries can be humorous to the spectators in the theater—while offering an opportunity to witness, vicariously, a transgression of boundaries— in a way that would be quite different if an actual dog jumped into the actual theater's audience.[8]

The work of framing is integral to children's socialization, to the processes of making and fitting them into the world. As a process of regimentation that ensures consistent internal dynamics in an event, framing can occur without explicit metanarrative or material structure.[9] Hope House taught children to attend to the norms expected during different situations. These involved implicit and explicit signaling, which might look like a restrictive form of disciplining—or of staging— but could also be conceived as a form of care, for the children's understanding of these frameworks enables them to engage in new forms of participation.

## Precious Pictures

Images of children get used for political and personal ends, part of their appeal coming from adults treating children as indexical icons of vulnerability and using their images to construct affective appeals to viewers. A "politics of pity" ensures that the image of the suffering child makes an impression on the spectator in ways that reports of numbers killed in battle, for example, fail to accomplish (Chouliaraki 2004). Yet drawing attention to certain images of pathos can take attention away from others. In the 1980s, missing children's faces appeared on American milk cartons, in hopes that someone would recognize them while eating breakfast in the morning and report their sightings to authorities. During this time, the rise of moral panic in the US surrounding individual acts of violence by kidnappers and pedophiles against children, especially white, middle-class children, garnered robust media attention. Meanwhile, structural violence through decreased social welfare systems and increased poverty went more easily overlooked. Ideologies of vulnerability extend to children's images as well, which then need to be protected from predatory gazes. Concomitant with the milk carton movement came a rise in paid services, in the US, for storing videos of children, promising parents a more reliable source of images that they could give to law enforcement officials should their child be abducted. These media providers, at the same time, promised to keep the videos securely locked away from the public, lest they fall into the hands of the imagined pedophiles from whom these parent customers were so vigilantly guarding their children.[10] Media companies thus doubly profited from parents' worries about child predators. The proliferation of new communication technologies and social media in the twenty-first century has given rise to new debates about sharing children's images—"sharenting"—raising questions about the risks of the practice and about the boundaries of the parent's "digital self" (Blum-Ross and Livingstone 2017).

At the same time that images of children in general are tied to ideologies surrounding childhood and image making—and often relate back to questions of children's vulnerability—adults treat the images of a specific child as precious objects, whether they cared for the child or if they once were that face, with fat cheeks and large eyes, looking back at them. Image-making technologies underscore and push against the ephemerality of childhood while infusing it with anticipatory nostalgia. Parents work to record a child's first steps, first day of school, and first birthday. These rituals of development are milestones that most children pass through, and thus act as markers and celebrations of the child's normativity. Nonetheless, because they will not happen again in this child's life, each of these moments is unique and precious.

In Kazakhstan, the image of the happy child, full of hope, promised a bright future for the nation-state. At the same time, children's images are powerful, vulnerable objects that should be protected from the dangerous gaze of the stranger. It is a Kazakh custom for parents to shield their newborns from the evil eye by keeping the child from the view of outsiders for the first forty days after birth. Images are included in this practice. On social media, friends would strategically hide the face of the child until the fortieth day had passed, sometimes using an emoji to cover the face while circulating images of the child's body. After this day had passed, images of children abounded.[11]

At Hope House, children were developing, growing, and passing through various milestones, but they did so while separated from the parents to whom such moments would presumably be the most dear. The children had not vanished, yet the circulation of images in and out of the home buffered against the loss of these years to their parents. The camera, as a framing technology, served as an actor in relationships of power into which children at Hope House were socialized. As discussed in chapter 3, adults at Hope House socialized the children to show themselves—to live audiences and to cameras. When I began my fieldwork at Hope House, I let everyone know about my plan to film, but the first couple of months I simply observed, played with the children, and took notes at the end of the day, afraid that the camera would put the children or the adults ill at ease. On the first day I brought in my camera, the kids pointed to the security camera high up in the corner and said, "Apai, there are two cameras now!" This did not neutralize my camera, for they did not treat these two cameras in the same way. Rather than imposing a power-laden relationship of technologies of surveillance where none had previously existed, I instead needed to come to terms with the way my camera entered a setting in which children and adults already responded to and made use of other technologies of framing in their daily lives.

While the security cameras were presumably to keep the children safe, visitors brought cameras to document the children and the home and to create evidence of their own copresence with the children, the recipients of their volunteer or corporate social responsibility efforts. I had a different set of goals and ideologies surrounding what I should be doing and how they should react to me. I wanted the children and the caregivers to let the camera fade into the background. In the group I visited most regularly, sheer repetition made this possible, eventually. This is a common technique described by documentary filmmakers, especially those working in traditions of observational or direct cinema—the fly on the wall with recording equipment.[12] Perhaps because of the frequency with which we work to gain this, to make the camera mundane, and perhaps as cameras proliferate in our own lives, we have forgotten the weirdness of this—of saying to a group of people, I'm interested in what you're doing, so I'm going to watch and record you, but I want you to forget that I'm here.

This became apparent when I tried, near the end of my fieldwork, to record the free play of the only Russian-speaking group in the home. I had been teaching them English for several months, so they knew me, but to them I was a teacher, not an observer. Nonetheless, because this mixed-age group included children the same age as those I had been studying for a year and a half already, I thought they could provide a useful comparison. After our English lesson ended, I told them to play, and I pulled out my camera. I told them to forget I was there. This was easy for some, especially for those who had largely ignored me during our English lessons. Other children competed for the attention of my camera and me. One girl, Anya, became so frustrated when other children stood between the camera and her that she pushed another child out of the frame. Anya ended up lying on her stomach, her face turned to the floor, crying. Other children—including the boy she had pushed—appealed to her to stop crying, insisting that the camera was, in fact, recording her.

Children have reduced rights over the circulation of their own images, but they can control the kind of face that the camera frames. They can even choose to hide their faces from the camera, as Anya does here. Anya generally strove to be the most attentive pupil and the hardest working performer—and to be recognized as such. At first, it struck me that her family situation, which I knew was complicated, had made her insecure and desperate to be recognized as good. But perhaps Anya simply understood more fully the expectations that most adults had of children—to pose, to smile, and to seek the camera's attention. Therefore, my violation of those norms was more confusing to her, to the point of temporarily unhinging her.

Aigul Apai was more straightforward than I in establishing expectations for those in front of the camera and in her vision of what would become of the audiovisual materials afterward. While I was gathering a corpus of footage for later analysis and editing, Aigul Apai seemed ready to think immediately about the usefulness of the camera. In my second year, she became more active in encouraging me to record the children's performances. These interested her more than the quotidian play that I preferred filming along with their daily lessons, so I worked to strike a balance among the three. She asked me to make disks (DVDs), requesting copies for her, for Hope House, and for the parents. She commissioned copies for all the parents in the group for two or three performances the children put on that seemed especially significant. For several other performances, she asked me to make DVDs specifically for Marlin's father. She would remind me that Marlin had a father, but no mother. His plight as a single father put him in a different category for Aigul Apai, whether she thought this reversal in gendered roles made it especially difficult for him, or whether she perhaps worried that it put Marlin in a more precarious position, more likely to end up in a long-term orphanage once he was old enough to go home.

Kashtanka's debut moved her from the frame of the little room into the frame of the circus ring surrounded by strangers, from a private space to a public one. In becoming more visible, Kashtanka also became susceptible to new encounters. Her increased visibility enabled the first master and his son to find her and to recuperate her. When she jumps into the crowd to make her way to these masters, Kashtanka gets passed from one pair of hands to another.

Children, vulnerable to displacement, frequently find themselves the objects of circulation, locally and transnationally, informally and mediated by states.[13] This is often experienced as an act of violation.[14] Young children's dependence on caregivers makes it difficult to imagine children having the right to determine their own movement. Instead, the guardianship of a child by an adult—especially by a parent—is considered not only desirable, but a basic right of children.[15] At the same time, temporary placement of children in state institutions and with extended kin can offer relief during times of hardship, so the circulation of children can, paradoxically, help families stay together, just as the institutionalization of children at Hope House helps prevent their permanent institutionalization (Leinaweaver 2008). Such movements can maintain ties even as they lead to separation. Nonetheless, in the circulation of children, there are manifold issues of inequality and power at play, such as states determining who is allowed to keep their children and under what conditions.

# Stepping out of the Ring

After Kashtanka's climactic escape from the ring, the trainer is left without his beloved Auntie, the stray dog he had worked to make into a character for his act. The children at Hope House did not flee the second home, but each child's departure was final. And while leaving was always anticipated, the exact day could arrive without warning. I was unable to say goodbye to most of the children in my group the first year. On a bright spring day, as described in chapter 3, the children greeted a business group that donated tricycles and scooters, dancing on a carpet that had been set down outside on the playground. After the children's performance, the children sat around the carpet and awaited their own entertainment. The business group had hired a small group of circus performers to put on a show for the children, complete with snakes, crocodiles, and a clown. For a magic trick, the clown chose Marlin as his volunteer. He pulled coins from Marlin's ear and mouth. We heard the sound of coins pouring out of Marlin's jeans, to his embarrassment and to everyone else's delight. At the end, he received a balloon sword, so envied by the other children that a teacher held onto it for safekeeping.

I wondered if all of this had been arranged beforehand. It was a year after the filming episode—when Aigul Apai had directed while I recorded her lessons. It was Marlin's birthday again. Today he was turning seven, the age he should go home. As in *Kashtanka*, a circus performance would coincide with a departure. Marlin's father would be coming in the afternoon to pick him up and take him home. Aigul Apai had assured me of the timing of this so that I could be there to see him off and to record his leaving. After the circus, the children performed for a second guest that morning. They ate a late lunch, took a quick nap, and then sat in front of the television and waited for Marlin's father to arrive. When his approach was announced, Marlin ran out to the hall. A minute later, he came bounding back, carrying a cake. He set it on the teacher's desk and began to change clothes.

Clothes at Hope House ceased belonging to the children when they outgrew them or went home. Marlin's father had brought new clothing for his departure—a plain white T-shirt and a pair of jeans. While Marlin changed his clothes, Aigul Apai seated his father at her desk, with a notebook and pen. She leaned over him, guiding him as he wrote a note of gratitude to her and to the children's home. While Marlin had to leave behind his old clothes, Aigul Apai began to load him down with other things that he was to take with him. Zhamilia, too, offered him trinkets—a plastic ring, for example—which he refused. Other children surrounded the father, begging to be picked up. He gathered three or four of them at one time into his arms, lifting them up and setting them back down again immediately. In the meantime, Marlin's hands had become full of things that Aigul Apai had given him—new toys, activity books, and the balloon sword he had received during the circus performance. His father put down the other children to help Marlin carry the things that were going home with them.

I followed Aigul Apai, Marlin, and his father as they made their way to the door leading out to the stairs. Aigul began to tell Marlin's father how much Marlin had learned at the school, motioning to me that I had taught him English. He thanked me. I realized, then, that they were already leaving. I stopped filming to get Marlin the small present I had for him. Marlin's father told him to go back into the classroom and kiss all of the children goodbye. This idea—of telling the other kids goodbye—had not seemed to occur to Aigul Apai, or to Marlin. Marlin ran back in, took each child's head in his hands, and kissed each cheek (See Illustration 22). He gave Ainura a kiss on each cheek, then one on the forehead, and then pressed his own forehead to hers. He did it just as quickly as the others, yet she beamed afterward. When he missed Zhamilia, she came up to him and kissed him on each cheek. The helper, Altyn Apai, told Marlin to be good and *molodets*—a Russian expression (often used in Kazakh as well) that tells a person that they have done well, that they are good. When it was my turn, I cut the camera for a moment to kiss him goodbye, then resumed documenting. The kids told Marlin goodbye—"*sau bol*"—as he and his father made their way to the hallway. The cake was left on the desk in the bedroom for the group to eat after Marlin and his father were gone.

I followed Marlin and his father outside. I wanted to get a shot of them walking through the gates that enclosed the home, but they turned back toward my camera. Marlin's father picked him up and put him back down. I told them goodbye again. Before they could leave, however, they were stopped—twice—by staff at Hope House who wanted to tell them goodbye and give them gifts, advice, or wishes. The camera's work of holding people in the frame was becoming an obstacle to their leaving, yet I could not bring myself to direct Marlin's father to walk away as I filmed, so I simply cut away and let them go.

As I walked back through the hall, I saw Anya sitting in the pedagogical director's office. I had noticed her earlier, returning to Hope House in one of the

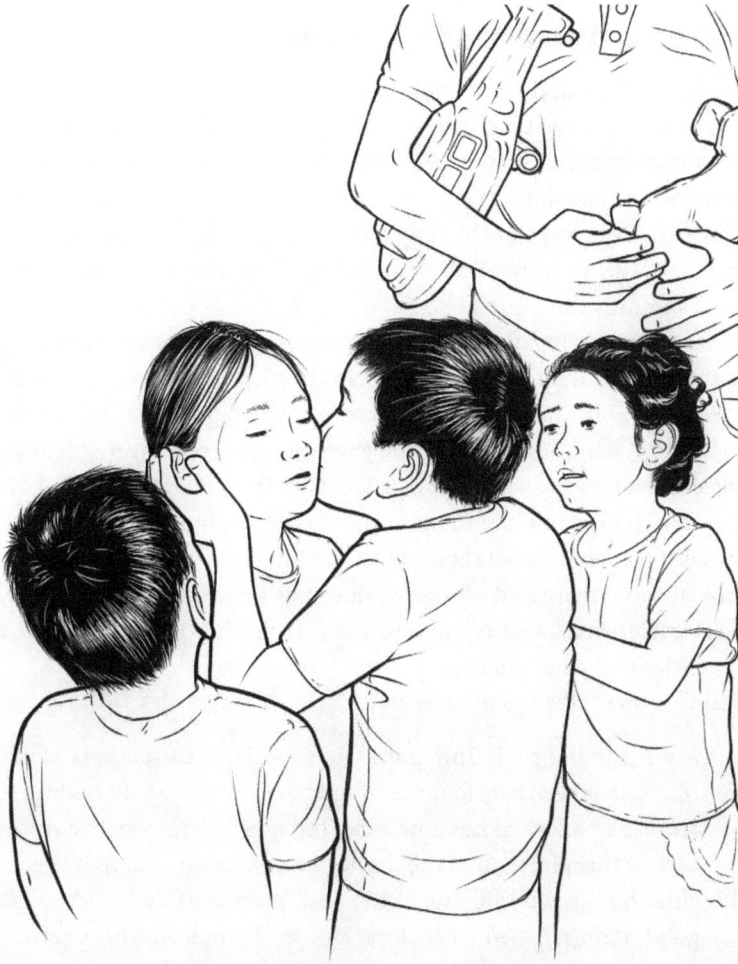

**ILLUSTRATION 22. MARLIN KISSES THE CHILDREN GOODBYE**   Marlin ran back in, took each child's head into his hands, and kissed each cheek. He gave Ainura a kiss on each cheek, then one on the forehead, and then pressed his own forehead to hers.

vans without any other children. A sponsor had arranged for her to take cello lessons. In the pedagogical director's cramped office, she offered me a short concert. She played a few simple melodies, using the bow and plucking the strings with her fingers. I said *molodets* many times. The pedagogical director asked me to help her with her computer. Anya stood up and said, *"Vsë"*—"That's all." She marked the end of her concert and directed me to stop filming, just as Aigul Apai had done.

# The Importance of Framing

When Aigul Apai found out I would soon be leaving, she had an idea. I should write an official letter of thanks, print it, have it framed, and give it to the director. She told me what to write in the letter. It should include a paragraph about her, about all she had done to help me with my project, and about how grateful I was for this. This was not the only letter of gratitude she requested at Hope House. A few weeks before Marlin's departure, his father and a few of the other children's mothers came to the home for a performance celebrating May 1.[16] It was the largest gathering of parents on one day that I had witnessed in my group. Before the parents went to watch their children's show, Aigul Apai first asked them to sit at the little tables in the classroom and complete questionnaires about Hope House. When they finished, she gave each parent a sheet of blank paper and asked them to write a letter of thanks. After the concert, she asked Marlin's father to talk to my camera. I thought she was arranging for an impromptu interview with me, but instead she instructed him:

"Look at the camera and say, now, what year he [Marlin] started here, then how he's developed a lot since you saw the disk of him. Please, mention all the good qualities that your son has."

Marlin's father talked to my camera:

> My name is Erbol. This pupil at Hope House's name is Marlin. . . . Marlin has been here four years, and next year he goes to study in school. He was small when he came here, and now he's grown. I've seen all the care of this place, all of the discipline and health. All of it is good. My child has grown into one of the best, most capable [children], it is all good. I am satisfied with Hope House. There is nowhere better, there are no quarrels, bad habits, bad characters. . . . They put on concerts, dance. We watch everything. We are given disks of recordings. I watched the last disk. . . . I would like to thank all of the employees here. They made all the opportunities for other people's children and look after them as they would their own child. I am thankful that they bring up children as their own and offer a good upbringing.

Still speaking to the camera, he offers gratitude to Hope House, wishing them good health and blessings for their families and their houses. Marlin's father offers, here, a hopeful narrative trajectory. He notes Marlin's physical and social growth, assuring the camera that this home has not impaired the child's development, that all has been good. He claims authority to judge this because, he assures the camera, he has seen it all. The camera made the children's actions into visual materials—the DVDs—that the father could view. This has enabled him to assess the home and to articulate this back to the camera and to the home.

When Aigul Apai requested a letter from me, I was about to head to Astana for a conference. I promised to bring it after I returned, on my last day in Kazakhstan. In the letter, I thanked the director and the institution for their help and cooperation in my research. I wrote a number of nice things about the institution, the teachers, and the children. In a separate paragraph, I said how especially pleasant it was to work with Aigul Apai, from beginning to end. I praised their work and wished them success. The letter was an adaptation of examples I found in my online search for "letter of gratitude" in Russian. I took cues from Erbol's address to my camera and from Aigul Apai's usual way of telling me goodbye, when she would assure me that she and the children always looked forward to my visits.

I printed the letter on the morning I was due at Hope House for the last time. The copy shop had no frames the size I needed, and I was running late, so I ran home, took a certificate I had been given (from a puppet festival) out of its frame and put the letter in its place. Just as I arrived at the children's home, I saw the director walking through the halls. She was a difficult person to catch, so I stopped her in the hallway to let her know it was my last day. Always awkward at presenting gifts, I handed her the letter, embarrassed at the self-importance that the frame implied. The director scanned it, took me into her office, and put the letter on a shelf. We chatted for a minute and said our goodbyes. I went upstairs to my group, relieved to have completed the most official order of business on my checklist of goodbyes that day.

Aigul Apai was astounded that I had given the letter to the director without letting her see it first. She sat me down in the kitchen, away from the children I was eager to see. She asked me to recite everything that was written in the letter. I tried my best to remember. I assured her that I had included an entire paragraph about her. She took me into the kids' bedroom, sat me down at her desk, gave me a notebook, and asked me to write, by hand, another letter of gratitude, this time addressed to her. I wrote one. Then she gave me a blank piece of loose-leaf paper and asked me to write another letter, again addressed to her. All of this letter writing piqued the children's curiosity. When I had finally finished writing the letters Aigul Apai had requested, the children started coming up to me with pieces of paper, asking me to write letters to them as well. These were short and simple, in Kazakh (whereas I had written Aigul's letters in Russian). I wrote things like:

"Dear (Child's name),

"My name is Meghanne. I am going to America. I will write a dissertation about you. You are my friend. I love you. Thank you. XOXOXO Meghanne"[17]

On Nurlan's last day, he was already imagining a time when I would take his picture to America and show people that he was my friend. On my last day, instead of a camera, a different mediating technology—writing—held me at the desk. It kept me from interacting as "directly" with the children as I had wanted, but it also prevented me from leaving and presumably left a trace of myself for after I was gone. Bekzhan asked me to write a letter to his mother rather than to him, so I did. We took pictures together. After eighteen months, the group was almost completely different from when I first arrived. Only Aigul Apai and Ainura were in this group from the beginning to the end of my fieldwork. Ainura was set to go home any day now. I gave the children hugs and kisses, along with temporary tattoos as farewell presents. Aigul Apai searched her shelves of extra gifts and presented me with a set of glass bowls. I protested that such a large, fragile gift would be difficult to transport back to the United States, especially since I would be traveling for several weeks to various destinations. Aigul instructed me, "Just be very careful." I said goodbye to the children, and Aigul Apai walked me to the hallway. I thanked her again for all she had done. "*Samoe glavnoe*," "The most important thing," Aigul Apai began her parting words in Russian, and she paused. Then she began again: "The most important thing—is that you wrote that letter, and you put it in a frame." Unsure how to respond, disappointed that the most important thing had not been my relationship with the children or with her, I agreed with her that yes, the plastic frame in which I had placed a formal letter of gratitude—which still contained a spelling error that I caught after I returned home to reread it on my computer—was the most important thing.

## The Circle of Blessings

Various materials and technological devices help make a frame—cameras, pencils and paper, broken toys, architectural structures such as gates and doors—but human bodies can also make up the frames they fill. In a rehearsal, described in chapter 2, Kuba compared himself to the master, and the animals to the actors, by describing them as *svoi*, a relationship of belonging. Because of this, he told them, it was expected that he would yell at them more than he would a new actor, just as the second master scolds the gander and cat more harshly than the dog on that first day, and just as the carpenter immediately curses Kashtanka when they are reunited. On the day before the premiere, described in chapter 4, Kuba proved this. He first reprimanded the actors, then Liuba, the puppet maker. He brought in the administrative director and a number of other employees. The administrative director lectured them for not understanding their responsibilities, for blaming others rather than simply executing their duties. The artistic director quit.

The unity of the group was ruptured. Vlad, the actor who played the first master and carpenter, admitted that they all felt shaken by the loud reprimand they had just received. He requested a five-minute pause so they could collect themselves before returning to rehearsal. As often happened, the five-minute smoke break turned into an hour-long lunch.

When rehearsal resumed, while the seamstresses were busy repairing the puppets, Kuba set to mending the rift he had helped make in the group that morning. Using a signal that I did not catch, Kuba and the actors began clearing the furniture to the walls of the room. With invisible brooms, they began sweeping, from the walls toward the center. Once they had all made their way to the middle, they pulled together to pick up the large invisible mass they had accumulated. Walking together, they carried it out the door of the performance hall, through the foyer, and out of the building. The pianist and I followed behind, watching. We looked at each other in wonder—eyes large, jaws slightly dropped. Neither of us had seen this behavior at their rehearsals before.

The actors returned to the hall and stood in a circle. Afraid to intrude on the intimacy of the exercise, but assured by now that everyone was calm, I resumed filming. In their circle, they looked at one another, smiled, and began, one by one, to hug each other, slowly (See Illustration 23). This moment resembled the children's routine of giving blessings in a circle, though the actors remained silent. Kuba calmly gave notes to each actor while they stood in their circle. These directions also articulated his wishes for them as artists. In the circle, they created a kind of frame—with nothing in the middle—that enabled them to look across at each other, to share each other's burdens and responsibilities. The rehearsal resumed. Later, when I interviewed Kuba, he explained that he was glad about what had happened earlier. This whole play, he said, was part of an ongoing process that he hoped would continue long after the premiere. He had used the circle of embraces to restore a temporary breach, and then they moved forward.[18]

When I looked back at the film of Marlin's sixth birthday, the day his father had been refused at the door, the wishes consoled me. The children often made wishes to one another—as part of their lessons, on holidays—or to me, if I had just given them a present. Usually, they did this as a chain, in a circle, each going around and making a wish to the person on their left or their right. But on Marlin's birthday, all the wishes were for him. Some of the children still did not understand how to make wishes properly, or they got nervous. Nurlan began to speak, then stopped in the middle to give the kiss, then resumed his wish. Bekzhan never managed to kiss Marlin. Olzhas made an elaborate wish for Marlin—not to get sick, to be rich and

**ILLUSTRATION 23. THE ARTISTS MAKE A CIRCLE OF EMBRACES**   The actors returned to the hall and stood in a circle. They looked at one another, smiled, and began, one by one, to hug each other, slowly.

happy, and to listen to the teachers. The wishes offered a way of making it known to Marlin that he was special, that a hopeful future awaited him.

# Filling the Empty Frame

Afterward, for some time, I wondered why the letter in the frame was the most important thing. Aigul Apai's collection—of videos, of letters of gratitude—suggested to me that she had plans to seek a promotion or a different job altogether. But when I visited three years later, she was still there, as dedicated to her teaching as ever. Recognition of her work was nonetheless important to her.[19] Wolof griots in Senegal sing praises of nobles, as nobles bragging about themselves would violate expectations that they be laconic and reserved. The affective animation of Wolof griots takes advantage of typifications of their volatile nature and eloquence in expression, even if this outpouring of excitement is not entirely spontaneous (Irvine 1996). Songhay elders consider ethnographers to be griots for the historical and cultural knowledge they acquire and share at gatherings of elders (Stoller 1997). Unlike the verbal artistry of griots, my own letters were far from eloquent, but my status as a student who had learned from Aigul Apai—like the parents whose children had lived with her at Hope House—gave me particular authority to testify to the value of her work.

The form of the letter only mattered insofar as it met standards of formality befitting an official letter. The physical frame, however, transformed its size, shape, and texture. Printed on paper, the letter was susceptible to getting stained or torn. It was a thing small enough to get mixed up in a pile of papers on the director's desk. With the frame, it was harder, more durable, more difficult to ignore, comparable to a certificate, readily available for display. Like the work of entextualization, it made the text a different kind of object, more portable and more subject to scrutiny in suggesting its display.[20] The objectification of talk, text, or other interactional experience through acts of framing, recording, and circulation offers a way to observe experience, including one's own. The letters of gratitude offered Aigul Apai an opportunity to see her work set apart so that it could be taken in.

The built environment and other spatial configurations can act as framing devices for social relationships, each space at once anticipating and producing social relations.[21] Loss creates an absence that empties this frame of social relations. Ritual mourning takes stock of this loss, grieving the failure of a dream of unity and marking the emptiness that follows. Mourning offers not only an expression of loss, but also an opportunity to gain new understanding, as Erik Mueggler describes regarding the emptiness left in a house when a member passes away:

> If loss emptied these frames, it also gave people opportunities to take on, partially and imperfectly, the perspective of another. In this way, houses could be a kind of material foundation for an inclusive ethics through which their inhabitants could share each other's burdens and responsibilities, despite the many differences of power and perspective that divided them. (Mueggler 2001, 94)

When I began coming to Hope House, Aigul Apai told me to put my jacket and purse in an empty locker that was assigned to a boy I had never seen, named Marlin. There were seven children and eight beds. All I knew, for my first couple of months, was that he was in a sanatorium. Then, one day, Marlin returned. No one explained his sanatorium stay. Kashtanka is hidden away until her debut, but this second home was far more public than the animals' little room, and Marlin had to perform for a visitor on his very first day back. In a short play about a group of animals, each vying to lead the others, Marlin played the mouse, the unlikely hero at the end. He seemed shy on that day, and the woman visiting told the children they should emote more when performing. His father's narrative—of Marlin gaining strength and confidence—was one I witnessed over the year that followed. I have a video of him hugging a tree and then insisting that I feel the strength of his biceps, and another of him catching ladybugs and sharing them with Zhamilia.

Once Marlin left with his father, another child would soon occupy his bed, would use his locker, and would wear the clothes he wore. Hope House, as a frame, would not offer clear traces of his absence, and teachers weren't encouraged to mourn a child's departure as a loss. The clown did not leave the gander's place empty for long; he rushed to replace him with Auntie, who then jumped at the chance to escape.

The frame should not be a work of art itself, Simmel warns us. It can only have style, which Simmel (1994, 15) describes as "an unburdening of the personality." The frame helps to typify the work of art, while the work itself is singular. Simmel sees the work of art as akin to the individual; we need to set ourselves apart as well in order to avoid being purely social creatures. There is, in this need for us to be in the world and apart from it, a delicate yet dynamic process of "advancing and retreating" faced not only in art, but also in what Simmel calls "the historical realm, in which the individual and society mutually wear one another down" (16–17). The individual and society, through advance and retreat, do not merely wear each other down. They mutually make one another up. The simple distinction between individual and society overlooks the many units of relationality—whether classified as kin, friends, or *svoi*—that appear in between. All of this work of framing produces an entity—a work of art, or an individual such as Marlin—that can then be taken in. An incredible amount of intersubjective work goes into this, mediated by objects. This, too, is a process of animation.

On the afternoon Marlin left, it struck me how, just as he was about to leave everything behind—clothes, toys, children, and caregivers—he showed no ambivalence. In everything he did, he moved quickly, impatiently, as if he was trying to steal away with his father, and people kept stopping him, weighing him down, asking for another goodbye. The camera too held them in. While I waited for them to turn and walk away, they would stand frozen in front of it until I put it down. The camera and the gifts mitigated absence, creating hope for a bond that would survive by tracing past copresence. The continual framing of the moment of goodbye through these media—letters, gifts, and videos—served to delay it as well. The most important gift that Aigul Apai sent home with Marlin's father was Marlin himself. When it was time for him to go, he was ready. This was the result of the work of Aigul Apai and the other caregivers at the home.

Baqytzhan, looking fully ridiculous in his clown costume as he calls out for the dog who has abandoned him, holds his large black bag. Fyodr Timofeyitch, the cat, must still be inside. It is Bolat, Kashtanka's puppeteer and the narrator of the play, who comes out last, truly empty-handed. He narrates to the audience the last lines of the story—describing how Kashtanka, once she rejoined her first masters, felt as if no time had passed since they had last been together. Her time with the clown, the gander, and the cat, the rehearsals and the meals—all of these seem, to Kashtanka, looking back on them, like "a long, mixed up and heavy dream."

Is that what Hope House became for Marlin, as soon as he left? I had no permission to follow them outside the gates. By directing me to film the children's performances and create the disks, Aigul Apai enabled a circulation of images to anchor connections between the parents and their children whom they sometimes did not see for weeks or months at a time. By engineering the video testimony addressed to my camera, she acted as a principal to Erbol's animation of gratitude addressed to her, to Hope House, and to me, for having enabled him to watch, from afar, his son's growth and development. Aigul Apai and the other teachers filled lessons and playtime, planned shows and coordinated art projects, all designed to maintain the children's ties with the parents who had left them there and had promised to come back. They helped foster feelings of responsibility for the children among visiting spectators. Amid these efforts to tie the children to parents and to sponsors, the connections between the teachers and children risked being overlooked. There was no one coordinating such an array of material, textual, and visual documentation that would link the teachers themselves to these children whom they had spent years rearing. Aigul Apai was not too shy to assemble proof of her work in the form of these mediating objects.

Aigul Apai, a temporary substitute for the children's parents, had to be prepared to say goodbye to these children and to be enthusiastic about their return home. She is not left alone, of course. More children would pass through to receive her lessons and care. The letters and videos did not merely present reminders of the children and the parents who had passed through the house. Like the notes the director gave the puppeteers, and like the instructions and evaluations the teachers conferred onto the children, these media objects gave teachers such as Aigul Apai a way to see and hear their work articulated back to them. Aigul Apai never suggested to me that she cared for the children as if they were her own. It was Marlin's father, the only single father I met at Hope House, who suggested for my camera that the employees had cared for his son in this way, as their own child. Erbol thanked all the teachers in his video, not mentioning Aigul Apai by name. But I did. Following Aigul Apai's careful direction, I wrote it in a separate paragraph, and I put it in a frame.

# CODA

I revisited Hope House almost three years after my fieldwork had ended. Aigul Apai introduced me to the children of her current group, including Tamilia and Zhamilia's younger brother, Alan. I had met him once, as a toddler. He had been living at home with his mother while the twins resided at Hope House. I was sorry to see that the girls' return home had meant their brother's placement here, their mother presumably unable to afford all three at once. I was nonetheless glad to meet someone connected to the twins, to be able to tell Alan that I had known his sisters and loved them. Aigul Apai told him to recite a poem to me, a poem about his mother. She told him to give me a card with a flower made of tissue paper on the front—handmade, probably by a teacher. The inside, written in pen by an adult, said, "Mama! For the 8th of March I congratulate you!" Their International Women's Day concert had taken place the day before, and this card was left over. I had helped make similar cards at Hope House. Children would pass them out to their mothers, if they were present, or to a director or visitor, if not.

Just as the children had allowed for ambiguity in categorizing caregivers, Aigul Apai allowed this blurring to happen for me. The message was written by a woman, not a child, and addressed to a woman who was not me. In an interaction coordinated by Aigul Apai, Alan in some sense substituted the twins for me and allowed me to be a stand-in for a mother. This act of replacement was safe because it was fleeting. It nonetheless offered a flash of familiarity between the two of us.

That summer, at the EXPO in Astana, I visited one pavilion in which I was invited to take a slow-moving ride on a short train, with the history of the earth projected on the walls. We moved through the Anthropocene into a dystopic near future in which the world was at the brink of collapse. As passengers, we needed to put our hands over an orb in front of us. Our energy would regenerate the heart of the earth. I was the only passenger, but my hands sufficed to take us to a bright future. There, giant children in a green field planted corn. They arranged windmills and solar panels, aided by a woman in a white dress with Kazakh ornament. At the end, we exited into a room whose walls were covered with pinwheels made by Kazakhstani schoolchildren.

The children will save us, as long as we save them first. Institutions, individuals, and the various social configurations in between employ familiarization techniques to bring people closer. Children play an integral role in these processes. They promise continuity and improvement. In order for children to animate hopeful figurations properly, they need apais to guide them, and they ask for our energies in projecting our hopes onto them.

In 2019, after almost thirty years as president of Kazakhstan, Nursultan Nazarbayev announced that he was stepping down. He appointed a temporary replacement, Kassym-Jomart Tokayev, who then ran virtually unopposed (and won). Tokayev renamed the capital city Nur-Sultan. Demonstrators protested that they were not given a meaningful choice. They were jailed, and Nazarbayev was assumed to continue to hold considerable power over his replacement. In January 2022, hikes in oil prices led to massive demonstrations around the country, with Tokayev eventually ordering security forces to shoot to kill without warning. At least ten thousand people were detained and 227 died. Soon after, Tokayev changed the name of the capital back to Astana, presumably in an effort to appear more independent from the first president.[1] The government continued to provide assurances of stability and growth, keeping the country in a state of anticipation.

Kuba left the theater not long after I finished my fieldwork. Two years later, Vlad, the actor who had played the carpenter, and who had been with the theater for decades, unexpectedly passed away. *Kashtanka* did not appear for a long time afterward. The first master was not easy to replace.

Chekhov writes that when Kashtanka rediscovered her old masters, her life picked up right where it had left off. The time Kashtanka had spent in that small room with the gander and the cat, the life with the clown, quickly seemed like just a dream to her. Yet even when the past feels more like a dream than a memory, when it feels more imagined than real, we continue trying to work out the difference, trying to make sense of the memory and of the possibilities that still exist for some kind of reconnection. We work to accept that certain reunions are impossible.

In 2023, as I was completing this manuscript, Hope House closed.[2]

The summer I spent in Astana in 2017, I went to a play staged by a troupe visiting from Almaty. The theater was large and mostly empty. The troupe performed in a combination of German and Kazakh. Not knowing the former and having forgotten much of the latter, I had trouble following along. In one of the last scenes, a tall man, nicely dressed, walked onstage. It was Kuba. He delivered a few lines, and the play was over.

# Notes

## NOTE ON TRANSLITERATION

1. After I finished my fieldwork, the government began rolling out a series of plans for orthographic reform of Kazakh, switching from the Cyrillic alphabet to a Latin one (Warburton and Barker 2018). This process has seen many drafts. The alphabet used here can be found on the Prime Minister of Kazakhstan's website (2021).

## INTRODUCTION

1. The children let the wolf off easy. In other versions of this widespread folktale, the wolf eats the kids, but they are eventually released from the wolf's stomach. The wolf meets an ill fate, whether his belly is burst open by sharp rocks or opened by the mother goat and filled with stones (Grimm and Grimm 2014; Afanas'ev 2014).

2. *Kashtanka* refers to the puppet play throughout this book, while "Kashtanka" refers to Chekhov's original text (a short story, first published in 1887 and now in the public domain). Kashtanka without italics or quotation marks refers to the character of the dog herself. For all quotes from "Kashtanka," I use my own translations of the original Russian text, but I have closely consulted translations by Constance Garnett and by Richard Pevear and Larissa Volokhonsky (Chekhov 2017; 2014).

3. As elaborated in other chapters, the cuteness of the children is iconic in their resemblance to other children, to young animals, and to cute objects. It is indexical in pointing to their future growth and development. The pragmatist Charles S. Peirce (1955) gives us a trichotomy of qualities that inhere in semiotic processes, emphasizing that they are rarely pure or exclusive, so that signification often involves a combination of iconic relations (based on resemblance), indexicality (involving some kind of real connection, pointing to the object), and symbolization (based on conventionality).

4. I use pseudonyms for everyone at Hope House and for all backstage artists and workers at the theater. Because the puppet artists and directors performed these roles publicly, and having asked their preference on the matter, I use their real names.

5. Margarethe Adams (2020) argues that holiday celebrations, performances, and popular media offer a unique lens for understanding the particular temporality of Kazakhstani culture, as one concerned with the persistent influence of Soviet culture, while the precarity of the present informs discourses of hopeful future.

6. My historical information regarding the Almaty State Puppet Theater comes from the theater's files (Fond 1241) at the Central State Archive of the Republic of Kazakhstan, dedicated to the Regional Puppet Theater of the Kazakh ASSR (*Kraevoi kukol'nyĭ teatr Kaz. ASSR*). Originally, the theater was comprised of two troupes, one for each language. During my fieldwork, one large troupe performed a bilingual repertoire. There was only one artist who was ethnically Russian and never performed in Kazakh, though he understood well enough to follow when meetings were held in Kazakh. Other artists varied in their bilingual fluency, but were mostly able to perform in either language. Directors attended to differences in artists' comfort in one language over the other. They cast accordingly and, when rehearsing a play in Russian, sometimes switched to Kazakh to give direction to a particular artist. Many artists had no problem switching between the two, however.

7. According to a 2017 UNICEF report, more than twice as many Russian children were classified as "orphans and children without parental care, in residential institutions" between 2013 and 2015, as compared to Kazakhs. See Committee on Statistics of the Ministry of National Economy of the Republic of Kazakhstan 2017. This is despite the fact that Russians under nineteen years old comprised only 13–16 percent of their respective age groups in 2013 (Laruelle, Royce, and Beyssembayev 2019), so that the overrepresentation of Russians in children's institutions was substantial. Nonetheless, these statistics belie the complexity of ethnic categorization in Kazakhstan (Edgar 2022). Moreover, language and ethnicity do not neatly map onto one another. A permanent children's home where I volunteered in Almaty in 2011 was reportedly bilingual, but children and teachers spoke mostly Russian, as did children and teachers at the children's homes I visited in East Kazakhstan in 2010 and 2011.

8. On the complex history of language politics in Kazakhstan, see Dave 2007; Smagulova 2008. Russia's invasion of Ukraine in 2022 apparently motivated Russian-speaking Kazakhstanis to learn Kazakh (Moldabekov 2022).

9. For relations between artists and patrons, see Nauruzbayeva 2011; Dubuisson 2014. For patronal politics in Eurasia, see Hale 2014.

10. There were other such homes in Kazakhstan that functioned as temporary homes for children, along with "hope" wards within baby houses.

11. The first were for children under three years of age, the second for ages three and older, and the third for school-age children who could stay with family on weekends and holidays. All still existed in Kazakhstan during my research. There were also various special boarding schools for children with impairments in hearing or vision, physical or learning disabilities, and for children who had been institutionalized because of behavioral or legal issues.

12. During this period, the gross national income dropped, outmigration of non-Kazakhs increased dramatically, and Kazakhstan's fertility declined by 29 percent between 1989 and 1999 (Agadjanian, Dommaraju, and Glick 2008). On transitions in post-Soviet Kazakhstan see Alexander 2007; Heyneman and DeYoung 2004; LoBue 2007.

13. For example, SOS Kinder Villages, an international organization founded in Austria after World War II, puts together a small collection of houses in an area to comprise a "village," each staffed by a "mother" and a few "aunts." Children live in mixed age groups so that they come to see one another as brothers and sisters. See the SOS Children's Villages website 2023. SOS has such villages in Kazakhstan. The state has also developed its own "family type" children's homes in the country, though the one I visited in East Kazakhstan consisted of a single building that looked more like a school than a home where a family might live.

14. For details on these figures, see Committee on Statistics of the Ministry of National Economy of the Republic of Kazakhstan 2017. On the prevention of social orphanhood, see Assylbekova, Abibulayeva, and Aimagambetova 2019.

15. *Tärbieshi*, in Kazakh (from the verb *tärbieleu*, "to rear," or *vospitatel'* in Russian, the verb relating to *vospitat'*, "to rear," which also hints at *pitat'*, "to feed"), the title was used for preschool or kindergarten teachers as well.

16. Other accounts of post-Soviet orphanages describe the work as grueling and the position of orphanage caregiver as embarrassing, below the status of schoolteacher (Fujimura, Stoecker, and Sudakova 2005). At Hope House, teachers and directors expressed pride in their work and commitment to pedagogical development, as evident in their regular teaching demonstrations and observations and the discussions that followed, discussed in chapter 3.

17. *Kömekshi*, in Kazakh, from the noun *kömek*, "help."

18. The relationship between power and pleasure perhaps emerges most clearly in Foucault's ([1961] 1988; [1984] 1990) later work on sexuality, yet he already anticipates the intimacy of the doctor-patient couple in his earlier work on madness.

19. In highlighting this aspect of Nazarbayev as leader (and discourses of kinship and power related to his leadership and legacy), I do not wish to reduce Kazakhstan's political and social history to a patriarchy that conflates family, patrilineality, nation, tradition, and Islam, as Roche (2020) argues scholars of central Asia have often done. However, the significance of Nazarbayev as a father figure for the nation arose in popular discourse during my fieldwork. See Isaacs 2010 on "Papa" Nazarbayev as a charismatic leader of a particularly post-Soviet character (Weber 1978).

20. On pre-Revolutionary and early Soviet puppetry in Russia, see Simonovich-Efimova 1935; Kelly 1990; Solomonik 1992; Barker 2021.

21. The region is known as the birthplace of the apple, *alma* in Kazakh. The capital moved to Alma-Ata (known as Vernyi under the Russian Empire) after two just chaotic years of Kyzyl-Orda as the capital (Shelekpayev 2018). In 1991, the name was changed to Almaty, thought to be closer to the original Kazakh form of the nearby settlement for which it was named.

22. As Goffman (1974; 1981) argues in introducing participation frameworks, a naive conception of communication as occurring between a simple speaker and hearer assumes that a single individual acts simultaneously as author, principal, and animator of an utterance. This can hardly be taken for granted. Humans often animate the words of others, whether as COSplayers or as praise-singing griots (Silvio 2006; Irvine 1996).

23. The makers of the puppets were carpenters who had begun carving these forms as a hobby. According to the theater director who organized the festival, while other forms of Kazakh traditional culture, such as the music itself, were supported during the Soviet period, *orteke* was suppressed because of its link to Zoroastrian spiritual beliefs. The spiritual power of *orteke* was apparently considered dangerous.

24. See Shklovsky 1965. While Shklovsky frames *ostranenie* as an aesthetic commitment, Brecht's defamiliarization sought more explicitly political effects (Mitchell 1974). Artists used the concept of alienation in the twentieth century with varied goals and methods, yet estrangement offers a useful "point of departure for reflecting on the relationship between aesthetics and politics" (Jestrovic 2018, 277).

25. See Meĭerkhol'd and Braun 1969. Meyerhold drew inspiration on the human-puppet relationship from the British theater artist Edward Gordon Craig's (1911) call for the artist to become an "über-marionette."

26. See Mamedov 2020, 234. For examples of central Asian queer and feminist science fiction, see Shatalova and Mamedov 2018.

27. A figure might be staged or natural: "Natural figures stand for themselves; being real, they can be imagined to be" (Goffman 1974, 525–526). See Silverstein 2005 on the interdiscursive movements between tokens and types.

28. See, for example Lemon 2008; Wirtz 2011. In her analysis of the future-oriented narratives of Eveni children in Siberia, Olga Ulturgasheva (2012) shows different chronotopes at work among forest versus village children, even as both trajectories involve a productive absence from home.

29. William Mazzarella (2017, 8) describes the "mimetic archive" as "residue, embedded . . . in built environments and material forms, in the concrete history of the senses, and in the habits of our shared embodiment."

30. On intertextuality in anthropology, see Bauman 2004; Prentice and Barker 2017. See Jakobson 1960 on the poetics of language. On the persistent tension between the real

and the represented that indexicality presents, see Nakassis 2018; Silverstein 1976. For arguments regarding why linguistic anthropology has never taken as narrow a conception of language or meaning as most outsiders assume, see Nakassis 2016b.

31. MacDougall describes social aesthetics within a total institution for children where he filmed their everyday lives. The devices studied in this book move across institutions and involve a social poetics of cocreating a story.

32. Sociologists and historians of childhood have worked to highlight and debate the agency of children, debunking assumptions of universality across racialized and class divisions (Ariès 1965; James 2007; R. Bernstein 2011; Zelizer 1985). Anthropologists and other social scientists not working on childhood often overlook excellent scholarship on the topic, even when examining relevant topics such as that of creativity or animation. In regional work on childhood, historical perspectives evince both the ideal visions of Soviet childhood and the grim realities, particularly of orphans—both of which are cited throughout the book. Children, if rarely the focus of ethnographic work in central Asia, feature in studies of migration and work, thus presenting their lives as intertwined with the struggles and aspirations of their family (Franz and Fitzroy 2006; Nasritdinov and Schenkkan 2012; Akilova 2017; Demintseva 2020). These studies reveal children as potential contributors to the household, as members of extended kin networks, and as vulnerable to exploitation and other negative outcomes when families struggle with poverty, social isolation, or environmental degradation.

33. This has been a key argument in Silvio's (2019) work, as well as that of Paul Manning (Hastings and Manning 2004; Manning 2009) on avatars, alterity, and related topics.

34. See Gell 1998; Latour 1999; Enfield and Kockelman 2017.

35. For key works in language socialization, see Schieffelin and Ochs 1986; Kulick 1992; Garrett and Baquedano-López 2002; Goodwin and Kyratzis 2007.

36. The term *Homo Sovieticus* gained traction at the end of the Cold War, at a time when the Soviet project was coming to be seen as an utter failure, and social science was employed to show this and to anticipate the "transition" beyond. Sharafutdinova (2019) describes a resurgence of the term around 2017 in popular anglophone press, in efforts to explain Putin's success in Russia as an inherited dependency on authoritarian rule. A more nuanced view of the Soviet and post-Soviet individual would allow for individual agency and pleasure and would consider the material factors that shape individuals' decisions, rather than relying on outdated social-psychological notions of an entire population possessing a characteristic "personality." See Krylova 2000; Sharafutdinova 2019 for comprehensive critiques of this easy division between the Western liberal subject and the simple, passive, duplicitous Soviet man.

37. See Volkov 2000, 226. While the concept of *kul'turnost* encompassed myriad codes of conduct and thus acted as a way to control individual behavior, it carried notions of self-righteousness and performatively helped to bestow on material possessions attributes of dignity and virtue (Dunham 1990, 22–23).

38. See Silvio 2006 on disembodiment and animation. Boellstorff (2011) sees avatars as a form of embodiment. However they describe the process, these scholars of virtuality and animation are generally concerned with an understanding of figures, characters, and selves as being more complex than mapping easily onto a single body. Animation offers a useful analytic for understanding virtual worlds and new media participation frameworks (Manning 2013; Manning and Gershon 2013).

39. See Postman 1982; Cook 2004. See chapter 4 for the Soviet context of the child consumer.

40. For work on race, class, and consumption of children's culture and commodities, see Seiter 1993; Chin 2001. For work on children and media see Heath 1982; Banet-Weiser 2007; Ito et al. 2009; Livingstone and Blum-Ross 2020.

41. See Lemon 2017 on phaticity and desire and ambivalence over contact, along with Lepselter 2016 and Mazzarella 2017 on resonance.

42. See Cole and Durham 2008 on tropes of hope and futurity surrounding childhood in various global contexts.

43. Alla Salnikova (2002) argues that children were actually rather opportunistic in their engagements with politics during the first decade of the Soviet Union, and that it was only later in the 1920s that they absorbed ideological commitments.

44. On the promises and disappointments of Soviet plans for orphanages, see A. M. Ball 1994; Kirschenbaum 2001; Green 2006; Kelly 2007.

45. See Berlant 2011 on optimism at the turn of the century, along with Miyazaki 2006 on hope.

## 1. GETTING LOST

1. Kathleen Stewart (2010, 353) writes, "It is the production and modulation of 'life itself' through worlding refrains." For work on worlding in terms of virtual spaces, see Boellstorff 2008; Jenkins 2006; Manning 2018.

2. A number of scholars have emphasized the uncanny nature of puppets (Cappelletto 2011; Gross 2011; Posner, Orenstein, and Bell 2014), while anthropologists have productively connected puppet worlds and the virtual (Manning 2009; Manning and Gershon 2013; Silvio 2019).

3. Central Asia is a prime site for asking questions about porous boundaries and supposed divisions between state and society. Madeleine Reeves's (2014, 5) ethnography of "border work" in the Ferghana Valley in Kyrgyzstan and Tajikistan describes ongoing, often contested acts of "fixing the bounds of the state" as "transforming space into territory." See also Mostowlansky 2017 on central Asian borders and crossing.

4. On ancestral monuments, sacred geography, and political and spiritual relations to the land, see Dubuisson 2017 and Tsyrempilov, Bigozhin, and Zhumabayev 2021.

5. Kazakhs were not the only indigenous, nomadic communities to be forcibly settled by Soviet authorities. For a comparable account of the settling and collectivization of reindeer herders in Siberia, see Vitebsky 2005.

6. On the histories of forced deportations to Kazakhstan, see G. Kim 2003, K. Brown 2004, Viola 2007, and Smagulova 2008.

7. *Kulak*, which means "fist" in Russian, was used to refer to citizens forced by the early Soviet government to give up land or, in Kazakhstan, livestock, and punished for withholding these.

8. Dostoevsky and Eliasberg 1917, 69. Dostoevsky does not go to a desert. He finds both friendship and love—even if the latter is not to last (Frank 2009).

9. On the nuclear testing carried out at the Semipalatinsk Polygon for forty years, see Werner and Purvis-Roberts 2014; Stawkowski 2016. The Baikonur launch site was three hundred kilometers away from the town for which it was named, in order to keep the location secret (Andrews and Siddiqi 2011).

10. "Baby boxes" exist in other countries—a system that allows a parent to leave an infant anonymously, without risking the child's health. These have been discussed as a possible "cradle of hope" for at-risk infants in Kazakhstan, but no such anonymity was policy at Hope House (Baimanov 2017).

11. On discourses and practices surrounding Soviet promises of women's emancipation, see Naiman 1997; Kiaer and Naiman 2006; LoBue 2007; Shatalova and Mamedov 2016. Regarding the particular push for unveiling in central Asia as an "emancipatory" act for women, see Northrop 2004 and Kamp 2006.

12. For popular press on the lack of preschools in Almaty and Kazakhstan, see, for example, Kenzhebekova 2012; Salmina and Zhumabayev 2019; MK-KZ 2020.

13. See Alexander 2007; LoBue 2007; Dugarova 2019.

14. See Freud [1920] 1990. These themes of loss and longing for recovery might resonate with psychoanalytic literature, whether it brings to mind the Freudian lost object (Freud 1949b) or the Lacanian *objet petit a* (Lacan 1966). I remain wary of treating the children's specific loss of their parents—and the ways the home worked to cultivate the children's awareness of this loss—as little more than a particular manifestation of a universal experience. Hope House can teach us about other types of loss, but only if we attend to the specificity of the children's situations and the institutional and personal reactions to them.

15. When I describe and analyze video footage, I often shift into present tense because the footage itself makes the events again present to me, each time I watch it.

16. Chapter 3 goes into greater detail regarding the connections between pedagogy and performance in post-Soviet childhood.

17. See U. G. Kim 2018 on registers of respect among Kazakh children in Xinjiang, China.

18. At the homes I visited in Almaty, Semey, and a small town in East Kazakhstan, residents called the directors "Mom," plus first name, plus patronymic, to show respect. Such practices resemble other extensions of kin terms, such as those used in the Catholic Church, except that they used this more informal term of "Mom."

19. In the US, I met American parents who had adopted from Kazakhstan, and who described their children's shock at meeting their adoptive father and having close contact with a man for the first time. At Hope House, the one father who visited regularly became the center of the children's attention, as described in chapter 6.

20. Besides blood, for example, anthropologists have shown the importance of milk and other substances in constituting kin, in addition to actions (Parkes 2004; Carsten 1997, 2000). Scholarship on language socialization arose out of concern regarding the focus on dyadic mother-child speech in developmental psychology (Ochs and Schieffelin 1984).

21. See Leinaweaver 2008 and Carpenter 2021.

22. For ethnographies of orphanage care in Russia, see Fujimura, Stoecker, and Sudakova 2005; Rockhill 2010.

23. Bakhtin and Voloshinov's writings on dialogism and reported speech have been incredibly productive in linguistic anthropology for thinking about the everyday multiplicity of voices that inhere in an utterance (Bakhtin 1981; Voloshinov 1986; Hill 1995; Inoue 2006).

24. One that I visited on Green Island, Taiwan, for example, offered model cells filled with faceless figures, all the same, perhaps inviting the visitor to project a specific face onto the simple forms. Another, on Phú Quốc Island, Vietnam, included detailed and graphic representations of torture.

25. Madeleine Reeves (2014, 14) offers the term "impersonation" as one of productive ambiguity between enactment and pretense, in order to underline "that being seen to embody state authority also requires a certain external recognition: recognition that is empirically variable and spatially contingent."

26. See Ulturgasheva 2012; Vitebsky 2005.

27. Kate Brown (2004, 187) notes that, despite Soviet efforts to force people and land into a productive agricultural relationship, agricultural communities never took hold. The land did not make good on its promises. At ALZhIR and at KarLag, nonetheless, exhibits boast the success of workers in meeting and exceeding their quotas.

28. Christopher Ball's (2014, 156) writing on dicentization is useful here, as it "applies to situations in which images are perceived to come alive, either through some external agency or our own, whereby relations of identity, otherness, and existence are invoked and made actual."

29. For Gaister's story, see Shikheeva-Gaister, Vetrova, and Frierson 2015; Slezkine 2017. She wrote Samizdat in the 1970s and 1980s. Her typewriter is now archived on the Virtual Gulag Museum website (2023).

30. *Zdravstvui̇ dorogaia*
*mamochka pochemu*
*ty mne pishish*
*pisma. mamochka*
*ty ne znaesh*
*gde papa. Mamochka*
*ia uchus' vo 2m klasi.*
*Mamochka ia ochen' dolgo*
*bolel striguchem*
*lishaem. Mamochka*
*ia zhyv i zdorovyi̇.*
*Momochka ty pisala*
*chto utebia, net bumagi*
*mamochka ia tebe prishln (?).*
*mamochka ia zatoboi̇*
*ochen' skuchil. Bolshe*
*pisat' necheva.*

In his handwriting, it is unclear when the first *m* is capitalized or lowercase. He uses the *i* that was eliminated in Russian in 1918 but still used in related languages like Ukrainian and Belorusian (and in Kazakh).

31. See Senderovich 1981; Finke 1994.

32. The children's removal from their family homes might have affected their memories. Psychologists are still working to untangle exactly how childhood trauma affects memories of particular events and overall memory functioning during childhood and into adulthood, along with the effects of being able to recall these events in a coherent manner. Early exposure to stress seems to make young brains behave more like mature ones, the heightened cortisol levels aiding the encoding of memory, based on studies of infant rats separated from their mothers (Callaghan and Richardson 2012). At the same time, long-term early exposure to stress results in impaired working memory in adults (Dodaj et al. 2017). One study suggests that children's memories of singular traumatic events are no better or worse than their memories of positive events (Bray et al. 2018). Other scholars have studied children ten to twelve years of age who experienced war, finding that peritraumatic dissociation causes dysfunctional, incoherent episodic memory, which then increases the likelihood of posttraumatic stress disorder (Peltonen et al. 2017). Psychoanalysts have noted that traumatic experience can give rise to compulsion to repeat; the work of psychoanalytic healing can involve turning this repetition into memory (Freud [1920] 1990, 13).

33. On footing and alignment, see Goffman 1981.

34. A number of scholars have taken up the topic of *oralman*. Alexander Diener (2009) traces different periods of movement to denaturalize a coupling of Kazakh people and "homeland." One result of this "return" has been the creation of "a viable cross-border community," rather than a permanent migration to Kazakhstan (Genina 2015, 1). Werner and Barcus (2015) examine the gendered inequalities of returnee experiences.

35. See Umirbekov 2019; tengrinews.kz 2020; Zhang and Tsakhirmaa 2022.

36. Abashin 2015. Kazakhstan was estimated to have almost 20 percent of its own citizens living abroad in 2015 (Roche 2020). It also increasingly acts as host to migrant labor from its neighbors (Najibullah 2021; Sharifzoda 2019).

37. For historical and ethnographic studies of the shifting identities of the Kazakhstani capital cities, see Bissenova 2013, 2017; Laszczkowski 2016.

## 2. MEETING A STRANGER

1. The proscenium is the point that marks the division between stage and audience. Alaina Lemon (2000) treats the proscenium as a potent symbol for the boundaries of the performance frame, with some accused of not understanding this dividing line between performance and real.

2. See Bowlby 1969. This literature continues to develop and find new popularity through twenty-first century uses of adult "attachment styles," with scholarly studies (reported in popular literature) using attachment style as a predictor for adult romantic relationships, work-life balance, and social media patterns. See, for example, Gillath, Karantzas, and Selcuk 2017; Lin 2015; Saunders 2018.

3. Goldfarb 1955, 108–111. Goldfarb's studies were influential to Bowlby's (Goldfarb 1945).

4. For attachment studies on Eastern European children, see Nelson, Fox, and Zeanah 2014; Stryker 2010. I discuss the post–Cold War studies in chapter 5. Kathie Carpenter (2021) shows how orphanage care is not always as starkly affectless as the stereotype describes, though she also contrasts her own ethnography of Cambodian orphanages to those of Eastern Europe, keeping the latter reputation intact.

5. For work on the dangers and promises of fleeting intimacies, on the role of poetic devices and mediating technologies on animating spaces as rife with opportunities for such connections, see Barker 2024.

6. See A. M. Ball 1994; Green 2006; Kelly 2007 on the history of Soviet orphanages.

7. See Schatz 2004; Werner 1997; Werner and Barcus 2015.

8. See Roche 2020; Schatz 2004; Nasritdinov, Gareyeva, and Efremenko 2015.

9. The city was renamed in order to distance itself from the Semipalatinsk Polygon, the nuclear testing site that shares its name. On the edge of the city is a memorial to the victims of the testing—a mother cradling an infant with a nuclear blast overhead—but museums such as the one dedicated to Dostoevsky and another dedicated to Abai Qunanbaiuly, Kazakhstan's most celebrated poet, focus on the city's legacy as an intellectual center in Kazakhstan under Russian rule.

10. The film begins in present-day Russia and then animates the past: a young woman visits the memorial museum and watches display dummies come to life, immersing her in her grandmother's world as a prisoner there.

11. Though ethnic Germans have largely left Kazakhstan, and though the troupe has lost its building, the theater still performs some of the most experimental work in the city. On Soviet minority theaters, see Doi 2002; Lemon 2002.

12. See Agbo and Pak 2017. During my second year at Hope House, in response to this call for trilingualism, teachers asked me to teach English to the eldest three groups at the home.

13. Stalin began promoting the metaphor of the Friendship of the Peoples in 1933. This shift from class to *narod* ("nation," in the sense of "ethnicity") was accompanied both by a notion of a primordial national ethnicity (thus creating new ethnic boundaries and unities in central Asia) and by forced displacement of these nationalities (Martin 2001). See also M. Adams 2020 on continued celebrations of this ideology through performance in Kazakhstan.

14. Performances often bordered on stereotype. Puppet artists discussed the particular gender dynamics of the Caucuses that needed to come through in their manipulation of marionettes for the "Armenian" number. The children of Hope House attempted to imitate a Tajik dance style by sliding their heads sideways.

15. See Trouillot 2015 on relationships of power and historical narrative. Indexicality works in two directions so that a statement, by presupposing, can have creative, entailing effects (Silverstein 1993).

16. The Kazakhstani government compensated victims of nuclear testing with a one-time payment of the equivalent of $50, as an example of a refusal of responsibility for Soviet actions (Stawkowski 2016) that stands in contrast with compensation to Chernobyl victims (Petryna 2002).

17. See Kelly 2007; Rockhill 2010.

18. They may have formed rigid ideas of the children at a certain point, as identities form and solidify over time in classrooms (Bucholtz et al. 2012; Wortham 2005).

19. This kind of "emotion management" is its own kind of "emotional labor" (Hochschild 1983). Adult caregivers might have to learn to treat infants and young children with a certain measure of emotional restraint (Rockhill 2010; Scheper-Hughes 1992). For capitalist service work, clients expect service workers to care about them, whereas emotional investment in children can prove a liability when a worker (or parent) is overwhelmed with everyday demands or is struggling to survive.

20. To return to Mazzarella's (2017, 5) discussion of the logic of constitutive resonance, "If 'I' and 'you' can appear as 'subject' and 'object' then it is only by means of a shared field of emergence in which no such boundaries can be taken for granted."

21. The production format of other media, such as cinema, should not be taken as a straightforward matter of active media-makers and passively receiving consumers (Nakassis 2023).

22. Meyerhold, like Freud, was interested in author E. T. A. Hoffman's ability to traverse the familiar and the strange. The effects of rupture depend on the habits of perception and the material and sensorial environments in which they unfold (Lemon 2017).

23. To make someone *svoi* is a process of adoption—*usvoit'* in Russian means "to adopt," though not for the adoption of children. Other terms are used for that (*udocherit'* or *usynovit'*—to make into one's daughter or son, respectively).

24. The first observer then apparently joined a second one in an adjacent room, where they watched the children through a one-way mirror and audio recorded what happened.

25. This was emphasized, as well, when a similar procedure was carried out at the American nursery school where I worked.

26. For a view of precursors to Ainsworth's Strange Situation, see Van Rosmalen, Van der Veer, and Van der Horst 2015. Some of these involved simply leaving a child alone in a strange place, designed to elicit a reaction of fear or anxiety, so as to observe the degree of anxiety the child seemed to experience when separated from their mother. With these, it was often difficult to judge whether a seemingly calm child might be hiding "undercurrents" of anxiety (Shirley and Poyntz 1941, 252).

27. Studies of adoption have underscored the processual nature of the ways families are made, reminding us again that family and kin are dynamic and imbricated in larger legal and political structures (Howell 2006; Yngvesson 2010; Frekko, Leinaweaver, and Marre 2015).

28. Adoptions declined relative to the total population of children ages 0–3 (Committee on Statistics of the Ministry of National Economy of the Republic of Kazakhstan 2017, 113). An and Kulmala (2020) describe a stagnant trend in adoption during this period, which might be accounting for the fact that total numbers of children lacking parental care also declined during this period.

29. For Goffman (1974, 38), primary frameworks enable us to form "conjectures as to what occurred before and expectations of what is likely to happen now." In other words, they are our basic sense of what is going on, whether it is a lesson or a performance, a real fight or an imagined kidnapping. These frameworks guide our behavior accordingly.

30. I heard the children use *mama* and *papa* in Kazakh (and Russian) more than the Kazakh terms for "mother" and "father," *ana* and *ata*, at Hope House.

31. They use the Kazakh verb *boiau*, meaning "to color" or "to paint" with the Russian noun *kraska*, or "paint." My research assistant insisted afterward that when they say they are painting the dolls, they are saying that they are putting makeup on them, though I always heard the puppet artists use other terms—*grym* (for stage makeup) or *kosmetika* (for everyday cosmetics). Either way, their way of making up their dolls—of painting them—extends beyond their faces, as they trace the lines of the doll and pony bodies. They call their doll and horse *böpeler*, "babies," rather than *balalar*, "children," though they have announced that these babies are six-and-a-half years old. They are making their babies, as they make them up.

32. See G. Wood 2002; Allison 2006.

33. When adults pose questions about imaginary friends, children often seem to make up answers on the spot (Taylor 1999).

## 3. JUMPING THROUGH HOOPS

1. For discussions of ideology, structure, and agency in childhood studies, see Jenkins 1998; A. James 2004; Spyrou, Rosen, and Cook 2018.

2. Performance is pervasive in other orphanages (Carpenter 2021). Many routines of childhood involve performative elements, such as when children act out the "scripts" of racialized power relations (R. Bernstein 2011) or "perform the nation" (Woronov 2007). See also Georgescu 2019. Gendered performance is citational, relying on past iterations, but with no origin point (Butler 1988). Butler's performativity can be useful in thinking about the effects that children's performances of childhood have on the world, rather than taking them as passive recipients of normativity. Nakassis (2016a) treats "citationality" as a semiotic form of performativity in which Tamil youths participate in order to reanimate, reflexively, forms of liminality and ambivalence that make up youth style. If performativity seems to focus on the individual in constituting categories of identity (Hastings and Manning 2004), these are nonetheless political and therefore relational. That is, performances of gender or age have consequences regarding belonging. At Hope House, effective performance secures care.

3. This ethnographic material and analysis of childhood and performance in Kazakhstan first appeared in Barker 2019a. I have expanded on the original discussion in various parts of this book, particularly this chapter and chapter 5.

4. See Lemon 2017; Sharafutdinova 2019.

5. See Deák 1975; Cassiday 2000; Oushakine 2016.

6. See Merchant 2009; L. Adams 2010; Bigozhin 2018; Klenke 2019.

7. Puppeteers in other contexts have characterized themselves as shy actors, hiding behind puppets or dummies in order to let these animated objects say and do things they would not dare. Silvio (2010) mentions this, and I encountered it various times in interviews with puppeteers from other theaters (Barker 2017b). Graham Jones (2011) describes a similar narrative of shy-youth-turned-performer among French magicians. The puppeteers I met in Kazakhstan never described shyness as a reason for pursuing puppetry. In fact, they argued that they were the ultimate performing artists because, besides manipulating the puppets, they also sometimes danced, sang, and played human roles onstage.

8. When they worked with rod or hand puppets, a curtain concealed the puppeteers as they controlled their instruments from below. In the musical revue they performed most frequently at the theater, however, the puppeteers wore sparkly white suits, lots of makeup, and smiled at the audience as they adroitly twirled and spun marionettes.

9. Puppeteers generally model gaze for the audience by focusing on their puppet rather than looking out at the audience (avoiding what an artist called the "four-eyes"

effect). However, in the Almaty theater, puppeteers do, at times, look out at the audience and smile.

10. This play between artist-as-character and artist-as-puppeteer was not in itself novel: Pulcinella puppeteers, ventriloquists, and the Soviet master puppeteer Sergei Obraztsov all offer examples of puppeteer-puppet interactions, but each often involves a certain regularity surrounding when and how this happens. For example, puppeteers often use interactions with puppets at the beginning and end of shows, thus framing the narrated event.

11. Armond Towns (2020, 6) has offered a compelling argument for thinking about definitions of media as they relate to the history of colonialism, with the Black body acting as "vehicle (or medium) toward the establishment of the West." As a technology of labor made invisible, the suffering of Black bodies gets disguised as white ingenuity in celebrations of "progress."

12. See websites of the Committee for Protecting Children's Rights (2023) and the UNICEF Child Friendly Cities Initiative (2023).

13. Regarding *vospitannye* in relation to Russian orphanages, see Rockhill 2010.

14. See Nozawa 2013 on characterization as an analytic for understanding the process of typification in animation by which people come to live surrounded by characters.

15. This movement from external animating forces to internal ones can make us think of Freud's ([1923] 1989) writing on the development of the superego as a kind of internal parental figure who not only represses inappropriate urges but also acts as a comfort. This internalization of external socializing forces also corresponds with Vygotsky's ([1934] 1986) argument—against Piaget's—that the "inner voice" comes after the child internalizes language, which is, at first, profoundly social. Sloterdijk (2014, 4), on the cultivation of "practicing life," focuses less on a trajectory of external to internal or vice versa, but notes instead the proliferation of cultures of habit, discipline, and exercise, which reveal "humans as the beings who result from repetition."

16. That is, biological anthropologists tie children's cuteness to strategies for survival and to basic processes of communication and learning. "Historical" factors include social, cultural, and political contexts that are, thus, highly variable.

17. Human infants in some ways resemble "altricial" newborns (like chicks) in their lacking locomotion, and yet are "precocial" (like colts) in that they are born with eyes open, can make eye contact, and are primed to prefer looking at human faces (Trevathan 2016). This has garnered biological anthropologists' attention working to consider evolutionary implications: Infants need care for a prolonged period of time after birth, creating an extended period of adults attending to infants, necessitating and giving way to relationships of joint attention. According to some, this condition of a prolonged period of care enabled new kinds of communication and created unique conditions for the evolution of intelligence, sociality, and language. On joint attention, see Citton 2017; Tomasello 2019. Humans' large brains (and narrow hips, enabling bipedalism) require premature birth. Their resultant helplessness means they need smart caregivers, so intelligence becomes a factor in selection (Piantadosi and Kidd 2016). Of course, not everyone sees this distinction from other animals as an unambiguous gain, as philosophers such as Rousseau ([1755] 2009) worked to imagine the unmediated access to the world that "natural man" must have enjoyed. Philosophical distinctions between man and animal, and their legacy in the myth of the feral child, become salient in chapter 5.

18. This "alloparenting" has important effects on sociality and communication according to some accounts of human evolution (Hrdy 2009; Isler and van Schaik 2012).

19. Most famous for describing the imprinting process of young animals such as newly hatched ducks, Lorenz (1943; 1970; 1981) introduced *kindenschema* in 1943.

20. Scholars taking up Lorenz's baby schema in their own research have examined humans' attraction to these features across age, species, and race. For example, some argue that even young children are attracted to these schema, and that they are attracted to baby animals (Borgi et al. 2014). Others explore racial bias regarding adult responsiveness to infant faces (Hodsoll, Quinn, and Hodsoll 2010; Proverbio et al. 2011). Some propose that adults might be less attracted to infants under three months old, despite infants' extreme helplessness during this period (Franklin, Volk, and Wong 2018). As they add detail and nuance to this proposition, however, they also risk naturalizing attitudes that could be an outcome of learned cultural norms, in the same way that evolutionary psychologists sometimes offer biological explanations for men prioritizing women's attractiveness (Burch 2020; Ruti 2015).

21. On Japanese *kawaii* culture and its links to ideal and exaggerated femininity, see Kinsella 1995; Okazaki and Johnson 2013; Yiu and Chan 2013. On cuteness in American consumer culture, see Harris 2000; Ngai 2012.

22. Puppets and other trivial objects serve to reinforce the trivialization of women (Shershow 1995). Children and women are compared to "dolls," affectionately referred to as "poppet" in British slang or as *lutka* in Bosnian/Croatian/Serbian.

23. See R. Bernstein 2011 on the exclusion of Black children from child innocence in America and Hannah Dyer (2019, 74) on "a refusal to learn" from children who have experienced violence and have therefore lost their innocence, in the eyes of many adults. Dyer notes that in failing to look at the experiences of difficult childhoods, we miss the "opportunity to forge empathy by prying open the edges of 'childhood' so that the affective resonances of war" can be shared (75). She draws from Stockton (2009) to consider the queerness of childhood.

24. The closest words in Russian and Kazakh, respectively, for "cute" seem to be *milyĭ* and *süikimdi*, but lexical mapping offers little understanding regarding aesthetic preferences surrounding children and childhood and their relation to material culture.

25. One example that achieved international attention was the characters from Yuri Norstein's *Hedgehog in the Fog* (1975). Anna Fishzon (2015, 572) describes late Soviet animation as offering a "voluptuous present" in the queer futurity of Brezhnev-era stagnation.

26. See Beumers 2007. While we might imagine that Stalin would have been opposed to fantastical themes presented by puppet theaters and animations, it was Lenin's wife, Nadezhda Krupskaia (1979), who advocated replacing silly fairy tales and nonsensical children's books with new tales that would teach children about contemporary life.

27. See Goldovskiĭ 2004; Obraztsov 1950.

28. For example, children watched programs such as *Nu, pogodi!* (Kandel et al. 1969) and *Chipollino* (Dyozhkin 1961) at Hope House and at the private kindergarten where I volunteered. The Almaty State Puppet Theater's windows featured characters from these animations alongside figures of Kazakh folklore and Disney. In public urban spaces in Astana, adults bring to life Soviet animations as part of a popular group game called "Encounter" that exists both offline and online (Laszczkowski 2016).

29. Milne's beloved character, first published in 1926, was adapted into a Soviet cel animation in 1969 (*Soyuzmultfilm*, directed by Fyodor Khitruk), which became another enduring favorite of Soviet animation. The Disney director Woolie Reitherman reportedly told Khitruk that he preferred the Soviet version to their own, which had just won an Academy Award (Moritz 1999).

30. Uspenskiĭ, Pshenichnaia, and Solin [1965] 1998.

31. Uspenskiĭ, Pshenichnaia, and Solin [1965] 1998.

32. For historical and anthropological work on socialist-era cultural institutions, see Grant 1995; Murawski 2019.

33. He offers a compromise between the two types of objects Boris Arvatov (1923; Arvatov and Kiaer 1997; Kiaer 1997) described just after the Bolshevik Revolution: the passive objects of the bourgeoisie, which can only be arranged on the shelf, and the production-oriented, dynamic objects that would destroy passive consumption and help build communism. Constructivist artists during the early Soviet period worked to create commodities that would be endowed with volition, which would stand in relationship to the worker-owner as "comrades," precisely because of their involvement in sensuous human activity (Kiaer 2005, 70).

34. Despite the success of these films, they were somewhat politically controversial. The Artistic Council overseeing the Cheburashka films expressed reservations at their tongue-and-cheek portrayal of Soviet institutions such as the Pioneers (Katz 2016).

35. James Baldwin (Baldwin and Jones [1963] 2012, 110), describing his young siblings being led up to gaze at the casket of their dead father, notes "something very gallant about children at such moments. . . . Their legs, somehow, seem *exposed*, so that it is at once incredible and terribly clear that their legs are all they have to hold them up." Here, Baldwin suggests both the urge to protect children and the limits to its possibility.

36. See Arns et al. 2016; Buck-Morss 2000; Oushakine 2016.

37. See Diderot 1883; Gell 1996. Diderot's (1883) paradox—that the actor moves the audience through calculated moves—influenced Meyerhold's (Meĭerkhol'd and Braun 1969) biomechanics. Though Kuba originally studied puppetry, he likely picked up a variation of these theories and others in his graduate studies of directing in Russia, which he then applied to his work in the puppet theater.

38. Sloterdijk (2011) offers a genealogy that connects Bruno's theory of bonding to Mesmer's animal magnetism to depth psychology, including Freud. His analysis focuses on duality, beginning with mother and child, and with all other relations acting as a substitute, an attempt to return to that primary relationship. Bruno's theorization is more open, reminding us that the relations that follow need not be mere substitutes. Each new instance can be modeled after previous experiences, but the bonds can also accumulate, transform, and create new possibilities to imagine what a relationship is.

39. Barker 2019b offers an extended discussion of the shows as traps and the intersubjective work of puppeteers imagining child spectators.

40. See Lipovskiĭ 1967 and Neirick 2012 on the Soviet circus, the Durovs, and Chekhov.

41. For a historical account of pre-Soviet Petrushka, see Kelly 1990. For a historical account of Soviet puppetry from a Soviet perspective, see Smirnova 1963. The remediation of Petrushka in early Soviet children's culture worked both in the puppet theater and in children's literature, while Buratino offered another beloved figure who traverses between puppet and boy, appearing in book, stage, and screen forms across Soviet periods and who is still popular today (Barker 2021).

42. Even in giving these instructions, puppet theaters employed a participatory style, asking the child audiences about these rules rather than telling them, as if they already knew and just needed to be reminded. At one theater, the emcee would take out an invisible key, prompting the children to do the same. Together, they put the key to their lips, turned it to lock their mouths shut, and then put the key safely in their pockets.

43. For example, Bambi Schieffelin (1990) describes Kaluli mothers holding their babies facing outward and then speaking for the young child to others rather than talking directly to the baby, in this way ventriloquizing as a way of scaffolding communication until the child becomes more competent at speaking for themselves.

44. Here I distinguish between "performative," in the sense of exhibiting citationality (Butler 1990) and generating effects (Austin 1962), and "theatricality" in the sense of

involving explicitly framed interactions of rehearsal, execution, and evaluation (Evreinov and Nazaroff 1927).

45. *Otkrytie zaniatiia* in Russian, *ashyq sabaq* in Kazakh, this practice existed in Soviet and post-Soviet schools in Kazakhstan, though according to friends' accounts, there was less preparation for them at schools.

46. Vitebsky (2005) describes an art class in Siberia which similarly seems to lack the creative openness that one might expect in an American or British setting. While certain classroom activities at Hope House aimed at training children to achieve mastery over particular skills, they were allowed to be free in their expression during play time.

47. See Barker 2019b. This division corresponds nicely to earlier discussions of Diderot and Meyerhold.

48. The *I* as metaphor, rather than deictic, enables transmission—of messages and of culture (Urban 1989). The two *Is* created by Kuba enable distance, treating the body as a thinking and planning artist and as an instrument that incorporates other instruments. It is not that the interior *I* is a self and the rest is mere matter, but that the two *Is* are key to one another's existence. Just as the anaphoric—and, in elaborations of possible framings, the theatrical—*I* in Urban's essay allows the *I* to become a metaphor for someone else, splitting the *first I* and *second I* enables the puppeteer's body to become a characterological figure onstage alongside the animated puppet, while the puppeteer maintains an awareness of a larger plan of action. In Western autobiographical traditions, there is an inevitable split between narrated and narrating *I* that generally gets ignored, but this split nonetheless creates the possibility for dialogical engagement (Crapanzano 1992).

49. See Peirce 1955 on dicent signs, C. Ball 2014 on dicentization, and Barker 2019b on puppet animation as a process of dicentization.

50. Carpenter (2021) describes the "voluntourism" that flourished in Cambodia in the early 2000s as having given rise to an orphanage "boom," these visits similarly involving an exchange of performances from the children with goods or entertainment from the foreign visitors. Hope House received, instead, mostly local visitors, allowing pedagogy students to practice organizing a New Year's celebration or providing oil companies a photo op to show off their corporate social responsibility campaigns.

51. *Meiırım* was used as the name of the festival, whether the text or speech surrounding it was in Russian or in Kazakh.

52. Agency emerges over time and gets distributed at different scales. As Kockelman (2006, 13) argues, "Agency may be shown not to necessarily (or even usually) adhere in specific people: the 'one' in question can be distributed over time (now and then), space (here and there), unit (super-individual and sub-individual), number (one and several), entity (human and nonhuman), and individual (Tom and Jane)."

53. Looking at responsibility helps identify attributions of agency (Hill and Irvine 1993).

54. On the book and its adaptations, see A. N. Tolstoy 1957; N. Tolstoy 1983; Lipovetsky 2011. The 1976 film was made by Belarusfilm (dir. Leonid Nechayev).

55. This is the process, for example, of enslavement (Kopytoff 1986). Slavery makes people into orphans in a way that can make recovery impossible, even for descendants (Hartman 2008).

56. Vladimir Propp's 1927 *Morphology of the Folk Tale*, which dissects Russian folktales along formalist principles, lists the functions of the *dramatis personae*. The first function is, "One of the members of a family absents himself from the home." In the subheadings of this function, Propp (1968, 26) adds, "An intensified form of abstention is represented by the death of parents."

57. For work on nostalgia and postsocialism, see Bloch 2005; Todorova and Gille 2010.

58. Struggles against forgetting subsided in the 1990s, replaced by a new desire for an imagined, ahistorical past when things were stable and normal. This period became one

of mass nostalgia (Boym 2001, 58). In Astana, longtime residents stigmatized migrants by referring to them as the mankurt's opposite, the *mambet* (Laszczkowski 2016, 58). While a mankurt (or *mangurt*, in Laszczkowski's transcription) has forgotten his past, the mambet clings to the uncultured ways of his village, even after moving to the city.

59. I looked for this quotation in Tolstoy's writings but was unable to locate it.

## 4. GETTING COMFORTABLE

1. Numerous scholars have underlined Soviet hostility toward *byt*. Translated as "everyday life," it was associated with the bourgeois trappings of materiality, the home, tradition and customs, and femininity, which socialism promised to transform (Kiaer 2005; Northrop 2004; Hirsch 2005). It is the opposite of *dusha*—"soul" (Pesmen 2000).

2. Sloterdijk (2014, 62) aligns Kafka's hunger artist and the acrobat, as both offer exemplary exercises in bodily discipline. And yet, Kafka's artist eventually reveals that it is easy for him to fast because he never found food he liked, whereas Kashtanka loves the dinners the new master offers her (Kafka 1983).

3. The sentimentality attributed to the carpenter's home, however, hardly corresponds with the descriptions Chekhov offers, in which he constantly curses the dog (Kataev 2003).

4. Puppeteers at the theater explained to me that the simple designs of the puppets made them better than actors in bringing to life figures of pure good and pure evil. Similar discourses can be found in Soviet-era writing on puppetry, such as when Nataliia Il'inichna Smirnova (1963, 6) argues that Soviet puppetry is especially equipped to express "types of life" (*tipy zhizni*). She describes "type" as "the artistic expression of an enormous fount of generalizations in life."

5. There were concerns that the end of Nazarbayev's presidency could give Russia an advantage over claiming the northern regions of Kazakhstan, where there were large populations of ethnic Russians (Brletich 2015). The official stance of Kazakhstan's leaders before Russia's 2022 invasion of Ukraine was that the Crimean Referendum was legal, and thus what happened was not an annexation, but the free will of the people (Current Time 2019). At the same time, Nazarbayev's successor, President Tokayev, stressed that ethnic Russians were an important part of Kazakhstan's multinational and multilingual history and culture and that majority Russian areas thus belonged in the Republic of Kazakhstan (*EADaily* 2020). Russia's invasion of Ukraine has triggered a number of shifts in relations between Russia and Kazakhstan and among Russians and Kazakhs within Kazakhstan (Begim 2022).

6. See, for example, Beckett et al. 2006; Nelson, Fox, and Zeanah 2014; Colvert et al. 2008.

7. On the political potency of grayness in postsocialist Hungary, see Fehérváry 2013. Regarding Cold War relations on either side of the Iron Curtain, Lemon (2011, 317, emphasis in original) writes: "Through qualic signs, it is *as if* materials and sensations give body to social contacts and political gaps." When reviewing adoption blogs of American parents adopting from Kazakhstan during the first decade of the 2000s, I found they had a tendency to describe, upon arrival, the gray landscape they found in postsocialist cities such as Almaty as an indication of the unfeeling nature of the Soviet regime from which adoptive parents were saving these innocent children. Nonetheless, adoptive parents I met also described the caregivers at the baby houses and children's homes from which they adopted as warm and caring.

8. See Cartwright 2005. Anthropologists working in other parts of the world have highlighted the ways children classified as orphans (and living with relatives) or those living in residential care (whether considered orphans or not) are not only affected by but also influence wider, kin-based economic conditions (Freidus 2010; Dahl 2014).

9. See Fujimura, Stoecker, and Sudakova 2005; Rockhill 2010.

10. In the late Soviet context, material conditions improved compared to the early years of famine and war, but the institutional system and the children living within it remained stigmatized. During the later period, "the orphanage system became the repository for children who were in one sense or another marginal, in particular sick and handicapped children; the children of sick, alcoholic, or otherwise incapable parents; and the offspring of single mothers, since the social stigma of birth outside marriage remained powerful" (Kelly 2007, 267).

11. In Russian-language literature on children without parents, the term "deprivation"—*lishenye*—is used to describe the condition on both sides: children have been deprived of their parents while parents whose children have been taken from them are "deprived" of their parental rights. See, for example, the Kazakhstani government's E-Gov website (2021).

12. She made little enough money to qualify for government welfare for single mothers, but she said the time and bus fare required to fill out and submit all of the required paperwork were not worth the meager payments they offered.

13. See Dubuisson 2017. These shrines have gained political significance through projects such as Sacred Geography of Kazakhstan, nonetheless, which some have argued contributes to a strengthening of an ethnonationalist conception of Kazakhstan, as the selection of sites as part of the "Sacred Geography" of national territory involves a "recoding of the semantics of space, by selecting, codifying, and articulating some symbols and practices, while leveling and 'forgetting' others" (Tsyrempilov, Bigozhin, and Zhumabayev 2021, 1). In this way, the shrines might enable connections to the land for some citizens of Kazakhstan while erasing others' historical engagements with the territory.

14. For a more extended treatment of this lesson, see Barker 2017a.

15. The main figures known as proponents for scaffolding children's learning are Vygotsky ([1934] 1986), who proposed "Zones of Proximal Development" and Bruner (D. Wood, Bruner, and Ross 1976, 197).

16. See Bateson ([1955] 1987) on the paradox of play as real and not real and Sidnell 2011 on children breaking the play frame in order to discuss it.

17. Vygotsky ([1966] 1978) describes the toy as a pivotal object toward children's understanding of the symbolic. Dolls can bring together high and low art (Shatirishvili and Manning 2011). In Peircian terms, toys can act as indexical icons, pointing to a real object through their resemblance to them, but as objects with their own qualia, they remain open to interpretation, such as when the girls in chapter 2 treated a horse and Barbie as their babies, or when Nurlan repurposed a helicopter as a musical instrument in chapter 1. For anthropological work on qualia, see Gal 2013; Lemon 2013; Chumley 2017.

18. Adults at least tend to *assume* that children animate dolls without any of the anxiety over the uncanny that they, adults, might feel when encountering automatons, dolls, or puppets. The intersubjectivity attributed to the doll acts as an extension of agency outside of one's own body and onto the body of another. That other's (assumed) lack of reason makes this extension a benevolent act. Unlike Kantian subjects, endowed with reason, who should *not* become objects, these objects can, at once, be treated as subjects and still anchor other social relations, becoming a means that does not violate their own subjectivity, which is but a temporary gift anyway and can be taken away (Kant [1785] 2018).

19. In my observations, children name their dolls far less often than adults expect. I have seen adults in the US and in Kazakhstan ask children the name of a doll or stuffed animal only to receive a puzzled look from the child.

20. The toy gun is unlikely to do either. Of course, it can be seen as a phallic symbol, but the iconic relationship between the gun and phallus is less prone to explicit commentary from the caregivers who give it to the child. Moreover, if we follow de Beauvoir's arguments regarding the double, the phallus itself is already a symbolic doubling

of the boy, rendering the gun an indexical icon of an object already overdetermined (Beauvoir [1949] 2011).

21. Key works include Appadurai 1986; Gell 1998; Latour 1993, 2005; B. Brown 2010.

22. See Gibson 1966 on "affordances." Historical concern over women's susceptibility to consumer culture—especially when they could get physically closer to commodities—likewise suggests that the agency of objects gets treated as dominant over humans perceived as fragile. Nineteenth-century department stores were imagined to present a danger to the woman shopper because "the sight and touch of so many highly desirable and readily accessible luxuries would make a woman lose her self-control and buy beyond her needs or means" (Classen 2012, 194). Regarding the fragile agency of children, we find such fears amplified regarding technological determinism, with concerns about the influence of media and technology on such malleable young minds. Working-class mothers are especially susceptible to outside criticism for allowing children too much screen time (Seiter 1993; Livingstone and Blum-Ross 2020).

23. After Teen Talk Barbie drew a backlash for her complaints about math, Mattel Inc. removed the phrase from her repertoire (Associated Press 1992).

24. Cinema scholars have explored the "haptic" elements of film in highlighting the ways that sounds and textures can evoke tactile elements of environments (Marks 2000, 2002).

25. Miriam Forman-Brunell (1993) argues for this starkly gendered difference between different approaches to American doll making at the turn of the twentieth century. Around this same time, pedagogues at an international toy congress in Russia discussed the dangers of walking, talking dolls and French dolls that encouraged consumption, arguing that the technologically advanced dolls impinged on children's imaginations, and that the French dolls would encourage girls' vanity (Hall and Ellis 1897; Peers 2004).

26. See, for example, D. W. Ball 1967; Kline 1993; Cross 1997; Rogers 1999.

27. See M. L. Jones 2016; Vlahos 2015.

28. See, for example, Hall and Ellis's 1897 wonderful survey of children's doll play in the US. Children queer Barbie, critique her body shape, and engage with questions of dolls' racialization beyond skin color (Rand 1995; Chin 2001).

29. See Bhat 2014 on late Soviet youth culture and consumerism, and see Reid and Crowley 2000; Patterson 2001; Fehérváry 2009 on consumer culture in various contexts of Eastern European state socialism.

30. Sociologists, focusing especially on American contexts, highlight the interrelationship between television shows and advertising targeting children with "commoditoys" that always keep children wanting more (Langer 2002).

31. Fehérváry (2013) calls us to attend not merely to questions of shortage versus choice in understandings of consumerism during and after state socialism, but insists that quality has always mattered, and that the qualities of goods have served to index relationships between the state and its citizens, along with qualities of the households who are able to consume the goods available (and those that are not).

32. The gender of my gifts brings me no pride; Maisa's play with her fake Barbie from her mother made me curious about how the girls would play among each other if given similar toys. I gave little thought to the boys' toys, except that they often played with cars.

33. Nakassis (2016a, 57) shows, in his fieldwork among youth in Tamil Nadu, that local ways of doing style do not rely on owning authentically branded products but rely on owning products that are "like" branded products, and in this way serve to distinguish those wearing such clothing, revealing an "ambivalent tension . . . between identity and quality." Whereas identity appears to be at the core of concerns among the youth of his field site (and though this identity is never devoid of a social field), the gifts the children received at Hope

House did not necessarily index individual identity (of the child recipient or adult giver) or the relationship between the two, but could be interpreted as any combination of these.

34. Lasseter, dir. 1996; Williams 1922.

35. See Mauss 1954. Connecting with children requires understanding their systems of valuing particular competencies, objects, and routines of exchange (Evans 2006). At the same time, children from particular class backgrounds gain a remarkably sophisticated understanding of the value of money for their families (Chin 2001), in a way that contrasts sharply with middle-class ideologies of innocence that lead parents to protect their children from financial knowledge (Zaloom 2019).

36. The lines between artist and technical worker can often be unclear in creative institutions and industries, such as film production (Kelly 2021).

37. Following the New Year's shows, they would have slow weeks of mending their own clothes, doing crossword puzzles, or napping at their workstations.

38. *The Velveteen Rabbit*, by the British author Margery Williams (1922) has, as an alternative title, *Or How Toys Become Real*. In this story, the stuffed rabbit goes to bed with a boy who develops scarlet fever. After he is well, all of his toys must be burned, including the rabbit, and it is then that the rabbit becomes a real rabbit. Here, as in Sania's story, the toys' main wish is to serve their child owner. Saltanat Apai, in warning the children about breaking their toys, focuses on the children's duty toward the objects.

## 5. LOSING A FRIEND

1. See Barker 2019b for earlier analysis of this seen in relation to discussions of the division of roles at the puppet theater.

2. See Althusser 1994; Kulick 2003 on the "bad subject" and Kulick and Schieffelin 2005 as it applies to language socialization. Barker 2019a looks at the case of Erlan, ideologies of cuteness, and the threat of the bad subject, within the context of Hope House.

3. Bunraku puppetry captured Roland Barthes' (1971, 79) attention, as well, for the way it separates act, voice, and movement, or act and gesture, because it banishes the concept of the soul "hidden behind all animation."

4. Mori wrote his essay when the humanoid robots against which he warns were only beginning to be designed. His placement of objects on the uncanny valley came largely from his own reactions to different phenomena. Jentsch (2008) and Freud's (1953) essays allow for individual variability concerning when the uncanny arises, yet we should expect cultural variation as well regarding who or what is familiar or strange to whom. The very recognition of similarity depends on the perspective of who is classifying two things as similar to one another (Goodman 1972); anything could, potentially, be familiar yet strange. The emergence of similarities as relevant to a given perspective requires considering how interactions between subjects and objects unfold.

5. Erich Heller (1978, 422) describes the conclusion of Kleist's essay thus: "If man succeeds in infinitely expanding his consciousness, natural grace will return."

6. On efforts to preserve and reanimate human remains in Soviet and post-Soviet Russia, see A. Bernstein 2019; Yurchak 2015.

7. E. T. A. Hoffman's (1967) stories served as paradigmatic examples for Jentsch and Freud's essays on the topic, while dolls and puppets who refuse to remain inanimate offer horror film fodder in the twentieth and twenty-first centuries. In 2016, I interviewed a New York–based performer who frequently used puppets and dressed as a clown in his shows for adults. The performance I saw included human organs made of foam, yet when I broached the question of the uncanniness of puppets, the artist insisted, with some frustration, that there was nothing inherently disturbing about puppets or clowns. Audiences interpreted his work as such due to cultural influences that they needed to overcome.

8. A report by Bakwin (1949, 512) describing infants' "listlessness" focuses especially on children abandoned and left to live for extended periods of time in hospitals. See Askeland 2005 and McKenzie 1998 on the decline of institutionalization in the US.

9. See Bluebond-Langner 1978 and Clemente 2015 on children and teenagers with terminal illnesses, for example.

10. See Kelly 1990; Barker 2021.

11. Sloterdijk (2011, 17) writes of the child blowing bubbles: "For the duration of the bubble's life the blower was outside himself, as if the little orb's survival depended on remaining encased in an attention that floated out with it." Children also love to pop bubbles.

12. See Foster and Sherr 2006; D. J. Johnson, Agbényiga, and Bahemuka 2013.

13. See Ellis and Hall 1897; Forman-Brunell 1993.

14. See Toren 2009 on childhood and intersubjectivity, and Ulturgasheva 2012 for work on personhood in Siberia, drawing from Strathern 1988. See Kharkhordin 1999 on the collective and the individual in twentieth-century Russia.

15. Children are born immobile, and most learn to walk. They are born mostly without teeth and acquire them. They do not talk, but usually they eventually do. Social, cultural, or historical factors might be considered as variables that shift expected timeframes. The rate at which children do these things compared with others justifies diagnoses and interventions.

16. In Lemon's (2009) description of theater students' efforts to become inanimate objects, the students gravitate toward enacting the objects' demise, as it offers a necessary element of *konflikt*. The breaking of an object gives it a personality; being broken makes the object come to life. This can remind us of the dying goose, who seems to take on a life of its own, beyond the puppeteer's control, just as it is dying.

17. I reviewed forty-two articles on institutions like *detdom*, from four popular outlets, and found them more than twice as likely to focus on the problems with such homes. Other topics included efforts to prevent placement in such institutions, outreach efforts to *detdoms* from celebrities or organizations, accounts of specific *detdoms* closing, and general discussions of the necessity and problems with continued reliance on institutionalization or on international adoption. Only one article focused on a positive aspect of children's homes themselves, arguing that within *detdoms*, children and workers created family.

18. Maria Kromidas (2014, 426) has argued that social scientists have kept children as figures of the savage or "less than fully human."

19. Works on children and infants treated as snakes, demons, or witches—and issues of infanticide—include Denham 2017; La Fontaine 2009; Sargent 1988.

20. The first word that one of the children uttered was interpreted as the Phrygian word for "bread." Similar experiments were reportedly attempted by later rulers (Herodotus, Beloe, and Valpy 1830, 160–161; Shattuck and Candland 1994, 44).

21. Eighteenth-century Enlightenment scholars used instances of feral children to explore questions of the nature and classification of humanity. Linnaeus created a separate category for feral man—*Homo ferus*—inspired by cases such as Peter the Wild Boy, found in Hanover, Germany, in 1724. Peter and Victor (of Aveyron, found in 1799) drew the interest of scholars as exemplars of the "natural man" romanticized by Rousseau ([1755] 2009). See Malson and Itard 1972; Douthwaite 2002. The latter half of the eighteenth century saw a diminishment of cases of European wild children and a rise of reported cases of wild native children in the colonies. The cases of wild children in the colonies presented a conundrum for classification, as they were doubly animallike, by nature of their behavior and their race (Nath 2009). Kipling's (1894) Mowgli offers a solution to the dilemma posed by feral native children, for he eventually becomes a loyal subject of the ruling whites rather

than part of the colonized locals. Based loosely on nonfiction accounts, *The Jungle Book* shows how easily authors of cultural texts move between fact and fiction.

22. See Montagu's (1943) review of Singh, Zingg, and Feuerbach ([1942] 1960).

23. The critical period for language acquisition is often thought to be sometime before the onset of puberty, by which time a child must acquire a language if they are to acquire it fluently (Lenneberg 1967).

24. See Malson and Itard 1972; Douthwaite 2002.

25. *Raised Wild*, Animal Planet, MacFarlane 2012.

26. See, for example, Solonevich 2009; "*Deti maugli*" (Mowgli children) 2013; "*Liudi— maugli*" (Mowgli people) 2005. While Russian-language press also refers to such children as "wild" (*dikie*)—or, more rarely, "feral" (*feral'noe*)—they more commonly use the term *syndrom Maugli* to describe their behaviors. "Mowgli syndrome" was coined by an American scholar, Wendy Doniger O'Flaherty ([1988] 1995), in the context of a cross-cultural study of myth and storytelling. Nonetheless, the term "Mowgli syndrome" appears in Russian popular press as if it were an established psychological diagnosis for real children.

27. The National Geographic documentary about feral children features Charles Nelson, a pediatrician who has spent decades studying institutionalized children in Romania. He points out that children such as Oxana must have fled abusive households to end up seeking animal affection, but this is edited into the last five minutes of the forty-five-minute program.

28. For example, see the "*Chelovecheskiĭ detenysh*" (Human cub) episode (2010) on the Russian TV talk show *Pust' govoriat'* (Let them speak).

29. Gidadhubli 1998, 1811. I am not suggesting that "normal" capitalism exists. Rather, characterizations of wild capitalism implicitly or explicitly blame the former Eastern Bloc's flawed or failed "transition" into a market economy on socialism's improper socialization of consumer citizens that left these postsocialist citizens ill-equipped to handle the open market. Inside the former Soviet Union, citizens would gradually come to terms with the potential that Perestroika and the early 1990s presented, followed by a realization of losses incurred with diminished social care (Aleksievich 2016). As Harper's (2006) ethnography of capitalism and environmental activism in postsocialist Hungary illustrates, the link between ecology and economy evoked by the term "wild capitalism" becomes more than a metaphor.

30. In the cases of Eastern European children adopted by Americans, it is as if the apparent whiteness of the children cloaks underlying deviance. In describing children from the region as "white," I refer to transnational stereotypes of Eastern European and Eurasian institutions and the children adopted from them. These outside perceptions often overlook racializing and ethnic distinctions within the region.

31. The eventual ban was interpreted in the US as a political maneuver by Putin to punish the US, rather than as a way to protect the children who were up for adoption (Shuster 2012).

32. The adoptive father claims his wife (at the time, for they since separated) pressured him into telling people the girl was older (Jensen 2019).

33. For ethnographic research on transnational adoption, see E. J. Kim 2010; Stryker 2010; Volkman et al. 2005. Domestic adoptions are complicated arrangements as well. In a 2017 survey in the UK conducted by the BBC and Adoption UK, more than 35 percent of adoptive parents said they felt they had not received "full and correct" information about their child at the time of adoption, and more than 60 percent said their child had exhibited aggressive behavior toward them, yet close to 90 percent answered that they were glad they had adopted. See Harte 2017; BBC and Adoption UK 2017.

34. By the late Soviet period, and into the early post-Soviet period in Ukraine, deaf culture became increasingly associated with a marginal societal position (Shaw 2017).

35. The stance of UNICEF, when I met with officials there at the beginning of my field-work and again in 2017, was that orphanages and other homes of substitute care should not be improved. They should simply close. Anthropologists working in other parts of the world have, nonetheless, argued that these forms of alternative care need not be uniformly condemned, as they can offer supportive networks of care within and provide a temporary solution for parents who wish eventually to resume care (G. A. Johnson 2011; Carpenter 2021; Leinaweaver 2008).

36. Roma in Moscow, for example, find themselves in an impossible position because of the stereotypes surrounding them regarding performance and authenticity. Authenticity requires a commitment to performance, which gets associated, in turn, with duplicity (Lemon 2000). Such tensions between authenticity and performance also unfold with relationships of tourists and "primitive" societies (Bruner and Kirshenblatt-Gimblett 1994) and in outsider evaluations of mass mourning of totalitarian leaders (Mazzarella 2015).

## 6. GOING HOME AGAIN

1. Regarding performance as creating the risks of approval or disapproval, of success or failure, see Bauman and Briggs 1990; Keane 1997; Yankah 1985.

2. *Osramimsia, provalimsia!*

3. *Osramitsia! Provalitsia!* The master's declaration—using "we"—is a direct quote from Chekhov's original text. Kuba has added this line in its adaptation for the stage. The third-person singular, without a subject, makes for a poetic parallel between Bolat's declaration and Baqytzhan's, as just one phoneme changes, the *m* to *t*. The statement, without an overt grammatical subject in the second case, makes it ambiguous who exactly will be a disgrace, a flop. We will soon see that it is indeed the clown who faces humiliation in the ring.

4. Each instance of the curse—at the beginning and end of the story—seems to be a misquoting of Psalm 50, line 7, "*I vo grekhe rodila menia mat' moia.*" Translators Pevear and Volokhonsky note that *utroba* could be translated as either "innards" or "womb," but they chose the latter to emphasize the absurdity of the master's curses (in Chekhov 2014, 131).

5. Laura Mulvey (2005) sees the moving image on film—made up of individual frames—as an uncanny object that always threatens to break down, like our own temporarily animated selves.

6. As many scholars have noted (and debated), photographs and film (and their digital counterparts) are often treated as standing in a primarily indexical relationship with the matter depicted within them (Bazin, Renoir, and Andrew 2004; D. Morgan 2006; Gunning 2007; Doane 2007; Barker and Nakassis 2020; Nakassis 2020; Lefebvre 2021). They can be manipulated during various stages in the process, but there are always elements beyond my control that sneak into the frame, surprises I didn't notice the first ten times I watched a clip, the semiotic bundling of infinite qualia leaving it up to me to decide what is most relevant to the questions I pose (Keane 2003). That is true of utterances and live performances as well, as Jakobson (1960, 354) notes when discussing the way an actor was asked to audition for Stanislavsky by uttering "this evening" (*segodnia vecerom*) forty different ways.

7. The tension between the represented and the real that has brought linguistic anthropologists to explore the productive ambivalence of indexicality, which enables movement between these (Silverstein 1976; Nakassis 2018).

8. People traverse such thresholds in both directions, such as when a theatergoer transgresses by approaching the stage (Lemon 2000).

9. For example, Shirley Brice Heath's (1982) study of reading practices between adults and children in three different communities reveals how adults of each group engage children with books and storytelling in distinct ways. This shapes children's literacy practices in school, with teachers and children often having divergent expectations of how to show their understanding of a story.

10. See Freedman 2010 on milk carton faces and a fascinating moment of mediation surrounding children's images. On the hypermediation of individual perpetrators over the structural violence of inequality, see Scheper-Hughes and Stein 1998.

11. Rituals surrounding particular milestones differ as well. For a child's first birthday, their feet are tied together and then untied by someone who walks quickly. This helps ensure that the baby will go places in life. Then a group of objects is placed before the child and the child chooses one; this will determine their priorities in life. I observed only one such ceremony, at a mother's house (*Dom mamy*) for young single mothers and their young children. Before the child, a girl, they placed cash, a book, car keys, and *bauyrsaq* (fried bread). After much hesitation, the baby chose some of the cash, but not all of it.

12. See Grimshaw and Ravetz 2009; Sandall 1972.

13. Children have also found themselves the objects of global circulation through transnational adoption (Yngvesson 2010; E. J. Kim 2010; Briggs 2012).

14. This is especially true in systems of slave trade or human trafficking. Rubin (1975, 171) rejects a conflation between the trafficking of women and objectification, since this creates a false dichotomy between objects and persons that does not hold up across cultures. However, she argues that we need to understand and acknowledge that kinship systems based on the exchange of women involve an unequal dynamic of power insofar as the exchange, described as such, serves as "a shorthand for expressing that the social relations of a kinship system specify that men have certain rights in their female kin, and that women do not have the same rights either to themselves or to their male kin."

15. For example, the United Nations Convention on the Rights of the Child (1989) states, in Article 7.1: "The child shall be registered immediately after birth and shall have the right from birth to a name, the right to acquire a nationality and, as far as possible, the right to know and be cared for by his or her parents." The use of "the child" throughout this document allows the reader to imagine a single child—as an individual and as a universal kind of child. This risks overlooking the great variety of interests and practices of children and of contexts in which they have specific needs and wants (James and James 2004). At the same time, Article 8 of the Convention preserves the child's "identity," which includes their nationality, name, and family relations.

16. Known as Unity Day, the holiday celebrates interethnic harmony between Kazakhs and non-Kazakhs. During Soviet times, as in many countries, May 1 was Day of the International Solidarity of Workers, but President Nazarbayev changed the holiday in 1996.

17. They read XOXOXO as Cyrillic, pronouncing it "ho ho ho," and found it very funny.

18. The artistic director returned in time for the premiere the following day.

19. The importance of official letters of gratitude could be a continuation of Soviet-era practices, when receiving such letters often served as a reward in and of itself as part of a larger economy of honorary awards (Guillebaud 1953; P. M. Morgan 1968).

20. Entextualization not only fixes or freezes but enables creative recontextualizations that exceed the intentions of creators. Meanings change and grow. See Bauman and Briggs 1990; Silverstein and Urban 1996.

21. On homologous relations between the built environment and local cosmologies and ideologies regarding social relations, see Bourdieu 1977; Fehérváry 2013.

## CODA

1. See Astrasheuskaya 2019; Begim 2022; Kumenov 2022; Pannier 2022.

2. A press announcement claimed this was so that social workers and nongovernment organizations could focus on preventing family separation. The numbers of children's homes and of children in them continue to decline, without disappearing. See DKN World News 2023; Ministry of Education 2021.

# References

Abashin, Sergey. 2015. *"Vozvrashchenie domoi: semeinye i migratsionnye stsenarii v Uzbekistane"* [Returning home: Family and migrant scenarios in Uzbekistan] *Ab Imperio* 2015 (3): 125–65. https://doi.org/10.1353/imp.2015.0064.

Adams, Laura L. 2010. *The Spectacular State: Culture and National Identity in Uzbekistan.* Durham, NC: Duke University Press.

Adams, Margarethe. 2020. *Steppe Dreams: Time, Mediation, and Postsocialist Celebrations in Kazakhstan.* Pittsburgh, PA: University of Pittsburgh Press. https://doi.org/10.2307/j.ctv125jsxn.

Adler, Nanci. 2012. *Keeping Faith with the Party.* Bloomington: Indiana University Press.

Afanas'ev, A. N. 2014. *The Complete Folktales of A. N. Afanas'ev Volume I.* Edited by Jack V. Haney. Jackson: University Press of Mississippi.

Agadjanian, Victor, Premchand Dommaraju, and Jennifer E. Glick. 2008. "Reproduction in Upheaval: Ethnic-Specific Fertility Responses to Societal Turbulence in Kazakhstan." *Population Studies* 62 (2): 211–33. https://doi.org/10.1080/02615470802045433.

Agbo, Seth A., and Natalya Pak. 2017. "Globalization and Educational Reform in Kazakhstan: English as the Language of Instruction in Graduate Programs." *International Journal of Educational Reform* 26 (1): 14–43. https://doi.org/10.1177/1056787 91702600102.

Ainsworth, Mary D. Salter, and Silvia M. Bell. 1970. "Attachment, Exploration, and Separation: Illustrated by the Behavior of One-Year-Olds in a Strange Situation." *Child Development* 41 (1): 49–67. https://doi.org/10.2307/1127388.

Akilova, Mashura. 2017. "Pathways to Child Work in Tajikistan: Narratives of Child Workers and Their Parents." *Central Asian Survey*, February, 1–16. https://doi.org /10.1080/02634937.2017.1281791.

Aleksievich, Svetlana. 2016. *Secondhand Time: The Last of the Soviets.* New York: Random House.

Alexander, Catherine. 2007. "Almaty: Rethinking the Public Sector." In *Urban Life in Post-Soviet Asia*, edited by Catharine Alexander, Victor Buchli, and Caroline Humphrey, 70–101. London: UCL Press.

Allison, Anne. 2006. *Millennial Monsters: Japanese Toys and the Global Imagination.* Berkeley: University of California Press. https://www.jstor.org/stable/10.1525/j .cttlppk4p.11.

Althusser, Louis. 1994. "Ideology and Ideological State Apparatuses." In *Mapping Ideology*, edited by Slavoj Žižek, 100–140. London: Verso.

An, Sofia, and Meri Kulmala. 2020. "Global Deinstitutionalisation Policy in the Post-Soviet Space: A Comparison of Child-Welfare Reforms in Russia and Kazakhstan." *Global Social Policy*, May. https://doi.org/10.1177/1468018120913312.

Andrews, James T., and Asif A. Siddiqi. 2011. *Into the Cosmos: Space Exploration and Soviet Culture.* Pittsburgh, PA: University of Pittsburgh Press.

Appadurai, Arjun, ed. 1986. *The Social Life of Things: Commodities in Cultural Perspective.* Cambridge, UK: Cambridge University Press.

Ariès, Philippe. 1965. *Centuries of Childhood: A Social History of Family Life*. New York: Vintage Books.

Arns, Inke, Sylvia Sasse, Igor Chubarov, Bernard Heise, David Riff, and Jordan Kee Schnee, eds. 2016. *Nikolai Evreinov & Others: "The Storming of the Winter Palace."* Zurich: Diaphanes.

Artaud, Antonin. (1938) 2010. *The Theatre and Its Double*. Translated by Victor Corti. Richmond, UK: Oneworld Classics.

Arvatov, B. 1923. *Iskusstvo I Klassy*. Moskva: Gosizdat.

Arvatov, Boris, and Christina Kiaer. 1997. "Everyday Life and the Culture of the Thing (Toward the Formulation of the Question)." *October* 81 (July): 119–28. https://doi.org/10.2307/779022.

Askeland, Lori. 2005. *Children and Youth in Adoption, Orphanages, and Foster Care: A Historical Handbook and Guide*. Westport, CT: Greenwood.

Associated Press. 1992. "Company News: Mattel Says It Erred; Teen Talk Barbie Turns Silent on Math." *New York Times*, October 21, 1992, Business Day.

Assylbekova, M. P., A. B. Abibulayeva, and R. H. Aimagambetova. 2019. "Prevention of Social Orphanhood: Kazakhstan Case Study." *Bulletin of the L.N. Gumilyov Eurasian National University*, Pedagogy. Psychology. Sociology, 3 (128): 15–24. Accessed June 28, 2023. http://dspace.enu.kz/handle/data/17827.

Astrasheuskaya, Nastassia. 2019. "Voters Sense Hand of Nazarbayev in Kazakh Presidential Poll." *Financial Times*, June 7, 2019, Kazakhstan. https://www.ft.com/content/9324b22e-883a-11e9-a028-86cea8523dc2.

Austin, J. L. 1962. *How to Do Things with Words*. Cambridge, MA: Harvard University Press.

Baimanov, Damir. 2017. "*Deputat Khamenova nazvala bebi-boksy kolybelíu nadezhdy*" [Deputy Khamenova called baby boxes a cradle of hope]. *Kazinform*, 15 March. https://www.inform.kz/ru/deputat-hamenova-nazvala-bebi-boksy-kolybel-yu-nadezhdy_a3008059.

Bakhtin, Mikhail M., and Michael Holquist. 1981. *Dialogic Imagination: Four Essays*. Austin: University of Texas Press.

Bakwin, Harry. 1949. "Emotional Deprivation in Infants." *Journal of Pediatrics* 35 (4): 512–21. https://doi.org/10.1016/S0022-3476(49)80071-0.

Baldwin, James, and Edward P. Jones. (1963) 2012. *Notes of a Native Son*. Boston: Beacon Press.

Ball, Alan M. 1994. *And Now My Soul Is Hardened: Abandoned Children in Soviet Russia, 1918–1930*. Berkeley: University of California Press.

Ball, Christopher. 2014. "On Dicentization." *Journal of Linguistic Anthropology* 24 (2): 151–73. https://doi.org/10.1111/jola.12046.

Ball, Donald W. 1967. "Toward a Sociology of Toys: Inanimate Objects, Socialization, and the Demography of the Doll World." *Sociological Quarterly* 8 (4): 447–58.

Bandey, Aijaz A., and Farooq Ahmad Rather. 2013. "Socio-Economic and Political Motivations of Russian Out-Migration from Central Asia." *Journal of Eurasian Studies* 4 (July): 146–53. https://doi.org/10.1016/j.euras.2013.03.004.

Banet-Weiser, Sarah. 2007. *Kids Rule!: Nickelodeon and Consumer Citizenship*. Durham, NC: Duke University Press. https://doi.org/10.2307/j.ctv1198x7x.

Barker, Meghanne. 2017a. "Belonging and Belongings: Kinship Narratives and Material Anchors at a Second Home in Kazakhstan." *Journal of the Anthropological Society of Oxford* 9 (1): 65–82.

Barker, Meghanne. 2017b. "Framing the Fantastic: Animating Childhood in Contemporary Kazakhstan." PhD diss., University of Michigan, 2017. https://search.proquest.com/docview/1989674220?pq-origsite=summon.

Barker, Meghanne. 2019a. "Dancing Dolls: Animating Childhood in a Contemporary Kazakhstani Institution." *Anthropological Quarterly* 92 (2): 311–43. doi:10.1353/anq.2019.0017.

Barker, Meghanne. 2019b. "Intersubjective Traps over Tricks on the Kazakhstani Puppet Stage: Animation as Dicentization." *Journal of Linguistic Anthropology* 29 (3): 375–96. https://doi.org/10.1111/jola.12227.

Barker, Meghanne. 2021. "From Stage to Page and Back Again: Remediating Petrushka in Early Soviet Children's Culture." *Russian Review* 80 (3): 375–401. https://doi.org/10.1111/russ.12318.

Barker, Meghanne. 2024. "You Have Been Misconnected. *Critical Inquiry* 50 (2): 201–224. https://doi.org/10.1086/727641

Barker, Meghanne, and Constantine V. Nakassis. 2020. "Images." *Semiotic Review* 9 (November). https://www.semioticreview.com/ojs/index.php/sr/article/view/61.

Barthes, Roland. 1971. "On Bunraku." *The Drama Review: TDR* 15 (2): 76–80. https://doi.org/10.2307/1144622.

Barthes, Roland. 1982. *Camera Lucida: Reflections on Photography*. Translated by Richard Howard. New York: Hill and Wang.

Bateson, Gregory. (1955) 1987. *Steps to an Ecology of Mind: Collected Essays in Anthropology, Psychiatry, Evolution, and Epistemology*. Northvale, N.J.; Aronson.

Bauman, Richard. 2004. *A World of Others' Words: Cross-Cultural Perspectives on Intertextuality*. Malden, MA: Blackwell.

Bauman, Richard, and Charles L. Briggs. 1990. "Poetics and Performances as Critical Perspectives on Language and Social Life." *Annual Review of Anthropology* 19 (October): 59–88. https://doi.org/10.1146/annurev.an.19.100190.000423.

Bazin, Andre, Jean Renoir, and Dudley Andrew. 2004. *What Is Cinema? Vol. 1*. Translated by Hugh Gray. 2nd ed. Berkeley: University of California Press.

BBC and Adoption UK. "BBC/Adoption UK Survey." 2017. Issuu. Last updated September 27. https://issuu.com/adoptionuk/docs/bbc_adoption_uk_survey_doc.

Beauvoir, Simone De. (1949) 2011. *The Second Sex*. Translated by Constance Borde and Sheila Malovany-Chevallier. New York: Vintage.

Becker, Charles M., and David D. Hemley. 1998. "Demographic Change in the Former Soviet Union during the Transition Period." *World Development* 26 (11): 1957–75. https://doi.org/10.1016/S0305-750X(98)00113-2.

Beckett, Celia, Barbara Maughan, Michael Rutter, Jenny Castle, Emma Colvert, Christine Groothues, Jana Kreppner, Suzanne Stevens, Thomas G. O'Connor, and Edmund J. S. Sonuga-Barke. 2006. "Do the Effects of Early Severe Deprivation on Cognition Persist into Early Adolescence? Findings From the English and Romanian Adoptees Study." *Child Development* 77 (3): 696–711. https://doi.org/10.1111/j.1467-8624.2006.00898.x.

Begim, Ainur. 2018. "How to Retire like a Soviet Person: Informality, Household Finances, and Kinship in Financialized Kazakhstan." *Journal of the Royal Anthropological Institute* 24 (4): 767–85. https://doi.org/10.1111/1467-9655.12916.

Begim, Ainur. 2022. "Surreal Events, 'TV Zombies,' and Social Media in Postsocialist Kazakhstan: Reflecting on Violence in Russia's Sphere of Influence." *HAU: Journal of Ethnographic Theory* 12 (3): 632–41. https://doi.org/10.1086/722633.

Berlant, Lauren. 1998. "Intimacy: A Special Issue." *Critical Inquiry* 24 (2): 281–88. https://doi.org/10.1086/448875.

Berlant, Lauren. 2011. *Cruel Optimism*. Durham, NC: Duke University Press.

Bernstein, Anya. 2019. *The Future of Immortality: Remaking Life and Death in Contemporary Russia*. Princeton, NJ: Princeton University Press.

Bernstein, Robin. 2011. *Racial Innocence: Performing American Childhood from Slavery to Civil Rights*. New York: New York University Press.

Beumers, Birgit. 2007. "Comforting Creatures in Children's Cartoons." In *Reading Russian and Soviet Children's Culture*, edited by Marina Balina and Larissa Rudova, 153–71. New York: Taylor and Francis.

Bhat, Mohd Aslam. 2014. "(Re)Experiencing the Now-Gone: Youth and Cultural Politics in Soviet and Post-Soviet Central Asia." *Asian Affairs* 45 (3): 467–83. https://doi.org/10.1080/03068374.2014.951562.

Bigozhin, Ulan. 2018. "Nation-Building and a School Play in a Kazakh Saint's Jubilee." *Central Asian Affairs* 5 (1): 16–31. https://doi.org/10.1163/22142290-00501002.

Bissenova, Alima. 2013. "The Master Plan of Astana: Between the 'Art of Government' and the 'Art of Being Global.'" In *Ethnographies of the State in Central Asia: Performing Politics*, edited by Madeleine Reeves, Johan Rasanayagam, and Judith Beyer, 127–48. Bloomington: Indiana University Press.

Bissenova, Alima. 2016. "*Davlenie metropolii i tikhi natsionalizm akamicheskikh praktik*" [The pressure of metropoles and the quiet nationalism of academic practices]. *Ab Imperio* 2016 (4): 207–255.

Bissenova, Alima. 2017. "The Fortress and the Frontier: Mobility, Culture, and Class in Almaty and Astana." *Europe-Asia Studies* 69 (4): 642–667.

Bloch, Alexia. 2005. "Longing for the Kollektiv: Gender, Power, and Residential Schools in Central Siberia." *Cultural Anthropology* 20 (4): 534–69. https://doi.org/10.1525/can.2005.20.4.534.

Bluebond-Langner, Myra. 1978. *The Private Worlds of Dying Children*. Princeton, NJ: Princeton University Press.

Blum-Ross, Alicia, and Sonia Livingstone. 2017. "'Sharenting,' Parent Blogging, and the Boundaries of the Digital Self." *Popular Communication* 15 (2): 110–25. https://doi.org/10.1080/15405702.2016.1223300.

Boellstorff, Tom. 2008. *Coming of Age in Second Life: An Anthropologist Explores the Virtually Human*. Princeton, NJ: Princeton University Press.

Boellstorff, Tom. 2011. "Virtuality: Placing the Virtual Body: Avatar, Chora, Cypherg." In *A Companion to the Anthropology of the Body and Embodiment*, edited by Frances E. Mascia-Lees, 504–20. Newark: Wiley. https://doi.org/10.1002/9781444340488.ch29.

Boltanski, Luc. 1999. *Distant Suffering: Morality, Media, and Politics*. Cambridge, UK: Cambridge University Press.

Borgi, Marta, Irene Cogliati-Dezza, Victoria Brelsford, Kerstin Meints, and Francesca Cirulli. 2014. "Baby Schema in Human and Animal Faces Induces Cuteness Perception and Gaze Allocation in Children." *Frontiers in Psychology* 5 (May, Article 411): 1–12. https://doi.org/10.3389/fpsyg.2014.00411.

Bourdieu, Pierre. 1977. *Outline of a Theory of Practice*. Cambridge, UK: Cambridge University Press.

Bowlby, John. 1969. *Attachment and Loss*. London: Hogarth Press and the Institute of Psycho-Analysis.

Boym, Svetlana. 1998. "On Diasporic Intimacy: Ilya Kabakov's Installations and Immigrant Homes." *Critical Inquiry* 24 (2): 498–524. https://doi.org/10.1086/448882.

Boym, Svetlana. 2001. *The Future of Nostalgia*. New York: Basic Books.

Bray, Jemma, Neil Brewer, Kate Cameron, and Reginald D. V. Nixon. 2018. "Comparing Children's Memories for Negative Versus Positive Events in the Context of Posttraumatic Stress Symptoms." *Behavior Therapy* 49 (1): 32–45. https://doi.org/10.1016/j.beth.2017.03.006.

Briggs, Laura. 2012. *Somebody's Children: The Politics of Transracial and Transnational Adoption*. Durham, NC: Duke University Press.

Brletich, Samantha. 2015. "The Crimea Model: Will Russia Annex the Northern Region of Kazakhstan?" *Geopolitics, History, and International Relations* 7 (1): 11–29. http://www.jstor.org/stable/26805275.

Brown, Bill. 2010. "Objects, Others, and Us (The Refabrication of Things)." *Critical Inquiry* 36 (2): 183–217. https://doi.org/10.1086/648523.

Brown, Kate. 2004. *A Biography of No Place: From Ethnic Borderland to Soviet Heartland*. Cambridge, MA: Harvard University Press.

Bruner, Edward M., and Barbara Kirshenblatt-Gimblett. 1994. "Maasai on the Lawn: Tourist Realism in East Africa." *Cultural Anthropology* 9 (4): 435–70. https://doi.org/10.1525/can.1994.9.4.02a00010.

Bruno, Giordano. 1998. *Cause, Principle, and Unity: And Essays on Magic*. Cambridge, UK: Cambridge University Press.

Bucholtz, Mary, Brendan Barnwell, Elena Skapoulli, and Jung-Eun Janie Lee. 2012. "Itineraries of Identity in Undergraduate Science." *Anthropology & Education Quarterly* 43 (2): 157–72. https://doi.org/10.1111/j.1548-1492.2012.01167.x.

Buck-Morss, Susan. 2000. *Dreamworld and Catastrophe: The Passing of Mass Utopia in East and West*. Cambridge, MA: MIT Press.

Burch, Rebecca L. 2020. "More than Just a Pretty Face: The Overlooked Contributions of Women in Evolutionary Psychology Textbooks." *Evolutionary Behavioral Sciences* 14 (1): 100–114. https://doi.org/10.1037/ebs0000166.

Butler, Judith. 1988. "Performative Acts and Gender Constitution: An Essay in Phenomenology and Feminist Theory." *Theatre Journal* 40 (4): 519–31. https://doi.org/10.2307/3207893.

Butler, Judith. 1990. *Gender Trouble: Feminism and the Subversion of Identity*. New York: Routledge.

Callaghan, B. L., and R. Richardson. 2012. "The Effect of Adverse Rearing Environments on Persistent Memories in Young Rats: Removing the Brakes on Infant Fear Memories." *Translational Psychiatry* 2 (7): e138. https://doi.org/10.1038/tp.2012.65.

Cameron, Sarah. 2018. *The Hungry Steppe: Famine, Violence, and the Making of Soviet Kazakhstan*. Ithaca, NY: Cornell University Press.

Cappelletto, Chiara. 2011. "The Puppet's Paradox: An Organic Prosthesis." *RES: Anthropology and Aesthetics*, no. 59/60: 325–36. https://www.jstor.org/stable/23647798

Carpenter, Kathie. 2021. *Life in a Cambodian Orphanage: A Childhood Journey for New Opportunities*. New Brunswick, NJ: Rutgers University Press.

Carsten, Janet. 1997. *The Heat of the Hearth: The Process of Kinship in a Malay Fishing Community*. Oxford, UK: Clarendon Press.

Carsten, Janet. 2000. *Cultures of Relatedness: New Approaches to the Study of Kinship*. Cambridge, UK: Cambridge University Press.

Carsten, Janet. 2004. *After Kinship*. Cambridge, UK: Cambridge University Press.

Cartwright, Lisa. 2005. "'Images of 'Waiting Children': Spectatorship and Pity in the Representation of the Global Social Orphan in the 1990s." In *Cultures of Transnational Adoption*, edited by Toby Alice Volkman, 185–212. Durham, NC: Duke University Press.

Cassiday, Julie A. 2000. *The Enemy on Trial: Early Soviet Courts on Stage and Screen*. DeKalb, IL: Northern Illinois University Press.

Chekhov, Anton. 2014. *Anton Chekhov's Selected Stories*. Edited by Cathy Popkin. New York: W. W. Norton.

Chekhov, Anton. 2017. *Kashtanka: Bilingual Edition*. Translated by Constance Garnett. Independently published.

Chernyaeva, Natalia. 2013. "'Upbringing à la Dr. Spock:' Child-Care Manuals and Constructing Normative Motherhood in the Soviet Union, 1954–1970." *Ab Imperio* 2: 223–251. https://doi.org/10.1353/imp.2013.0048.

Chin, Elizabeth M. Liew Siew. 2001. *Purchasing Power: Black Kids and American Consumer Culture*. Minneapolis: University of Minnesota Press.

Chouliaraki, Lilie. 2004. "Watching 11 September: The Politics of Pity." *Discourse & Society* 15 (2–3): 185–98. https://doi.org/10.1177/0957926504041016.

Chouliaraki, Lilie. 2006. *The Spectatorship of Suffering*. London: SAGE Publications.

Chumley, Lily. 2017. "Qualia and Ontology: Language, Semiotics, and Materiality; an Introduction." *Signs and Society* 5 (S1): S1–20. https://doi.org/10.1086/690190.

Citton, Yves. 2017. *The Ecology of Attention*. Translated by Barnaby Norman. Cambridge, UK: Polity Press.

Classen, Constance. 2012. *The Deepest Sense: A Cultural History of Touch*. Urbana: University of Illinois Press.

Clemente, Ignasi. 2015. *Uncertain Futures: Communication and Culture in Childhood Cancer Treatment*. Chichester, UK: Wiley-Blackwell.

Cole, Jennifer, and Deborah Durham, eds. 2008. *Figuring the Future: Globalization and the Temporalities of Children and Youth*. Santa Fe, NM: School for Advanced Research Press.

Collodi, Carlo. (1883) 2020. *The Adventures of Pinocchio*. Translated by Ann Lawson Lucas. Oxford: University Press.

Colvert, Emma, Michael Rutter, Celia Beckett, Jenny Castle, Christine Groothues, Amanda Hawkins, Jana Kreppner, Thomas G. O'Connor, Suzanne Stevens, and Edmund J. S. Sonuga-Barke. 2008. "Emotional Difficulties in Early Adolescence Following Severe Early Deprivation: Findings from the English and Romanian Adoptees Study." *Development and Psychopathology* 20 (2): 547–67. https://doi.org/10.1017/S0954579408000278.

Committee for Protecting Children's Rights, of the Ministry of Education and Science of the Republic of Kazakhstan. 2023. Last accessed June 1, 2023. https://bala-kkk.kz/gorod-druzhestvennyj-k-rebenku/.

Committee on Statistics of the Ministry of National Economy of the Republic of Kazakhstan. 2017. "Children of Kazakhstan Statistical Yearbook." July. Last accessed June 21, 2023. https://www.unicef.org/kazakhstan/en/reports/children-kazakhstan-statistical-yearbook.

Condillac, Etienne Bonnot de, and Margaret Geraldine Spooner Carr. 1930. *Condillac's Treatise on the Sensations*. London: The Favil Press.

Convention on the Rights of the Child. November 20, 1989. Treaty no. 27531. *United Nations Treaty Series*, 1577, pp. 3–178. https://treaties.un.org/doc/Treaties/1990/09/19900902%2003-14%20AM/Ch_IV_11p.pdf.

Cook, Daniel Thomas. 2004. *The Commodification of Childhood: The Children's Clothing Industry and the Rise of the Child Consumer*. Durham, NC: Duke University Press.

Craig, Edward Gordon. 1911. *On the Art of the Theatre*. Chicago: Browne's bookstore.

Crapanzano, Vincent. 1992. "'Self'-Centering Narratives." *Yale Journal of Criticism* 5 (3): 61–79.

Crary, David. 2009. "Advocates of Adoption Upset by 'Orphan' Film." *Los Angeles Times*, July 19, 2009, Movies.

Cross, Gary. 1997. *Kids' Stuff: Toys and the Changing World of American Childhood*. Cambridge, MA: Harvard University Press.

Current Time. 2019. "*Prezident Kazakhstana zaiavil, chto ne schitaet anneksiei 'to, chto proizoshlo v Krymu'*" [President of Kazakhstan announced that he does not consider 'what happened in Crimea' annexation]. *Nastoiashchee Vremia* [Current Time], December 4, 2019. https://www.currenttime.tv/a/crimea-russia-ukraine -kazakhstan/30307356.html.

Curtiss, Susan. 1977. *Genie: A Psycholinguistic Study of a Modern-Day "Wild Child."* Perspectives in Neurolinguistics and Psycholinguistics. New York: Academic Press.

Dahl, Bianca. 2014. "'Too Fat to Be an Orphan': The Moral Semiotics of Food Aid in Botswana." *Cultural Anthropology* 29 (4): 626–47. https://doi.org/10.14506/ca29.4.03.

Dave, Bhavna. 2007. *Kazakhstan: Ethnicity, Language and Power*. London: Routledge.

Deák, František. 1975. "Russian Mass Spectacles." *Drama Review: TDR* 19 (2): 7–22. https://doi.org/10.2307/1144942.

Debord, Guy. (1967) 1977. *Society of the Spectacle*. Translated by Black & Red. Detroit, MI: Black & Red.

Demintseva, Ekaterina. 2020. "Educational Infrastructure Created in Conditions of Social Exclusion: 'Kyrgyz Clubs' for Migrant Children in Moscow." *Central Asian Survey* 39 (2): 220–35. https://doi.org/10.1080/02634937.2019.1697643.

Denham, Aaron R. 2017. *Spirit Children: Illness, Poverty, and Infanticide in Northern Ghana*. Madison: University of Wisconsin Press.

Diderot, Denis. 1883. *The Paradox of Acting*. Translated by Walter Herries Pollock. London: Chatto & Windus.

Diener, Alexander C. 2009. *One Homeland or Two?: The Nationalization and Transnationalization of Mongolia's Kazakhs*. Stanford, CA: Stanford University Press.

DKN World News. 2023. "*V Almaty zakrylsia Dom Nadezhdy s 30-letnei istoriei*" [In Almaty Hope House with 30-year history has closed]. *DKN World News*, April 11, 2023. https://dknews.kz/ru/dk-life/282054-v-almaty-zakrylsya-dom-nadezhdy -s-30-letney-istoriey.

Doane, Mary Ann. 2007. "Indexicality: Trace and Sign: Introduction." *Differences* 18 (1): 1–6. https://doi.org/10.1215/10407391-2006-020.

Dodaj, Arta, Marijana Krajina, Kristina Sesar, and Nataša Šimić. 2017. "The Effects of Maltreatment in Childhood on Working Memory Capacity in Adulthood." *Europe's Journal of Psychology*, no. 4: 618–732. https://doi.org/10.5964/ejop.v13i4.1373.

Doi, Mary Masayo. 2002. *Gesture, Gender, Nation: Dance and Social Change in Uzbekistan*. Westport, CT: Bergin & Garvey.

Dostoevsky, Fyodor, and Alexander Eliasberg. 1917. *Letters of Fyodor Michailovitch Dostoevsky to His Family and Friends*. New York: Macmillan.

Douthwaite, Julia V. 2002. *The Wild Girl, Natural Man, and the Monster: Dangerous Experiments in the Age of Enlightenment*. Chicago: University of Chicago Press.

Dubuisson, Eva-Marie. 2010. "Confrontation in and through the Nation in Kazakh Aitys Poetry." *Journal of Linguistic Anthropology* 20 (1): 101–15. https://doi.org/10.1111 /j.1548-1395.2010.01051.x.

Dubuisson, Eva-Marie. 2014. "Dialogic Authority: Kazakh Aitys Poets and Their Patrons." In *Ethnographies of the State in Central Asia*, edited by Madeleine Reeves, Johan Rasanayagam, and Judith Beyer, 55–77. Bloomington: Indiana University Press.

Dubuisson, Eva-Marie. 2017. *Living Language in Kazakhstan: The Dialogic Emergence of an Ancestral Worldview*. Pittsburgh: University of Pittsburgh Press.

Dugarova, Esuna. 2019. "Gender, Work, and Childcare in Kazakhstan, Mongolia, and Russia." *Social Policy & Administration* 53 (3): 385–400. https://doi.org/10.1111 /spol.12479.

Dunham, Vera Sandomirsky. 1990. *In Stalin's Time: Middleclass Values in Soviet Fiction*. Durham, NC: Duke University Press.

Durkheim, Émile. (1912) 1995 *The Elementary Forms of the Religious Life*. Translated by Karen E. Fields. New York: The Free Press.

Dyer, Hannah. 2019. *The Queer Aesthetics of Childhood: Asymmetries of Innocence and the Cultural Politics of Child Development*. New Brunswick, NJ: Rutgers University Press.

E-Gov Website for Government Services and Information Online. 2021. "Deprivation of Parental Rights in Kazakhstan." Last updated August 27. https://egov.kz/cms/ru/articles/child/lisheniye-rod-prav.

*EADaily*. 2020. *"Tokaev: Kazakhstan ne planiruet prisoedinitsya k soyuznomu gosudarstvu"* [Tokaev: Kazakhstan does not plan to join a union state]. June 3, 2020. https://eadaily.com/ru/news/2020/06/03/tokaev-kazahstan-ne-planiruet-prisoedinitsya-k-soyuznomu-gosudarstvu.

Ebert, Roger. 2009. "And When She Was Bad, She Was Very, Very Bad." Last updated July 22. http://www.rogerebert.com/reviews/orphan-2009.

Edgar, Adrienne. 2022. *Intermarriage and the Friendship of Peoples: Ethnic Mixing in Soviet Central Asia*. Ithaca, NY: Cornell University Press. https://doi.org/10.1515/9781501762956.

Enfield, N. J., and Paul Kockelman. 2017. *Distributed Agency*. New York: Oxford University Press.

Evans, Gillian. 2006. *Educational Failure and Working Class White Children in Britain*. Houndmills, UK: Palgrave Macmillan.

Evreinov, N. N., and Alexander I. Nazaroff. 1927. *The Theatre in Life*. New York: Brentano's.

Fehérváry, Krisztina. 2009. "Goods and States: The Political Logic of State-Socialist Material Culture." *Comparative Studies in Society and History* 51 (2): 426.

Fehérváry, Krisztina. 2013. *Politics in Color and Concrete: Socialist Materialities and the Middle Class in Hungary*. Bloomington: Indiana University Press.

Finke, Michael. 1994. "The Hero's Descent to the Underworld in Chekhov." *Russian Review* 53 (1): 67. https://doi.org/10.2307/131295.

Fishzon, Anna. 2015. "The Fog of Stagnation: Explorations of Time and Affect in Late Soviet Animation." *Cahiers Du Monde Russe* 56 (2/3): 571.

Forman-Brunell, Miriam. 1993. *Made to Play House: Dolls and the Commercialization of American Girlhood, 1830–1930*. New Haven, CT: Yale University Press.

Foster, Geoff, and Lorraine Sherr. 2006. "Vulnerability and Resilience of Children and Youth." *Vulnerable Children & Youth Studies* 1 (1): 1. https://doi.org/10.1080/17450120600793645.

Foucault, Michel. (1961) 1988. *Madness and Civilization: A History of Insanity in the Age of Reason*. Translated by Richard Howard. New York: Vintage Books.

Foucault, Michel. (1984) 1990. *The Use of Pleasure: Volume 2 of The History of Sexuality*. Translated by Robert Hurley. New York: Vintage Books.

Frank, Joseph. 2009. *Dostoevsky: A Writer in His Time*. Princeton, NJ: Princeton University Press.

Franklin, Prarthana, Anthony A. Volk, and Irisa Wong. 2018. "Are Newborns' Faces Less Appealing?" *Evolution and Human Behavior* 39 (3): 269–76. https://doi.org/10.1016/j.evolhumbehav.2018.01.003.

Franz, Jennifer, and Felix Fitzroy. 2006. "Child Mortality in Central Asia: Social Policy, Agriculture and the Environment." *Central Asian Survey* 25 (4): 481–98. https://doi.org/10.1080/02634930701210476.

Freedman, Eric. 2010. *Transient Images: Personal Media in Public Frameworks*. Philadelphia, PA: Temple University Press.

Freidus, Andrea. 2010. "'Saving' Malawi: Faithful Responses to Orphans And Vulnerable Children." *NAPA Bulletin* 33 (1): 50–67. https://doi.org/10.1111/j.1556-4797.2010.01040.x.

Frekko, Susan E., Jessaca B. Leinaweaver, and Diana Marre. 2015. "How (Not) to Talk about Adoption: On Communicative Vigilance in Spain." *American Ethnologist* 42 (4): 703–19. https://doi.org/10.1111/amet.12165.

Freud, Sigmund. 1949a. *An Outline of Psychoanalysis*. Translated by James Strachey. New York: W. W. Norton.

Freud, Sigmund. 1949b. *Three Essays on the Theory of Sexuality*. Translated and edited by James Strachey. London: Imago Pub. Co.

Freud, Sigmund. 1953. "The Uncanny (1919)." *The Standard Edition of the Complete Psychological Works of Sigmund Freud, Vol. XVII*. Translated under the general editorship of James Strachey, in collaboration with Anna Freud, assisted by Alix Strachey and Alan Tyson, 219–252. London: Hogarth.

Freud, Sigmund. 1989. "The Ego and the Id (1923)." *TACD Journal* 17 (1): 5–22. https://doi.org/10.1080/1046171X.1989.12034344.

Freud, Sigmund. (1920) 1990. *Beyond the Pleasure Principle*. Edited by James Strachey. New York: W. W. Norton.

Friedrich, Paul, and Anwar S. Dil. 1979. *Language, Context, and the Imagination: Essays*. Stanford, CA: Stanford University Press.

Fujimura, Clementine K., Sally W. Stoecker, and Tatyana. Sudakova. 2005. *Russia's Abandoned Children: An Intimate Understanding*. Westport, CT: Praeger Publishers.

Gal, Susan. 2013. "Tastes of Talk: Qualia and the Moral Flavor of Signs." *Anthropological Theory* 13 (1–2): 31–48. https://doi.org/10.1177/1463499613483396.

Garrett, Paul B., and Patricia Baquedano-López. 2002. "Language Socialization: Reproduction and Continuity, Transformation and Change." *Annual Review of Anthropology* 31 (January): 339–61. https://doi.org/10.1146/annurev.anthro.31.040402.085352.

Gaskins, Suzanne. 2013. "The Puzzle of Attachment: Unscrambling Maturational and Cultural Contributions to the Development of Early Emotional Bonds." In *Attachment Reconsidered: Cultural Perspectives on a Western Theory*, edited by Naomi Quinn and Jeannette Marie Mageo, 33–64. New York: Palgrave Macmillan. https://doi.org/10.1057/9781137386724_2.

Gell, Alfred. 1996. "Vogel's Net: Traps as Artworks and Artworks as Traps." *Journal of Material Culture* 1, no. 1 (March): 15–38. https://doi.org/10.1177/135918359600100102.

Gell, Alfred. 1998. *Art and Agency*. Oxford, UK: Oxford University Press.

Genina, Anna. 2015. "Claiming Ancestral Homelands? Mongolian Kazakh Migration in Inner Asia." PhD diss., University of Michigan.

George, Donna St., and Philip P. Pan. 2010. "Adoptions from Russia Plunged into Uncertainty; Tennessee Case Infuriates Foreign Officials and Pulls State Department into Dispute." *Washington Post*, April 16.

Georgescu, Diana. 2019. "Small Comrades as Historians and Ethnographers: Performativity, Agency, and the Socialist Pedagogy of Citizenship in Ceaușescu's Romania, 1969–1989." *Slavic Review* 78 (1): 74–102. https://doi.org/10.1017/slr.2019.9.

Gibson, James Jerome. 1966. *The Senses Considered as Perceptual Systems*. Boston: Houghton Mifflin.

Gidadhubli, R. G. 1998. "Resolving Financial Crisis." *Economic and Political Weekly* 33 (28): 1811–14.

Gillath, Omri, Gery C. Karantzas, and Emre Selcuk. 2017. "A Net of Friends: Investigating Friendship by Integrating Attachment Theory and Social Network Analysis." *Personality and Social Psychology Bulletin* 43 (11): 1546–65. https://doi.org/10.1177/0146167217719731.

Goffman, Erving. 1961. *Asylums: Essays on the Social Situation of Mental Patients and Other Inmates*. Garden City, NY: Anchor Books / Doubleday.

Goffman, Erving. 1974. *Frame Analysis: An Essay on the Organization of Experience*. Cambridge, MA: Harvard University Press.

Goffman, Erving. 1981. *Forms of Talk*. Philadelphia: University of Pennsylvania Press.

Goldfarb, William. 1945. "Effects of Psychological Deprivation in Infancy and Subsequent Stimulation." *American Journal of Psychiatry* 102: 18–33. https://doi.org/10.1176/ajp.102.1.18.

Goldfarb, William. 1955. "Emotional and intellectual consequences of psychologic deprivation in infancy: a revaluation." In *Psychopathology of Childhood*, Hoch, Paul H., and Joseph Zubin, eds. Proceedings of the 44th Annual Meeting of the American Psychopathological Association, 1954, 105–119. New York: Grune & Stratton.

Golding, William. 1962. *Lord of the Flies*. New York: Coward-McCann.

Goldovskiĭ, Boris. 2004. *Kukly: entsiklopediia*. Moskva: Vremia.

Goodman, Nelson. 1972. *Problems and Projects*. Indianapolis, IN: Bobbs-Merrill.

Goodwin, Marjorie Harness, and Amy Kyratzis. 2007. "Children Socializing Children: Practices for Negotiating the Social Order Among Peers." *Research on Language and Social Interaction* 40 (4): 279–89. https://doi.org/10.1080/08351810701471260.

Grant, Bruce. 1995. *In the Soviet House of Culture: A Century of Perestroikas*. Princeton, NJ: Princeton University Press.

Green, Rachel Faircloth. 2006. "'There Will Not Be Orphans among Us': Soviet Orphanages, Foster Care, and Adoption, 1941–1956." PhD diss., University of Chicago. https://search.proquest.com/docview/304954749?pq-origsite=primo.

Grice, Elizabeth. 2006. "Cry of an Enfant Sauvage." *Telegraph*, July 16. http://www.telegraph.co.uk/culture/tvandradio/3653890/Cry-of-an-enfant-sauvage.html.

Grimm, Jacob, and Wilhelm Grimm. 2014. "The Wolf and the Seven Kids." In *The Original Folk and Fairy Tales of the Brothers Grimm*, translated and edited by Jack Zipes, illustrated by Andrea Dezsö, 23–25. Princeton, NJ: Princeton University Press. https://www.jstor.org/stable/j.ctt6wq18v.12.

Grimshaw, Anna, and Amanda Ravetz. 2009. "Rethinking Observational Cinema." *Journal of the Royal Anthropological Institute* 15 (3): 538–56. https://doi.org/10.1111/j.1467-9655.2009.01573.x.

Gross, Kenneth. 2011. *Puppet: An Essay on Uncanny Life*. Chicago: University of Chicago Press.

Guillebaud, Philomena. 1953. "The Role of Honorary Awards in the Soviet Economic System." *American Slavic and East European Review* 12 (4): 486–505. https://doi.org/10.2307/3004226.

Gunning, Tom. 2007. "Moving Away from the Index: Cinema and the Impression of Reality." *Differences* 18 (1): 29–52. https://doi.org/10.1215/10407391-2006-022.

Hale, Henry E. 2014. *Patronal Politics: Eurasian Regime Dynamics in Comparative Perspective*. Cambridge, UK: Cambridge University Press. https://doi.org/10.1017/CBO9781139683524.

Hales, Molly. 2019. "Animating Relations: Digitally Mediated Intimacies between the Living and the Dead." *Cultural Anthropology* 34 (2): 187–212. https://doi.org/10.14506/ca34.2.02.

Hall, Granville Stanley, and Alexander Caswell Ellis. 1897. *A Study of Dolls*. New York: E. L. Kellogg.

Harper, Krista. 2006. *Wild Capitalism: Environmental Activists and Post-Socialist Political Ecology in Hungary*. New York: Columbia University Press.

Harris, Daniel. 2000. *Cute, Quaint, Hungry, and Romantic: The Aesthetics of Consumerism*. New York: Basic Books.

Harte, Alys, and Jane Drinkwater. 2017. "Over a Quarter of Adoptive Families in Crisis, Survey Shows." *BBC News*, 26 September, 2017, UK. https://www.bbc.com/news/uk-41379424.

Hartman, Saidiya. 2008. *Lose Your Mother: A Journey Along the Atlantic Slave Route.* New York: Farrar, Straus and Giroux.

Hastings, Adi, and Paul Manning. 2004. "Introduction: Acts of Alterity." *Language & Communication* 24: 291–311. https://doi.org/10.1016/j.langcom.2004.07.001.

Heath, Shirley Brice. 1982. "What No Bedtime Story Means: Narrative Skills at Home and School." *Language in Society* 11 (1): 49–76. https://www.jstor.org/stable/4167291.

Heller, Erich. 1978. "The Dismantling of a Marionette Theater; Or, Psychology and the Misinterpretation of Literature." *Critical Inquiry* 4 (3): 417–32.

Herodotus, William Beloe, and Abraham John Valpy. 1830. *Herodotus*. London: Henry Colburn and Richard Bentley.

Heyneman, Stephen P., and Alan J. DeYoung. 2004. *The Challenges of Education in Central Asia*. Greenwich, CT: Information Age Pub.

Hill, Jane. 1995. "The Voices of Don Gabriel: Responsibility and Self in a Modern Mexicano Narrative." In *The Dialogic Emergence of Culture*, edited by Dennis Tedlock and Mannheim, 97–147. Urbana: Univ. of Illinois Press.

Hill, Jane H., and Judith T. Irvine. 1993. *Responsibility and Evidence in Oral Discourse.* Cambridge, UK: Cambridge University Press.

Hirsch, Francine. 2005. *Empire of Nations: Ethnographic Knowledge & the Making of the Soviet Union*. Ithaca, NY: Cornell University Press.

Hochschild, Arlie Russell. 1983. *The Managed Heart: Commercialization of Human Feeling*. Berkeley: University of California Press.

Hodsoll, John, Kimberly A. Quinn, and Sara Hodsoll. 2010. "Attentional Prioritization of Infant Faces Is Limited to Own-Race Infants." Edited by Jan Lauwereyns. *pLoS ONE* 5 (9): e12509. https://doi.org/10.1371/journal.pone.0012509.

Hoffmann, E. T. A. 1967. *The Best Tales of Hoffmann*. Selections. Edited by Everett Franklin Bleiler. New York: Dover Publications.

Howell, Signe. 2006. *The Kinning of Foreigners: Transnational Adoption in a Global Perspective*. New York: Berghahn Books.

Hrdy, Sarah Blaffer. 2009. *Mothers and Others: The Evolutionary Origins of Mutual Understanding*. Cambridge, MA: Belknap Press of Harvard University Press.

Inoue, Miyako. 2006. *Vicarious Language: Gender and Linguistic Modernity in Japan.* Berkeley: University of California Press.

Irvine, Judith. 1996. "Shadow Conversations: The Indeterminacy of Participant Roles." In *Natural Histories of Discourse*, edited by Michael Silverstein and Greg Urban, 131–59. Chicago: University of Chicago Press.

Isaacs, Rico. 2010. "'Papa'–Nursultan Nazarbayev and the Discourse of Charismatic Leadership and Nation-Building in Post-Soviet Kazakhstan." *Studies in Ethnicity and Nationalism* 10 (3): 435–52. https://doi.org/10.1111/j.1754-9469.2011.01089.x.

Isler, Karin, and Carel P. van Schaik. 2012. "Allomaternal Care, Life History and Brain Size Evolution in Mammals." *Journal of Human Evolution* 63 (July): 52–63. https://doi.org/10.1016/j.jhevol.2012.03.009.

Ito, Mizuko, Heather A. Horst, Judd Antin, Megan Finn, Arthur Law, Annie Manion, Sarai Mitnick, David Schlossberg, and Sarita Yardi. 2009. *Hanging Out, Messing Around, and Geeking Out: Kids Living and Learning with New Media*. Cambridge, MA: MIT Press.

Jakobson, Roman. 1960. "Closing Statement: Linguistics and Poetics." In *Style in Language*, edited by Thomas A. Sebeok, 350–77. Cambridge, MA: MIT.

James, Allison. 2004. *Constructing Childhood: Theory, Policy and Social Practice.* 2004 ed. Houndmills, UK: Palgrave.

James, Allison. 2007. "Giving Voice to Children's Voices: Practices and Problems, Pitfalls and Potentials." *American Anthropologist* 109 (2): 261–72. https://doi.org/10.1525/aa.2007.109.2.261.

Jenkins, Henry. 1998. *The Children's Culture Reader.* New York: New York University Press.

Jenkins, Henry. 2006. *Convergence Culture: Where Old and New Media Collide.* New York: New York University Press.

Jensen, K. Thor. 2019. "Woman Charged with Abandoning Adopted 11-Year-Old Claims Girl Was Really 22-Year-Old Sociopath." *Newsweek*, September 18, 2019.

Jentsch, Ernst. 2008. "On the Psychology of the Uncanny (1906)." In *Uncanny Modernity: Cultural Theories, Modern Anxieties*, edited by Jo Collins and John Jervis, 216–28. Basingstoke, UK: Palgrave Macmillan.

Jestrovic, Silvija. 2018. "Seeing Better: Modernist Estrangement and Its Transformations." *Social Research* 85 (2): 275–299. https://doi.org/10.1353/sor.2018.0016.

Johnson, Barbara. 2010. *Persons and Things.* Cambridge, MA: Harvard University Press.

Johnson, Deborah J., DeBrenna LaFa Agbényiga, and Judith Mbula Bahemuka. 2013. "Vulnerable Childhood in a Global Context: Embracing the Sacred Trust." In *Vulnerable Children: Global Challenges in Education, Health, Well-Being, and Child Rights*, edited by Deborah J. Johnson, DeBrenna LaFa Agbényiga, and Robert K. Hitchcock, 1–10. New York: Springer. https://doi.org/10.1007/978-1-4614-6780-9_1.

Johnson, Ginger A. 2011. "A Child's Right to Participation: Photovoice as Methodology for Documenting the Experiences of Children Living in Kenyan Orphanages." *Visual Anthropology Review* 27 (2): 141–61. https://doi.org/10.1111/j.1548-7458.2011.01098.x.

Jones, Graham M. 2011. *Trade of the Tricks: Inside the Magician's Craft.* Berkeley: University of California Press.

Jones, Meg Leta. 2016. "Your New Best Frenemy: Hello Barbie and Privacy Without Screens." *Engaging Science, Technology, and Society* 2 (August): 242. https://doi.org/10.17351/ests2016.84.

Kafka, Franz. 1983. *The Complete Stories and Parables.* Edited by Nahum N. Glatzer. New York: Quality Paperback Book Club.

Kamp, Marianne. 2006. *The New Woman in Uzbekistan: Islam, Modernity, and Unveiling under Communism.* Seattle: University of Washington Press.

Kant, Immanuel. (1785) 2018. *Groundwork for the Metaphysics of Morals.* Translated and edited by Allen W. Wood. New Haven, CT: Yale University Press.

Kataev, Vladimir. 2003. *If Only We Could Know!: An Interpretation of Chekhov.* Edited by Harvey Pitcher. Chicago: Ivan R Dee, Inc.

Katz, Maya Balakirsky. 2016. *Drawing the Iron Curtain: Jews and the Golden Age of Soviet Animation.* New Brunswick, NJ: Rutgers University Press.

Keane, Webb. 1997. *Signs of Recognition: Powers and Hazards of Representation in an Indonesian Society.* Berkeley: University of California Press.

Keane, Webb. 1999. "Voice." *Journal of Linguistic Anthropology* 9 (1–2): 271–73. https://doi.org/10.1525/jlin.1999.9.1-2.271.

Keane, Webb. 2003. "Semiotics and the Social Analysis of Material Things." *Language & Communication* 23 (3–4): 409–25. https://doi.org/10.1016/S0271-5309(03)00010-7.

Kelly, Catriona. 1990. *Petrushka, the Russian Carnival Puppet Theatre.* Cambridge, UK: Cambridge University Press.

Kelly, Catriona. 2005. "Riding the Magic Carpet: Children and Leader Cult in the Stalin Era." *Slavic and East European Journal* 49 (2): 199. https://doi.org/10.2307/20058260.

Kelly, Catriona. 2007. *Children's World: Growing up in Russia, 1890–1991*. New Haven, CT: Yale University Press.

Kelly, Catriona. 2021. *Soviet Art House: Lenfilm Studio under Brezhnev*. Oxford, UK: Oxford University Press. https://doi.org/10.1093/oso/9780197548363.001.0001.

Kenzhebekova, Alma. 2012. *"Ocheredi v detsad v Almaty zhdut bolee 22 tysiach detei"* [More than 22,000 children wait for a spot in an Almaty nursery]. *Radio Azattyk*, May 8, 2012. https://rus.azattyq.org/a/detsad_babybum_esimov_zhunusova_seilova_/24572782.html.

Kharkhordin, Oleg. 1999. *The Collective and the Individual in Russia: A Study of Practices*. Berkeley: University of California Press.

Kiaer, Christina. 1997. "Boris Arvatov's Socialist Objects." *October* 81 (July): 105–18. https://doi.org/10.2307/779021.

Kiaer, Christina. 2005. *Imagine No Possessions: The Socialist Objects of Russian Constructivism*. Cambridge, MA: MIT Press.

Kiaer, Christina, and Eric Naiman. 2006. *Everyday Life in Early Soviet Russia: Taking the Revolution Inside*. Bloomington: Indiana University Press.

Kim, Eleana Jean. 2010. *Adopted Territory: Transnational Korean Adoptees and the Politics of Belonging*. Durham, NC: Duke University Press.

Kim, German. 2003. "Koryo Saram, or Koreans of the Former Soviet Union: In the Past and Present." *Amerasia Journal* 29 (3): 23–29. https://doi.org/10.17953/amer.29.3.xk2111131165t740.

Kim, U. Gene. 2018. "Ethical Management of Speech among Kazak Nomads in the Chinese Altai." PhD diss., University of Michigan.

Kindler, Robert. 2018. *Stalin's Nomads: Power and Famine in Kazakhstan*. Pittsburgh, PA: University of Pittsburgh Press.

Kinsella, Sharon. 1995. "Cuties in Japan." In *Women, Media, and Consumption in Japan*, edited by Lise Skov and Brian Moeran, 220–54. Richmond, Surrey: Curzon Press.

Kipling, Rudyard. 1894. *The Jungle Book*. London: Macmillan and Co.

Kirschenbaum, Lisa A. 2001. *Small Comrades: Revolutionizing Childhood in Soviet Russia, 1917–1932*. New York: RoutledgeFalmer.

Kleist, Heinrich von. (1810) 1982. *An Abyss Deep Enough: Letters of Heinrich von Kleist, with a Selection of Essays and Anecdotes*. Edited and translated by Philip B. Miller. New York: Dutton.

Klenke, Kerstin. 2019. *The Sound State of Uzbekistan: Popular Music and Politics in the Karimov Era*. London: Routledge.

Kline, Stephen. 1993. *Out of the Garden: Toys, TV, and Children's Culture in the Age of Marketing*. London: Verso.

Knox, Hannah. 2017. "Affective Infrastructures and the Political Imagination." *Public Culture* 29, no. 2 (82): 363–84. https://doi.org/10.1215/08992363-3749105.

Koch, Natalie. 2010. "The Monumental and the Miniature: Imagining 'Modernity' in Astana." *Social & Cultural Geography* 11 (8): 769–87. https://doi.org/10.1080/14649365.2010.521854.

Kockelman, Paul. 2006. "Agent, Person, Subject, Self." *Semiotica* 162 (1–4): 1–18. https://doi.org/10.1515/SEM.2006.072.

Kopytoff, Igor. 1986. "The Cultural Biography of Things: Commoditization as Process." In *The Social Life of Things: Commodities in Cultural Perspective*, edited by Arjun Appadurai, 64–92. Cambridge, UK: Cambridge University Press. https://doi.org/10.1017/CBO9780511819582.004.

Kozlovskaya, Angelina, and Anna Kozlova. 2020. "Children's Agency as a Theoretical Problem and a Practical Concern (an Anthropological Remark)." *Antropologicheskij Forum* 16 (45): 11–25. https://doi.org/10.31250/1815-8870-2020-16-45-11-25.

Kromidas, Maria. 2014. "The 'Savage' Child and the Nature of Race: Posthuman Interventions from New York City." *Anthropological Theory* 14 (4): 422–41. https://doi.org/10.1177/1463499614552739.

Krupskaia, N. K. 1979. *N.K. Krupskaia o detskoĭ literature i detskom chtenii: izbrannoe* [N. K. Krupskaia on children's literature and children's reading: Selected works]. Edited by N. B. Medvedeva. Moskva: Detskaia literatura.

Krylova, Anna. 2000. "The Tenacious Liberal Subject in Soviet Studies." *Kritika: Explorations in Russian and Eurasian History* 1 (1): 119–46. https://doi.org/10.1353/kri.2008.0092.

Kudaibergenova, Diana T. 2017. "'My Silk Road to You': Re-Imagining Routes, Roads, and Geography in Contemporary Art of 'Central Asia.'" *Journal of Eurasian Studies* 8 (1): 31–43. https://doi.org/10.1016/j.euras.2016.11.007.

Kulick, Don. 1992. *Language Shift and Cultural Reproduction: Socialization, Self, and Syncretism in a Papua New Guinean Village*. Cambridge, UK: Cambridge University Press.

Kulick, Don. 2003. "No." *Language & Communication* 23 (2): 139–51. https://doi.org/10.1016/S0271-5309(02)00043-5.

Kulick, Don, and Bambi B. Schieffelin. 2004. "Language Socialization." In *A Companion to Linguistic Anthropology*, edited by Alessandro Duranti, 347–68. Malden, MA: Blackwell. https://doi.org/10.1002/9780470996522.ch15.

Kumenov, Almaz. 2022. "Kazakhstan: Capital Reverts to Astana, Ending Brief Stint as Nur-Sultan." *Eurasianet*, September 13, 2022. https://eurasianet.org/kazakhstan-capital-reverts-to-astana-ending-brief-stint-as-nur-sultan.

La Fontaine, J. S. 2009. *The Devil's Children: From Spirit Possession to Witchcraft: New Allegations That Affect Children*. Farnham, UK: Ashgate Pub Ltd.

Lacan, Jacques. 1966. *Écrits*. Paris: Seuil.

Lancy, David F. 2008. *The Anthropology of Childhood: Cherubs, Chattel, Changelings*. Cambridge, UK: Cambridge University Press.

Langer, Beryl. 2002. "Commodified Enchantment: Children and Consumer Capitalism." *Thesis Eleven* 69 (1): 67–81. https://doi.org/10.1177/0725513602069001005.

Laruelle, Marlene, Dylan Royce, and Serik Beyssembayev. 2019. "Untangling the Puzzle of 'Russia's Influence' in Kazakhstan." *Eurasian Geography and Economics* 60 (2): 211–43. https://doi.org/10.1080/15387216.2019.1645033.

Laszczkowski, Mateusz. 2016. *"City of the Future": Built Space, Modernity and Urban Change in Astana*. New York: Berghahn Books.

Latour, Bruno. 1993. *We Have Never Been Modern*. Translated by Catherin Porter. New York: Harvester Wheatsheaf.

Latour, Bruno. 1999. *Pandora's Hope: Essays on the Reality of Science Studies*. Cambridge, MA: Harvard University Press.

Latour, Bruno. 2005. *Reassembling the Social an Introduction to Actor-Network-Theory*. Oxford, UK: Oxford University Press.

Lefebvre, Martin. 2021. "A Peircean Lens on Cinematic Special Effects," *Semiotic Review* no. 9 (April). https://www.semioticreview.com/ojs/index.php/sr/article/download/71/129?inline=1.

Leinaweaver, Jessaca B. 2008. *The Circulation of Children: Kinship, Adoption, and Morality in Andean Peru*. Durham, NC: Duke University Press.

Lemon, Alaina. 2000. *Between Two Fires: Gypsy Performance and Romani Memory from Pushkin to Postsocialism*. Durham, NC: Duke University Press.

Lemon, Alaina. 2002. "'Form' and 'Function' in Soviet Stage Romani: Modeling Metapragmatics through Performance Institutions." *Language in Society* 31 (1): 29–64.

Lemon, Alaina. 2008. "Hermeneutic Algebra: Solving for Love, Time/Space, and Value in Putin-Era Personal Ads." *Journal of Linguistic Anthropology* 18 (2): 236–67. https://doi.org/10.1111/j.1548-1395.2008.00021.x.

Lemon, Alaina. 2009. "The Emotional Lives of Moscow Things." *Russian History* 36 (2): 201–18. https://doi.org/10.1163/187633109X412843.

Lemon, Alaina. 2011. "Sensations to Superpowers." *Ab Imperio*, no. 3 (2011): 313–329. https://doi.org/10.1353/imp.2011.0104

Lemon, Alaina. 2013. "Touching the Gap: Social Qualia and Cold War Contact." *Anthropological Theory* 13 (1–2): 67–88. https://doi.org/10.1177/1463499613483400.

Lemon, Alaina. 2017. *Technologies for Intuition: Cold War Circles and Telepathic Rays*. Oakland: University of California Press.

Lenneberg, Eric H. 1967. *Biological Foundations of Language*. New York: Wiley.

Lepselter, Susan Claudia. 2016. *The Resonance of Unseen Things: Poetics, Power, Captivity, and UFOs in the American Uncanny*. Ann Arbor: University of Michigan Press.

Lillis, Joanna. 2018. *Dark Shadows*. London: I. B. Tauris.

Lin, Jih-Hsuan. 2015. "The Role of Attachment Style in Facebook Use and Social Capital: Evidence from University Students and a National Sample." *Cyberpsychology, Behavior and Social Networking* 18 (3): 173–80. https://doi.org/10.1089/cyber.2014.0341.

Lipovetsky, Mark. 2011. *Charms of the Cynical Reason: The Trickster's Transformations in Soviet and Post-Soviet Culture*. Boston, MA: Academic Studies Press.

Lipovskiĭ, Aleksandr Il'ich, ed. 1967. *The Soviet Circus: A Collection of Articles*. Moscow: Progress Publishers.

Livingstone, Sonia, and Alicia Blum-Ross. 2020. *Parenting for a Digital Future: How Hopes and Fears about Technology Shape Children's Lives*. Oxford, UK: Oxford University Press.

LoBue, Elise Helen. 2007. *Kazakhstan's Soviet Past, Globalized Present, and "Emancipated Women": A Case for a New Gender and Development Domain*. PhD diss., University of Iowa. http://gateway.proquest.com/openurl?url_ver=Z39.88-2004&rft_val _fmt=info:ofi/fmt:kev:mtx:dissertation&res_dat=xri:pqdiss&rft_dat =xri:pqdiss:3301725.

Lorenz, Konrad. 1943. "Die Angeborenen Formen Möglicher Erfahrung." *Zeitschrift Für Tierpsychologie* 5 (2): 235–409. https://doi.org/10.1111/j.1439-0310.1943.tb00655.x.

Lorenz, Konrad. 1970. *Studies in Animal and Human Behaviour*. Translated by Robert Martin. Cambridge, MA: Harvard University Press.

Lorenz, Konrad. 1981. *The Foundations of Ethology*. Translated by Konrad Z. Lorenz and Robert Warren Kickert. New York: Springer-Verlag New York.

Luria, A. R. 1973. *The Working Brain: An Introduction to Neuropsychology*. Translated by Basil Heigh. London: Penguin Books.

MacDougall, David. 2006. *The Corporeal Image: Film, Ethnography, and the Senses*. Princeton, NJ: Princeton University Press.

MacFadyen, David. 2005. *Yellow Crocodiles and Blue Oranges: Russian Animated Film since World War Two*. Montreal: McGill-Queen's University Press.

Madsen, Heather Bronwyn, and Jee Hyun Kim. 2016. "Ontogeny of Memory: An Update on 40 Years of Work on Infantile Amnesia." *Behavioural Brain Research*, Vol. 298 (Part A): 4–14. https://doi.org/10.1016/j.bbr.2015.07.030.

Malson, Lucien, and Jean Marc Gaspard Itard. 1972. *Wolf Children and the Problem of Human Nature*. Translated by Edmund Fawcett, Peter Ayrton, and Joan White. New York: Monthly Review Press.

Mamedov, Georgy. 2020. "Radical Imagination Can Only Be Collective: Political (Re)Discovery of Soviet Dialectical Pedagogy." In *Collectively*, edited by Anne Klontz and Johan Pousette, 230–37. Stockholm: Art and Theory Publishing.

Manning, Paul. 2009. "Can the Avatar Speak?" *Journal of Linguistic Anthropology* 19 (2): 310–25. https://doi.org/10.1111/j.1548-1395.2009.01036.x.

Manning, Paul. 2013. "Altaholics Anonymous." *Semiotic Review* no. 1 (March). https://www.semioticreview.com/ojs/index.php/sr/article/view/30.

Manning, Paul. 2018. "Animating Virtual Worlds: Emergence and Ecological Animation of Ryzom's Living World of Atys." *First Monday* 23 (6). http://firstmonday.org/ojs/index.php/fm/article/view/8127.

Manning, Paul, and Ilana Gershon. 2013. "Animating Interaction." *HAU: Journal of Ethnographic Theory* 3 (3): 107–37. https://doi.org/10.14318/hau3.3.006.

Marks, Laura U. 2000. *The Skin of the Film: Intercultural Cinema, Embodiment, and the Senses*. Durham, NC: Duke University Press Books.

Marks, Laura U. 2002. *Touch: Sensuous Theory and Multisensory Media*. Minneapolis: University of Minnesota Press.

Martin, Terry. 2001. *The Affirmative Action Empire: Nations and Nationalism in the Soviet Union, 1923–1939*. Ithaca, NY: Cornell University Press.

Maslinsky, Kirill. 2020. "The Ghost of Pedocracy in the Puppet Theater: On School Self-Government and the Subjectivity of Children in the First Decades of Soviet Power." *Antropologicheskij Forum* 16 (45): 50–74. https://doi.org/10.31250/1815-8870-2020-16-45-50-74.

Mauss, Marcel. 1954. *The Gift; Forms and Functions of Exchange in Archaic Societies*. London: Cohen & West.

Mazzarella, William. 2015. "Totalitarian Tears: Does the Crowd Really Mean It?" *Cultural Anthropology* 30 (1): 91–112. https://doi.org/10.14506/ca30.1.06.

Mazzarella, William. 2017. *The Mana of Mass Society*. Chicago: University of Chicago Press.

McKenzie, Richard B. 1998. *Rethinking Orphanages for the 21st Century*. Thousand Oaks, CA: SAGE Publications, Inc.

McLuhan, Marshall. 2001. *Understanding Media: (Routledge Classics): The Extension of Man*. 2nd ed. London: Routledge.

Meĭerkhol'd, V. È., and Edward. Braun. 1969. *Meyerhold on Theatre*. New York: Hill and Wang.

Merchant, Tanya. 2009. "Popping Tradition: Performing Maqom and Uzbek 'National' Estrada in the 21st Century." *Popular Music and Society* 32 (3): 371–86. https://doi.org/10.1080/03007760902985817.

Michaels, Paula A. 2001. "Motherhood, Patriotism, and Ethnicity: Soviet Kazakhstan and the 1936 Abortion Ban." *Feminist Studies* 27 (2): 307–33.

Miller, Daniel. 2010. *Stuff*. Cambridge, UK: Polity Press.

Milne, A. A. 1926. *Winnie-the-Pooh*. Illustrated by Ernest H. Shepard. London: Methuen.

Ministry of Education. 2021. "*Kolichestvo detskikh domov umen'shilos' v Kazakhstane*" [The number of children's homes has decreased in Kazakhstan]. gov.egov.kz. 1 June 2021. https://betaegov.kz/memleket/entities/edu/news/details/kolichestvo-detskih-domov-umenshilos-v-kazahstane. Last updated June 1.

Mitchell, Stanley. 1974. "From Shklovsky to Brecht: Some Preliminary Remarks towards a History of the Politicisation of Russian Formalism." *Screen* 15 (2): 74–81. https://doi.org/10.1093/screen/15.2.74.

Miyazaki, Hirokazu. 2006. *The Method of Hope: Anthropology, Philosophy, and Fijian Knowledge*. Stanford, CA: Stanford University Press.

MK-KZ. 2020. "*Desiatki tysiach detei po vsemu Kazakhstanu ozhidaiut svoei ocheredi v detskii sad*" [Tens of thousands of children in all of Kazakhstan await a spot in a kindergarten]. January 15, 2020, Society. https://mk-kz.kz/social/2020/01/15

/desyatki-tysyach-detey-po-vsemu-kazakhstanu-stoyat-v-ocheredi-v-detskiy
-sad.html.

Moldabekov, Daniyar. 2022. "Kazakhstan: Ukraine War Motivates Russian-Speakers
to Learn Kazakh." *EurasiaNet*, October 31, 2022. https://eurasianet.org/kazakhstan
-ukraine-war-motivates-russian-speakers-to-learn-kazakh.

Montagu, M. F. Ashley. 1943. "Asia and Africa: Wolf-Children and Feral Man. J. A. L.
Singhs and Robert M. Zingg." *American Anthropologist* 45 (3): 468–72. https://doi
.org/10.1525/aa.1943.45.3.02a00170.

Morgan, Daniel. 2006. "Rethinking Bazin: Ontology and Realist Aesthetics." *Critical
Inquiry* 32 (3): 443–81. https://doi.org/10.1086/505375.

Morgan, Patrick Michael. 1968. "The System of Formal Honorary Awards in the Soviet
Union." PhD diss., Yale University. https://search.proquest.com/docview
/302376300?pq-origsite=primo.

Mori, Masahiro. (1970) 2012. "The Uncanny Valley." Translated by Karl F. MacDorman
and Norri Kageki. *IEEE Spectrum*, June 12, 2012. https://spectrum.ieee.org/the
-uncanny-valley

Moritz, William. 1999. "The Spirit of Genius: Feodor Khitruk." *Animation World Network*,
1 March. https://www.awn.com/animationworld/spirit-genius-feodor-khitruk.

Mostowlansky, Till. 2017. *Azan on the Moon: Entangling Modernity Along Tajikistan's
Pamir Highway*. Pittsburgh, PA: University of Pittsburgh Press.

Mueggler, Erik. 2001. *The Age of Wild Ghosts: Memory, Violence, and Place in Southwest
China*. Berkeley: University of California Press.

Mulvey, Laura. 2005. *Death 24X A Second: Stillness and the Moving Image*. London: Reak-
tion Books.

Murawski, Michał. 2019. *The Palace Complex: A Stalinist Skyscraper, Capitalist Warsaw,
and a City Transfixed*. Bloomington: Indiana University Press.

Naiman, Eric. 1997. *Sex in Public: The Incarnation of Early Soviet Ideology*. Princeton,
NJ: Princeton University Press.

Najibullah, Farangis. 2021. "Central Asian Migrant Workers Choosing Kazakhstan
Over Russia Despite Lower Pay." *RadioFreeEurope/RadioLiberty*, June 3. https://
www.rferl.org/a/kazakhstan-central-asia-workers/31288542.html.

Nakassis, Constantine V. 2016a. *Doing Style: Youth and Mass Mediation in South India*.
Chicago: University of Chicago Press.

Nakassis, Constantine V. 2016b. "Linguistic Anthropology in 2015: Not the Study of Language." *American Anthropologist* 118 (2): 330–45. https://doi.org/10.1111/aman
.12528.

Nakassis, Constantine V. 2018. "Indexicality's Ambivalent Ground." *Signs and Society*
6 (1): 281–304. https://doi.org/10.1086/694753.

Nakassis, Constantine V. 2020. "Deixis and the Linguistic Anthropology of Cinema."
*Semiotic Review* 9 (November). https://www.semioticreview.com/ojs/index.php/sr
/article/view/65.

Nakassis, Constantine V. 2023. *Onscreen/Offscreen*. Toronto, ON: University of Toronto
Press.

Nasritdinov, Emil. 2016. "'Only by Learning How to Live Together Differently Can We
Live Together at All': Readability and Legibility of Central Asian Migrants' Presence in Urban Russia." *Central Asian Survey* 35 (2): 257–75. https://doi.org/10.1080
/02634937.2016.1153837.

Nasritdinov, Emil, Yelena Gareyeva, and Tatiana Efremenko. 2015. "How Small Kitch-
ens Become Smaller: Social Life of Soviet Micro-Districts in Bishkek." In *Un-
bounded: On the Interior and Interiority*, edited by Dolly Daou, D. J. Huppatz, and

Dinh Quoc Phuong. Newcastle upon Tyne, UK: Cambridge Scholars Publishing. https://www.academia.edu/11577851/How_small_kitchens_become_smaller _Social_life_of_Soviet_micro_districts_in_Bishkek.

Nasritdinov, Emil, and Nate Schenkkan. 2012. "Portrayal of Absence: Households of Migrants in Kyrgyzstan." Bishkek: Open Society Institute and HelpAge International, Kyrgyzstan. https://www.academia.edu/4370835/Portrayal_of_Absence _Households_of_Migrants_in_Kyrgyzstan.

Nath, Dipika. 2009. "Feral Disorders and Colonial Exclusions: Animal Reared Feral Children, Discourses of Animality, and the Treatment of Animals in Colonial India." PhD diss., University of Washington.

Nauruzbayeva, Zhanara. 2011. "Portraiture and Proximity: 'Official' Artists and the State-Ization of the Market in Post-Soviet Kazakhstan." *Ethnos* 76 (3): 375–97. https://doi.org/10.1080/00141844.2011.580355.

Neirick, Miriam. 2012. *When Pigs Could Fly and Bears Could Dance: A History of the Soviet Circus*. Madison: The University of Wisconsin Press.

Nelson, Charles A., Nathan A. Fox, and Charles H. Zeanah. 2014. *Romania's Abandoned Children: Deprivation, Brain Development, and the Struggle for Recovery*. Cambridge, MA: Harvard University Press.

Ngai, Sianne. 2012. *Our Aesthetic Categories: Zany, Cute, Interesting*. Cambridge, MA: Harvard University Press.

Northrop, Douglas Taylor. 2004. *Veiled Empire: Gender & Power in Stalinist Central Asia*. Ithaca, NY: Cornell University Press.

Nozawa, Shunsuke. 2013. "Characterization." *Semiotic Review* no. 3 (November). https://www.semioticreview.com/ojs/index.php/sr/article/view/16.

Obraztsov, S. V. 1950. *Moia professiia* [My profession]. Moskva: Iskusstvo.

Ochs, Elinor, and Bambi B. Schieffelin. 1984. "Language Acquisition and Socialization: Three Developmental Stories and Their Implications." In *Culture Theory: Essays on Mind, Self, and Emotion*, edited by Richard Shweder and Robert LeVine, 276–320. Cambridge, UK: Cambridge University Press.

O'Flaherty, Wendy Doniger. (1988) 1995. *Other Peoples' Myths: The Cave of Echoes*. Chicago: University of Chicago Press.

Okazaki, Manami, and Geoff Johnson. 2013. *Kawaii!: Japan's Culture of Cute*. Munich: Prestel.

Oushakine, Serguei Alex. 2016. "Translating Communism for Children: Fables and Posters of the Revolution." *Boundary* 2 43 (3): 159–219. https://doi.org/10.1215/01903659 -3572478.

Pannier, Bruce. 2022. "After Kazakhstan's 'Bloody January,' Can Toqaev Ever Gain the People's Support?" *Radio Free Europe/Radio Liberty*, January 25, 2022, *Qishloq Ovozi* (Archive). https://www.rferl.org/a/kazakhstan-toqaev-bloody-january /31671033.html.

Parkes, Peter. 2004. "Milk Kinship in Southeast Europe. Alternative Social Structures and Foster Relations in the Caucasus and the Balkans." *Social Anthropology* 12 (3): 341–58.

Parkhomenko, Marina. 2016. "*Deti—eto budushchee mira*" [Children—the Future of the World]. *Novosti Kazakhstana*, November 22. https://www.kazpravda.kz /fresh/view/deti—eto-budushchee-mira/.

Patterson, Patrick Hyder. 2001. *The New Class: Consumer Culture under Socialism and the Unmaking of the Yugoslav Dream, 1945–1991*. PhD diss., University of Michigan.

Peers, Juliette. 2004. *The Fashion Doll: From Bébé Jumeau to Barbie*. Oxford, UK: Berg.

Peirce, Charles S. 1955. *Philosophical Writings of Peirce / Selected and Edited with an Introduction by Justus Buchler*. New York: Dover.

Peltonen, Kirsi, Samuli Kangaslampi, Jenni Saranpää, Samir Qouta, and Raija-Leena Pu-
namäki. 2017. "Peritraumatic Dissociation Predicts Posttraumatic Stress Disorder Symptoms via Dysfunctional Trauma-Related Memory among War-Affected
Children." *European Journal of Psychotraumatology* 8 (Suppl 3): 1–8. https://doi
.org/10.1080/20008198.2017.1375828.

Pesmen, Dale. 2000. *Russia and Soul: An Exploration.* Ithaca, NY: Cornell University Press.

Petryna, Adriana. 2002. *Life Exposed: Biological Citizens after Chernobyl.* Princeton, NJ:
Princeton University Press.

Pianciola, Niccolò. 2001. "The Collectivization Famine in Kazakhstan, 1931–1933."
*Harvard Ukrainian Studies* 25 (3/4): 237–51. https://www.jstor.org/stable/41036834.

Piantadosi, Steven T., and Celeste Kidd. 2016. "Extraordinary Intelligence and the Care
of Infants." *Proceedings of the National Academy of Sciences* 113 (25): 6874–79.
https://doi.org/10.1073/pnas.1506752113.

Posner, Dassia N., Claudia Orenstein, and John Bell. 2014. *The Routledge Companion to
Puppetry and Material Performance.* London: Routledge.

Postman, Neil. 1982. *The Disappearance of Childhood.* New York: Delacorte Press.

Prentice, Michael, and Meghanne Barker. 2017. *Intertextuality and Interdiscursivity.* Oxford,
UK: Oxford University Press. https://doi.org/10.1093/obo/9780199766567-0171.

Prime Minister of Kazakhstan website. 2021. Last updated January 28. https://primemin
ister.kz/ru/news/a-mamin-provel-zasedanie-nackomissii-po-perevodu-alfavita
-kazahskogo-yazyka-na-latinskuyu-grafiku-280497.

Propp, V. IA. 1968. *Morphology of the Folktale.* Translated by Laurence Scott. Austin:
University of Texas Press.

Proschan, Frank. 1981. "Puppet Voices and Interlocutors: Language in Folk Puppetry."
*Journal of American Folklore* 94 (374): 527–55. https://doi.org/10.2307/540504.

Proverbio, Alice Mado, Valeria De Gabriele, Mirella Manfredi, and Roberta Adorni.
2011. "No Race Effect (ORE) in the Automatic Orienting toward Baby Faces: When
Ethnic Group Does Not Matter." *Psychology* 02 (09): 931–35. https://doi.org/10
.4236/psych.2011.29140.

Rand, Erica. 1995. *Barbie's Queer Accessories.* Durham, NC: Duke University Press.

Reeves, Madeleine. 2014. *Border Work: Spatial Lives of the State in Rural Central Asia.*
Ithaca, NY: Cornell University Press.

Reeves, Madeleine. 2017. "Infrastructural Hope: Anticipating 'Independent Roads'
and Territorial Integrity in Southern Kyrgyzstan." *Ethnos* 82 (4): 711–37. https://
doi.org/10.1080/00141844.2015.1119176.

Reid, Susan, and David Crowley. 2000. *Style and Socialism: Modernity and Material Culture in Post-War Eastern Europe.* Oxford, UK: Berg.

Roche, Sophie. 2020. *The Family in Central Asia: New Perspectives.* Berlin: De Gruyter.

Rockhill, Elena Khlinovskaya. 2010. *Lost to the State: Family Discontinuity, Social Orphanhood and Residential Care in the Russian Far East.* New York: Berghahn Books.

Rogers, Mary F. 1999. *Barbie Culture.* London: SAGE Publications.

Rosenthal, Miriam K. 1967. "The Generalization of Dependency Behaviour from Mother
to Stranger." *Journal of Child Psychology and Psychiatry* 8 (2): 117–33. https://doi
.org/10.1111/j.1469-7610.1967.tb02187.x.

Rousseau, Jean-Jacques. (1755) 2009. *Discourse on Inequality.* Edited by Patrick Coleman.
Translated by Franklin Philip. Oxford: Oxford University Press.

Rubin, Gayle. 1975. "The Traffic in Women: Notes on the 'Political Economy' of Sex." In
*Toward an Anthropology of Women,* edited by Rayna R. Reiter, 157–210. New York:
Monthly Review Press.

Ruti, Mari. 2015. *The Age of Scientific Sexism: How Evolutionary Psychology Promotes Gender Profiling and Fans the Battle of the Sexes.* New York: Bloomsbury Academic.

Rutter, Michael, Emma Colvert, Jana Kreppner, Celia Beckett, Jenny Castle, Christine Groothues, Amanda Hawkins, Thomas G O'Connor, Suzanne F. Stevens, and Edmund J. S Sonuga-Barke. 2007. "Early Adolescent Outcomes for Institutionally-Deprived and Non-Deprived Adoptees. I: Disinhibited Attachment." *Journal of Child Psychology and Psychiatry and Allied Disciplines (Print)* 48 (1): 17–30.

Salmina, Aleksandra, and Serzhan Zhumabayev. 2019. *Detskie sady stanoviatsia ne po karmanu almatintsam* [Kindergartens are unaffordable for Almaty residents]." *Khabar 24*, August 22, 2019. https://24.kz/ru/news/social/item/336073-detskie -sady-stanovyatsya-ne-po-karmanu-almatintsam.

Salnikova, Alla. 2002. *"Geenna Ognennaia": Deskoe vospriiatie rannego sovetskogo perioda* ['The Gehenna of fire': children's perceptions of the early Soviet period]. *Ab Imperio*, 3: 321–352. https://doi.org/10.1353/imp.2002.0007.

Sandall, Roger. 1972. "Observation and Identity." *Monthly Film Bulletin; London*, Autumn 1972.

Sargent, Carolyn F. 1988. "Born to Die: Witchcraft and Infanticide in Bariba Culture." *Ethnology* 27 (1): 79–95. https://doi.org/10.2307/3773562.

Saunders, Elizabeth Grace. 2018. "The 4 'Attachment Styles,' and How They Sabotage Your Work-Life Balance." *The New York Times*, December 19, 2018, sec. Smarter Living. https://www.nytimes.com/2018/12/19/smarter-living/attachment-styles -work-life-balance.html.

Schatz, Edward. 2004. *Modern Clan Politics: The Power of "Blood" in Kazakhstan and Beyond*. Seattle: University of Washington Press.

Scheper-Hughes, Nancy. 1992. *Death without Weeping: The Violence of Everyday Life in Brazil*. Berkeley: University of California Press.

Scheper-Hughes, Nancy, and Howard F. Stein. 1998. "Child Abuse and the Unconscious in American Popular Culture." In *The Children's Culture Reader*, edited by Henry Jenkins, 178–96. New York: New York University Press. https://www.jstor.org /stable/j.ctt9qfn8r.13.

Schieffelin, Bambi B. 1990. *The Give and Take of Everyday Life: Language Socialization of Kaluli Children*. Cambridge, UK: Cambridge University Press.

Schieffelin, Bambi B., and Elinor Ochs. 1986. "Language Socialization." *Annual Review of Anthropology* 15 (January): 163–91.

Seiter, Ellen. 1993. *Sold Separately: Children and Parents in Consumer Culture*. New Brunswick, NJ: Rutgers University Press.

Senderovich, Marena. 1981. 'The Implicit Semantic Unities in Chekhov's Work of 1886–1889." (Russian Text). PhD diss., New York University. https://search.proquest .com/docview/303156544?pq-origsite=primo.

Seymour, Tom. 2015. "Silent Horror: The Director of *The Tribe* on His Brutal Film about Life in a Deaf School." *The Guardian*, 13 May 2015. http://www.theguardian .com/film/2015/may/13/the-tribe-deaf-school-drama-myroslav-slaboshpytskiy.

Sharafutdinova, Gulnaz. 2019. "Was There a 'Simple Soviet' Person? Debating the Politics and Sociology of 'Homo Sovieticus.'" *Slavic Review* 78 (1): 173–95. https://doi .org/10.1017/slr.2019.13.

Sharifzoda, Khamza. 2019. "Why Is Kazakhstan a Growing Destination for Central Asian Migrant Workers?" *The Diplomat*, June 13. https://thediplomat.com/2019/06/why -is-kazakhstan-a-growing-destination-for-central-asian-migrant-workers/.

Sharipova, Dina. 2020. "Perceptions of National Identity in Kazakhstan: Pride, Language, and Religion." *Muslim World* 110 (1): 89–106. https://doi.org/10.1111/muwo.12320.

Shatalova, Oksana. 2016. *"Shtab: kvir-metod"* [Shtab: queer method]. In *Kvir-kommunizm eto etika*, edited by Oksana Shatalova and Georgii Mamedov, 104–15. Novye Krasnye. Bishkek: Svobodnoe marksistskoe izdatel'stvo.

Shatalova, Oksana, and Georgy Mamedov, eds. 2016. *Kvir-Kommunizm Eto Etika* [Queer communism is ethics] Novye krasnye. Bishkek: Svobodnoe marksistskoe izdatel'stvo.

Shatalova, Oksana, and Georgy Mamedov, eds. 2018. *Sovsem drugie: sbornik feministskoi i kvir-fantastiki* [Completely different: a collection of feminist and queer fantasy]. Bishkek: Shtab Press.

Shatirishvili, Zaza, and Paul Manning. 2011. "Why Are the Dolls Laughing? Tbilisi between Intelligentsia, Culture and Socialist Labor." In *Urban Spaces After Socialism: Ethnographies of Public Places in Eurasian Cities*, edited by Tsypylma Darieva, Wolfgang Kaschuba, and Melanie Krebs, 207–25. Frankfurt: Campus Verlag.

Shattuck, Roger, and Douglas Keith Candland. 1994. *The Forbidden Experiment: The Story of the Wild Boy of Aveyron*. Reprint. New York: Kodansha Globe.

Shaw, Claire L. 2017. *Deaf in the USSR: Marginality, Community, and Soviet Identity, 1917–1991*. Ithaca, NY: Cornell University Press.

Shelekpayev, Nari. 2018. "Astana as Imperial Project?: Kazakhstan and Its Wandering Capital City in the Twentieth Century." *Ab Imperio* 2018 (1): 157–89. https://doi .org/10.1353/imp.2018.0006.

Shershow, Scott Cutler. 1995. *Puppets and "Popular" Culture*. Ithaca, NY: Cornell University Press.

Shikheeva-Gaister, Inna Aronovna, Elena Vetrova, and Cathy A. Frierson. 2015. "'And We Began to Live There in Twenty-Six Square Meters; There Were Thirteen of Us.'" In *Silence Was Salvation: Child Survivors of Stalin's Terror and World War II in the Soviet Union*, by Cathy A. Frierson, 37–66. New Haven, CT: Yale University Press.

Shirley, Mary Margaret, and Lillian Poyntz. 1941. "Influence of Separation from the Mother on Children's Emotional Responses." *Journal of Psychology* 12 (October): 251–82.

Shklovsky, Viktor. 1965. "Art as Technique." In *Russian Formalist Criticism: Four Essays*, translated by Lee T. Lemon and Marion J. Reis, 3–24. Lincoln: University of Nebraska Press.

Shuster, Simon. 2012. "Why Has Moscow Passed a Bill to Ban U.S. Adoption of Russian Orphans?" *Time*. Dec. 20, 2012. http://world.time.com/2012/12/20/why-has -moscow-passed-a-law-to-ban-u-s-adoption-of-russian-orphans/.

Sidnell, Jack. 2011. "The Epistemics of Make-Believe." In *The Morality of Knowledge in Conversation*, edited by Jakob Steensig, Lorenza Mondada, and Tanya Stivers, 131– 56. Cambridge, UK: Cambridge University Press. https://doi.org/10.1017/CBO97805 11921674.007.

Silverstein, Michael. 1976. "Shifters, Linguistic Categories, and Cultural Description." In *Meaning in Anthropology*, edited by Keith Basso and Henry A. Selby, 11–55. Albuquerque: University of New Mexico Press.

Silverstein, Michael. 1993. "Metapragmatic Discourse and Metapragmatic Function." In *Reflexive Language: Reported Speech and Metapragmatics*, edited by John A. Lucy, 33–58. Cambridge, UK: Cambridge University Press. https://doi.org/10.1017 /CBO9780511621031.004.

Silverstein, Michael. 2005. "Axes of Evals: Token versus Type Interdiscursivity." *Journal of Linguistic Anthropology* 15 (1): 6–22.

Silverstein, Michael, and Greg Urban. 1996. *Natural Histories of Discourse*. Chicago: University of Chicago Press.

Silvio, Teri. 2006. "Informationalized Affect: The Body in Taiwanese Digital Video Puppetry and COSplay." In *Embodied Modernities Corporeality, Representation, and Chinese Cultures*, edited by Fran Martin and Larissa Heinrich, 195–217. Honolulu: University of Hawai'i Press.

Silvio, Teri. 2010. "Animation: The New Performance?" *Journal of Linguistic Anthropology* 20 (2): 422–38. https://doi.org/10.1111/j.1548-1395.2010.01078.x.

Silvio, Teri. 2019. *Puppets, Gods, and Brands: Theorizing the Age of Animation from Taiwan.* Honolulu: University of Hawai'i Press.

Simmel, Georg. 1950. *The Sociology of Georg Simmel.* Translated by Kurt H. Wolff. Glencoe, IL: The Free Press.

Simmel, Georg. 1994. "The Picture Frame: An Aesthetic Study." *Theory, Culture & Society* 11 (1): 11–17. https://doi.org/10.1177/026327694011001003.

Simonovich-Efimova, Nina. 1935. *Adventures of a Russian Puppet Theatre: Including Its Discoveries in Making and Performing with Hand-Puppets, Rod-Puppets and Shadow-Figures, Now Disclosed for All.* Translated by Elena Mitcoff. Birmingham, MI: Puppetry Imprints.

Singh, Joseph Amrito Lal, Robert M. Zingg, and Paul Johann Anselm Feuerbach. (1942) 1960. *Wolf-Children and Feral Man.* New York: Harper & Brothers.

Slezkine, Yuri. 2017. *The House of Government: A Saga of the Russian Revolution.* Princeton, NJ: Princeton University Press.

Sloterdijk, Peter. 2011. *Bubbles: Spheres Volume I: Microspherology.* Translated by Wieland Hoban. Los Angeles, CA: Semiotext.

Sloterdijk, Peter. 2014. *You Must Change Your Life.* Translated by Wieland Hoban. Cambridge, UK: Polity.

Smagulova, Juldyz. 2008. "Language Policies of Kazakhization and Their Influence on Language Attitudes and Use." *International Journal of Bilingual Education and Bilingualism* 11 (3–4): 440–75. https://doi.org/10.1080/13670050802148798.

Smirnova, Nataliia Il'inichna. 1963. *Sovetskiĭ teatr kukol* [The Soviet puppet theatre]. *1918–1932.* Moskva: Izd-vo Akademii nauk SSSR.

Smith, Adam. (1759) 2011. *The Theory of Moral Sentiments.* Kapaau, HI: Gutenberg Publishers.

Solomonik, Inna. 1992. "Puppet Theatre in the Home in Pre-Revolutionary Russia." *Contemporary Theatre Review* 1 (1): 25–30. https://doi.org/10.1080/10486809208568243.

Sontag, Susan. (1977) 2001. *On Photography.* New York: Farrar, Straus and Giroux.

Sontag, Susan. 2004. *Regarding the Pain of Others.* New York: Picador.

SOS Children's Villages. 2023. Support for children and young people. Last accessed May 30. https://www.soschildrensvillages.org.uk/how-we-help/support-for-children/.

Spyrou, Spyros, Rachel Rosen, and Daniel Thomas Cook, eds. 2018. *Reimagining Childhood Studies.* London: Bloomsbury Academic.

Stasch, Rupert. 2009. *Society of Others: Kinship and Mourning in a West Papuan Place.* Berkeley: University of California Press.

Stawkowski, Magdalena E. 2016. "'I Am a Radioactive Mutant': Emergent Biological Subjectivities at Kazakhstan's Semipalatinsk Nuclear Test Site." *American Ethnologist* 43 (1): 144–57. https://doi.org/10.1111/amet.12269.

Stewart, Kathleen. 2010. "Afterword: Worlding Refrains." In *The Affect Theory Reader,* edited by Melissa Gregg and Gregory J. Seigworth, 339–53. Durham, NC: Duke University Press.

Stewart, Susan. 1984. *On Longing: Narratives of the Miniature, the Gigantic, the Souvenir, the Collection.* Baltimore, MD: John Hopkins University Press.

Stockton, Kathryn Bond. 2009. *The Queer Child, or Growing Sideways in the Twentieth Century.* Durham, NC: Duke University Press.

Stoller, Paul. 1997. *Sensuous Scholarship.* Philadelphia: University of Pennsylvania Press.

Strathern, Marilyn. 1988. *The Gender of the Gift: Problems with Women and Problems with Society in Melanesia.* Berkeley: University of California Press.

Stryker, Rachael. 2010. *The Road to Evergreen: Adoption, Attachment Therapy, and the Promise of Family.* Ithaca, NY: Cornell University Press.

Suyarkulova, Mohira. 2020. "'Nobody Is Going to Want Her like This:' Disability, Sexuality, and Un/Happiness in Kyrgyzstan." *Kohl: A Journal for Body and Gender Research* 6 (2): 187–200.

Taylor, Marjorie. 1999. *Imaginary Companions and the Children Who Create Them.* New York: Oxford University Press.

Tengrinews.kz. 2020. "*Termin 'oralman' zamenili na 'kandas' v Kazakhstane*" [The term "*oralman*" is replaced by "*kandas*" in Kazakhstan], September 3. https:// tengrinews.kz/kazakhstan_news/termin-oralman-zamenili-na-kandas-v -kazahstane-413101/.

Tikhonova, Ekaterina. 2019. "*Neiuchennyi urok*" [A lesson not learned], *Vremia*, February 22. https://time.kz/articles/chastnyj/2019/02/22/nevyuchennyj-urok.

Tizard, Barbara, and Jill Hodges. 1978. "The Effect of Early Institutional Rearing on the Development of Eight Year Old Children." *Journal of Child Psychology and Psychiatry* 19 (2): 99–118. https://doi.org/10.1111/j.1469-7610.1978.tb00453.x.

Todorova, Mariîa Nikolaeva, and Zsuzsa Gille. 2010. *Post-Communist Nostalgia.* New York: Berghahn Books.

Tolstoy, Aleksey Nikolayevich. 1957. *Zolotoĭ kliuchik: ili prikliucheniia Buratino* [The golden key: or the adventures of Buratino]. Leningrad: Gos. Izd-vo Detskoi Literatury.

Tolstoy, Nikolai. 1983. *The Tolstoys: Twenty-Four Generations of Russian History, 1353– 1983.* London: H. Hamilton.

Tomasello, Michael. 2019. *Becoming Human: A Theory of Ontogeny.* Cambridge, MA: The Belknap Press of Harvard University Press.

Toren, Christina. 2009. "Intersubjectivity as Epistemology." *Social Analysis* 53 (2): 130–46.

Toren, Christina. 2012. "Imagining the World That Warrants Our Imagination: The Revelation of Ontogeny." *Cambridge Journal of Anthropology* 30 (1): 64–79. https:// doi.org/10.3167/ca.2012.300107.

Towns, Armond R. 2020. "Toward a Black Media Philosophy." *Cultural Studies* 34 (6): 851–73. https://doi.org/10.1080/09502386.2020.1792524.

Trevathan, Wenda. 2016. *Costly and Cute: Helpless Infants and Human Evolution.* Albuquerque: University of New Mexico Press.

Trouillot, Michel-Rolph. 2015. *Silencing the Past: Power and the Production of History.* Boston, MA: Beacon Press.

Tsivian, Yuri. 1995. "The Case of the Bioscope Beetle: Starewicz's Answer to Genetics." *Discourse* 17 (3): 119–25.

Tsyrempilov, Nikolay, Ulan Bigozhin, and Batyrkhan Zhumabayev. 2021. "A Nation's Holy Land: Kazakhstan's Large-Scale National Project to Map Its Sacred Geography." *Nationalities Papers* (May): 1–18. https://doi.org/10.1017/nps.2021.22.

Ulturgasheva, Olga. 2012. *Narrating the Future in Siberia: Childhood, Adolescence and Autobiography Among Young Eveny.* New York: Berghahn Books.

Umarekova, Gul'nara and Mukhi Kudykbaev. 2015. "*Festival' detskogo tvorchestva Meiırım-2015 proveli v Almaty*" [The 2015 Meiırım Festival of Children's Creativity took place in Almaty]. *24 KZ*, May 22, 2015.

Umirbekov, Darkhan. 2019. "Words Mean Everything in Ethnic Kazakh Debate." *EurasiaNet*, October 10, 2019. https://eurasianet.org/kazakhstan-words-mean -everything-in-ethnic-kazakh-debate.

UNICEF Child Friendly Cities Initiative. "Building a Child Friendly City." 2023. Last accessed June 1. https://www.childfriendlycities.org/building-child-friendly-city.

Urban, Greg. 1989. "The 'I' of Discourse in Shokleng." In *Semiotics, Self, and Society*, edited by Benjamin Lee and Greg Urban, 27–51. Berlin: Mouton de Gruyter.

Urciuoli, Bonnie. 1996. *Exposing Prejudice: Puerto Rican Experiences of Language, Race, and Class*. Boulder, CO: Westview Press.

Uspenskiĭ, Ė., I. Pshenichnaia, and A Solin. (1965) 1998. *Krokodil Gena i ego druz'ia͡: povest'-skazka*. Moskva: Rosman.

Van Rosmalen, Lenny, René Van der Veer, and Frank Van der Horst. 2015. "Ainsworth's Strange Situation Procedure: The Origin of an Instrument." *Journal of the History of the Behavioral Sciences* 51 (3): 261–84. https://doi.org/10.1002/jhbs.21729.

Viola, Lynne. 2007. *The Unknown Gulag: The Lost World of Stalin's Special Settlements*. Oxford, UK: Oxford University Press.

Virtual Museum of the Gulag. 2023. Last accessed June 20. http://www.gulagmuseum.org/showObject.do?object=334298&language=2.

Vitebsky, Piers. 2005. *Reindeer People: Living with Animals and Spirits in Siberia*. London: HarperCollins.

Vlahos, James. 2015. "Barbie Wants to Get to Know Your Child." *New York Times*, September 16, 2015. http://www.nytimes.com/2015/09/20/magazine/barbie-wants-to-get-to-know-your-child.html.

Volkman, Toby Alice. 2005. *Cultures of Transnational Adoption*. Durham, NC: Duke University Press.

Volkov, Vadim. 2000. "The Concept of Kul'turnost': Notes on the Stalinist Civilizing Process." In *Stalinism: New Directions*, edited by Sheila Fitzpatrick, 210–30. London: Routledge.

Voloshinov, V. N. 1986. *Marxism and the Philosophy of Language*. Translated by Ladislav Matejka and I. R. Titunik. Cambridge, MA: Harvard University Press.

Vygotsky, L. S. (1934) 1986. *Thought and Language*. Cambridge, MA: MIT.

Vygotsky, L. S. (1966) 1978. "The Role of Play in Development." In *Mind in Society: The Development of Higher Psychological Processes*, edited by Michael Cole, Vera John-Steiner, Sylvia Scribner, and Ellen Souberman, 92–104. Cambridge, MA: Harvard University Press.

Walker, Shaun. 2016. "'Here I Have Nobody': Life in a Strange Country May Be Worse than Guantánamo." *Guardian*, September 30, 2016, World News. https://www.theguardian.com/world/2016/sep/30/worse-than-guantanamo-ex-prisoner-struggles-with-new-life-in-kazakhstan.

Warburton, Alex, and Meghanne Barker. 2018. "Putting an End to the Rain of Apostrophes." *Anthropology News* 59 (6): e221–e225. https://doi.org/10.1111/AN.1043.

Weber, Max. 1978. *Economy and Society: An Outline of Interpretive Sociology*. Edited by Guenther Roth and Claus Wittich. Oakland, University of California Press.

Weld, Sara Pankenier. 2014. *Voiceless Vanguard: The Infantilist Aesthetic of the Russian Avant-Garde*. Evanston, Illinois: Northwestern University Press.

Werner, Cynthia. 1997. "Marriage, Markets, and Merchants: Changes in Wedding Feasts and Household Consumption Patterns in Rural Kazakhstan." *Culture & Agriculture* 19 (1–2): 6–13. https://doi.org/10.1525/cag.1997.19.1-2.6.

Werner, Cynthia, and Holly Barcus. 2015. "The Unequal Burdens of Repatriation: A Gendered View of the Transnational Migration of Mongolia's Kazakh Population." *American Anthropologist* 117 (2): 257–71. https://doi.org/10.1111/aman.12230.

Werner, Cynthia, and Kathleen Purvis-Roberts. 2014. "Cold War Memories and Post–Cold War Realities: The Politics of Memory and Identity in the Everyday Life of Kazakhstan's Radiation Victims." In *Ethnographies of the State in Central Asia: Performing Politics*, edited by Madeleine Reeves, Johan Rasanayagam, and Judith

Beyer, 285–310. Bloomington: Indiana University Press. https://www.jstor.org /stable/j.ctt16gzghd.18.

Williams, Margery. 1922. *The Velveteen Rabbit: Or How Toys Become Real*. Illustrated by William Nicholson. London: Heinemann.

Winnicott, D. W. 1971. *Playing and Reality*. New York: Basic Books.

Wirtz, Kristina. 2011. "Cuban Performances of Blackness as the Timeless Past Still Among Us." *Journal of Linguistic Anthropology* 21 (August): E11–34. https://doi .org/10.1111/j.1548-1395.2011.01095.x.

Wood, David, Jerome S Bruner, and Gail Ross. 1976. "The Role of Tutoring in Problem Solving." *Journal of Child Psychology and Psychiatry* 17 (2): 89–100. https://doi .org/10.1111/j.1469-7610.1976.tb00381.x.

Wood, Gaby. 2002. *Edison's Eve: A Magical History of the Quest for Mechanical Life*. New York: Knopf.

Woolard, Kathryn A. 1998. "Simultaneity and Bivalency as Strategies in Bilingualism." *Journal of Linguistic Anthropology* 8 (1): 3–29. https://doi.org/10.1525/jlin.1998 .8.1.3.

Woronov, T. W. 2007. "Performing the Nation: China's Children as Little Red Pioneers." *Anthropological Quarterly* 80 (3): 647–72. https://doi.org/10.1353/anq.2007.0052.

Wortham, Stanton E. F. 2005. "Socialization beyond the Speech Event." *Journal of Linguistic Anthropology* 15 (1): 95–112. https://doi.org/10.1525/jlin.2005.15.1.95.

Yankah, Kwesi. 1985. "Risks in Verbal Art Performance." *Journal of Folklore Research* 22 (2/3): 133–53.

Yiu, Wai-hung, and Alex Ching-shing Chan. 2013. "'Kawaii' and 'Moe'—Gazes, Geeks (Otaku), and Glocalization of Beautiful Girls (Bishōjo) in Hong Kong Youth Culture." *Positions: East Asia Cultures Critique* 21 (4): 853–84. https://doi.org/10 .1215/10679847-2346032.

Yngvesson, Barbara. 2010. *Belonging in an Adopted World: Race, Identity, and Transnational Adoption*. Chicago: University of Chicago Press.

Yurchak, Alexei. 2005. *Everything Was Forever, Until It Was No More: The Last Soviet Generation*. Princeton, NJ: Princeton University Press.

Yurchak, Alexei. 2015. "Bodies of Lenin: The Hidden Science of Communist Sovereignty." *Representations* 129 (1): 116–57. https://doi.org/10.1525/rep.2015.129.1.116.

Zaloom, Caitlin. 2019. *Indebted: How Families Make College Work at Any Cost*. Princeton, NJ: Princeton University Press. https://doi.org/10.2307/j.ctv182jt8b.

Zelizer, Viviana A. Rotman. 1985. *Pricing the Priceless Child: The Changing Social Value of Children*. New York: Basic Books.

Zhang, Zhe, and Sansar Tsakhirmaa. 2022. "Ethnonationalism and the Changing Pattern of Ethnic Kazakhs' Emigration from China to Kazakhstan." *China Information* 36 (3): 318–43. https://doi.org/10.1177/0920203X221092686.

## FILMS AND TELEVISION PROGRAMS

Baigazin, Emir Kenzhegazyuly, dir. 2013. *Uroki garmonii*; [Harmony lessons]. Kazakhstan, Germany: Kazakhfilm Studios.

"*Chelovecheskii detenysh*" [Human cub]. *Pust'govoriat'* [Let them speak]. Aired 2010 on Pervyĭ Kanal.

Collet-Serra, Jaume, dir. 2009. *Orphan*. Dark Castle Entertainment, Appian Way Productions, Studio Babelberg Motion Pictures, Studio Canal.

"*Deti maugli*" [Mowgli children]. Episode 191. *Dokumental'noe rassledovanie* [Documentary investigations]. Aired 2013 on *Sovershenno sekretno* [Totally secret] TV.

Dyozhkin, Boris, dir. 1961. *Chipollino*. Moscow: Soyuzmultfilm.

Garmon, Linda, dir. *Nova*. Season 21, episode 12, "The Secret of the Wild Child." Aired October 18, 1994 on PBS.

Kachanov, Roman, animator. 1969. *Krokodil Gena* [Gena the crocodile]. Moscow: Soyuzmultfilm.

Kandel, Felix, Arkady Khai and Aleksandr Kurlandsky. 1969. *Nu, pogodi!* [Well, just you wait!]. Moscow: Soyuzmultfilm.

Khitruk, Fyodor, animator. 1969. *Vinni-Pukh* [Winnie-the-Pooh]. Moscow: Soyuzmultfilm.

Lasseter, John, dir. 1996. *Toy Story*. Emeryville, CA: Walt Disney Pictures, Pixar Animation Studios.

*"Liudi—maugli"* [Mowgli people]. Season 1, episode 8. *Neob"iasnimo, no fakt* [Inexplicable but true]. 2005. TNT.

MacFarlane, Adrian and Gillian Pachter, dirs. 2012. *Raised Wild*. Animal Planet.

Matthews, Vicky and Heidi Christenson, writers. *Is It Real?* Season 3, episode 8, "Feral Children." Aired April 17, 2007 on National Geographic Channel.

Nechayev, Leonid, dir. 1976. *Priklyucheniya Buratino* [The adventures of Buratino]. Minsk: Belarusfilm.

*Neob"iasnimo, no fakt* [Inexplicable but true]. 2005-2008. TNT.

Norstein, Yuri, animator. 1975. *Yozhik v tumane* [Hedgehog in the fog]. Moscow: Soyuzmultfilm.

Raibaev, Anuar, dir. 2017. *ALZhIR: Blood, Washed by Snow*. Astana: RTRK Kazakhstan, Independent Producer Center KazTeleFilm. DCP, DVD9.

Ršumović, Vuk, dir. 2014. *Ničije dete* [No one's child]. Distributed by Art & Popcorn, BaBoon Production, Kinorama.

Slaboshpytskiy, Myroslav, dir. 2014. *Plemya* [The tribe]. Harmata Film Production; Ukrainian Film Agency; Hubert Bals Fund; Foundation for Development of Ukraine.

Solonevich, Andrei, dir. 2009. *Dikie deti* [Wild children]. Channel 1 Russia.

Švankmajer, Jan, dir. 1988. *Něco z Alenky* [Alice]. Czechoslovakia, Switzerland, United Kingdom, West Germany: Film Four International, Condor Films.

Toziya, Vardan, dir. 2016. *Amok*. Republic of North Macedonia: Ognen Antov—Dream Factory Macedonia.

# Index

References to endnotes consist of the page number followed by the letter 'n' followed by the number of the note. References to illustrations are indicated in italics.

Abashin, Sergey, 50
abortion, 35
absence: mitigation of, 149–50. *See also* loss; separation
acting: and mask/strangeness, 63–4; and projection, 18, 64; as trap, 90. *See also* performance
Adams, Laura L., 19
adoption: 2017 survey (BBC and Adoption UK), 190n33; in Kazakhstan, 8, 15, 68, 179n28; transnational adoptions, 192n13; in United States, 128; by US citizens of Eastern European children, 140–2, 143, 185n7
aesthetics: social aesthetics, 18. *See also* childhood aesthetics
affect: and infrastructural/institutional hope, 10; and power relations, 10
agency: of children, 20, 21, 22, 174n32; of objects, 12, 111–14; and power, 22; and responsibility, 97–8
Ainsworth, Mary, 66, 67, 71
*aitys* (competitive Kazakh poetry), 19
*Aldar Kose* (play), 5, 15
alienation theories, 31, 173n24. *See also* defamiliarization (or estrangement); *ostranenie* (defamiliarization/estrangement)
Almaty (formerly Alma-Ata): as capital of Kazakhstan, 51, 173n21; "Child Friendly City" (UNICEF designation), 84–5
Almaty State Puppet Theater: beginnings in Soviet era, 11; bilingual (Kazakh/Russian) programming, 4–5, 12; childhood, promotion of as key to nation's future, 15; childhood, universality of, 133; childhood as collective project, 78; expressiveness of entertainers, 129; fantasy, role of, 16, 19; "Friendship of the People" ideology, 58; Hope House children's visit to, 14; musical about wolf adopting baby chick, 141; pedagogy and socialization, 12, 102; performance, techniques and ideologies of, 14–15; political regime, subtle questioning of, 12;

power relations through affective means, 10; properly performing subject as goal, 20–1; puppeteers, number/training of, 11–12; puppet makers, 119–21, *120*; renovation and overhaul of repertoire, 12–14; shows in theater and on visits, 12; as site for adults to recuperate lost childhood, 99; Soviet bureaucratic organisation, 13; Soviet puppetry (no Kazakh *orteke*), 13; staff besides puppeteers, 12; warm-up games, 91–2. *See also Kashtanka* (Almaty State Puppet Theater); puppetry
Altshuller, Genrich, 16
ALZhIR (Akmolinsk Camp of Women of Traitors of the Country) museum: ALZhIR prison camp, 40; breaking-up of families, 15, 51; deportees' contributions to Soviet Kazakhstan, 58; description of museum exhibits, 41–3; Inna Aronovna Gaister case, 43; letter of child to mother with drawing, 44–5, *45*; Mania's letter to her relatives, 104–5; nearby villagers' hospitality, 57; Raibaev's film about, 57
amnesia, infantile amnesia, 46
*Amok* (Vardan Toziya), 143
animation: animation defined, 19; cel animation, 87, 182n29; deanimation, 64, 125–6, 127; and manipulation, 62–3; and photography, 42–3; and power, 62; and sentiment, 62; Soviet animation, 5, 87, 182n28; stop motion animation, 127. *See also* intimacy, animation of
anthropomorphism, 89
art: and picture frames, 151–2, 166; as trap, 90
Artaud, Antonin, 31, 32
Arvatov, Boris, 183n33
Astana: city's reinvention and renaming, 51; EXPO Astana, 51, 168–9
attachment theories, 21, 53, 55, 57; "disinhibited attachment" notion, 71; Reactive Attachment Disorder, 141; "strange situation" as experimental condition, 66–7, 75

"auntie" (*tëtka*), 58, 65, 149
automatons, 31, 74
Aveyron. *See* Victor of Aveyron

baby house (*dom rebënka*), 6, 88
"baby schema" concept, 86–7, 134
"bad subject" notion, 125
Baigazin, Emir Kenzhegazyuly, *Harmony Lessons* (*Uroki garmonii*), 143
Bakhtin, Mikhail, 17–18, 30–1, 176n23
balloons: vs. bubbles, 130; a girl gets all the balloons, 130–1, *130*
Barbie dolls, 72, 111–12, 113, 114, 187n28
Barthes, Roland, 42–3, 188n3
Bateson, Gregory, 152
belonging, 54, 78, 94, 105; and *svoi* ("our own"), 65, 75, 149, 162
Berlant, Lauren, 62, 75
blessings, 60, 163
boarding school (*internat*), 6, 10, 35, 97
bonding, 90–1, 96, 107, 108
Boym, Svetlana, 76
Brezhnev, Leonid, 35
Bruno, Giordano, 90
Bunraku-style puppets, 11, 126–7
*Buratino*, 15, 98–9, 115, 183n41
*byt* ("everyday life"), 185n1

camera: filming children at Hope House, 150–1, 152, 154–6; filming Marlin's departure from Hope House, 26, 157–9, *159*, 160–1, 166–7; "fly on the wall" technique, 155; as framing technology, 152, 154; as instrument to frame social relations, 151; and mitigation of absence, 149–50; and performance frames, 149; security cameras, 155; and socialization at Hope House, 154–5. *See also* films; photography
camps. *See* gulag (labour camps)
"capacity to call" notion, 44
capitalism: and *Cheburashka*, 88; and commoditization of childhood/cuteness, 87; "wild capitalism" concept, 140
care: animating care playing with dolls, 72, *73*, 74–6; and attachment theories in children's institutions, 55, 67; and control, 21, 32; and framing, 153; and manipulation, 61; and materiality, 89, 101–2, 107; from mothers vs. from strangers, 68; from nonparents/strangers, 69, 71, 86; overlapping roles of, 54; state care, 85; toy care, 115–18. *See also* adoption; foster care
Carpenter, Kathie, 178n4, 184n50

cel animation, 87, 182n29
*Cheburashka*, 87–9, 99, 115, 134
Chekhov, Anton. *See* "Kashtanka" (Anton Chekhov)
childhood: commoditization of, 87; narrative of and conflict, 135; and nostalgia, 22, 99; as political site, 15, 22; as public/collective affair, 10–11, 22, 78, 84–5; universality of, 133. *See also* childhood, ideologies of; childhood aesthetics; children; children's institutions; gender
childhood, ideologies of: and birth vs. death, 128, 131; and children on margins of humanity, 136–7; and children's actual experience, 79–80; and children's performances, 96–8; and "Mowgli children," 139–40; and state interests, 6
childhood aesthetics, 96, 128. *See also* competence; cuteness; helplessness; hopefulness; innocence; *Kashtanka* 3 - jumping through hoops; potential; vulnerability
children: agency of, 20, 21, 22, 174n32; circulation of, 156–7; collective child-rearing in early Soviet era, 22, 35; comparison with toys, 121–2; and consumer culture, 21, 87, 113; and death, 128, 131–2, 133; as evil/demonic/marginally human, 125–6, 136–7; feral children, 126, 137–8, 142, 143, 144, 146, 181n17; feral children and "Mowgli syndrome," 138–40; frame of children's play, 47, 48, 71, 109; iconicity of, 4, 22, 107, 153, 171n3; images of, 153–6; infantile amnesia, 46; and media objects/technologies, 21, 113, 187n22; orphaned child as salient figure, 28; and performance, 80–3, 85–6; and puppetry, 89–90, 91–2; as symbols of state paternalism, 85. *See also* childhood
children's home (*detdom*), 6, 34, 38, 59, 88, 136–7, 143
children's hospital, Pulcinella show, 128–32, *130*
children's institutions: different types of, 6, 8, 9, 172n13; in Eastern European fiction films, 142–3; institutionalization of "social orphans," 8; institutionalization raising likelihood of children's death, 128; number of children without parental care, 8; overrepresentation of ethnic Russians, 5; reliance on state and private support, 5–6; and theories of attachment, 55, 67. *See also* *detdom* (children's home); *dom rebënka* (baby house); Hope House; *internat* (boarding school); orphanages
chronotope. *See* creative chronotope

circus: circus performers at Hope House, 157, 158; circus ring as frame, 151, 153, 156; Durov brothers' shows, 91; *Kashtanka* circus scene, 65, 103, 146, 147, *148*, 149, 157

Committee Protecting the Rights of Children (Kazakhstan), 15

compatriots (*kandas*), 50, 58

competence: and cuteness, 94, 96; and performance, 86, 92, 144; and vulnerability, 96, 98–9. *See also* potential

conflict, and narrative of childhood, 135

consumer culture: and children, 21, 87, 113; in late Soviet era, 113; and women, 187n22

control: and care, 21, 32; photographs and institutional control, 42. *See also* manipulation

creative chronotope, 4, 17–19; at EXPO Astana, 51

Crimea, Russia's occupation of (2014), 104, 185n5

Curtiss, Susan, 138

cuteness: "baby schema" concept, 86–7, 134; and *Cheburashka*, 87–9, 99, 134; children mimicking cuteness of dolls, 15; children's animation of, 19, 26; children's strategies to appear cute, 133–4; and commoditization of childhood, 87; and competence, 94, 96; cute child as ideal figure, 17; cute costumes for children, 4, 86, 100; and indexicality, 171n3; and innocence, 87; in late Soviet children's culture, 78, 87; in narratives of national optimism, 3; and performance, 85–6; and potential, 79, 86, 100, 125, 144; and vulnerability, 79, 86, 89, 98, 100, 125, 144

deanimation, 64, 125–6, 127

death: and childhood aesthetics, 128; and children, 128, 131–2, 133; and orphaned child as salient figure, 28; of a parakeet at Hope House, 132–3; and puppets/dolls, 132; and the uncanny, 125, 127, 144

Debord, Guy, 19

defamiliarization (or estrangement), 16, 21, 56, 76. *See also* destrangement

deportations, 11, 15, 18, 28, 33, 50, 57–8. *See also* gulag (labour camps); imprisonment

destrangement, 4, 21–2, 53–8. *See also* *Kashtanka* 2 - meeting a stranger

*detdom* (children's home), 6, 34, 38, 59, 88, 136–7, 143

determinism: material determinism, 112; technological determinism, 187n22

dialectical materialism, 16

dicent signs, 95

Diderot, Denis, 90, 184n47

"digestive duck" automaton, 74

digital sharing (of images), 154

disembodiment, 21

"disinhibited attachment" notion, 71

displacement, 4, 21, 27–30, 34–5. *See also* *Kashtanka* 1 - getting lost

dolls: and agency of objects, 12, 111–14; and animation of intimacy, 19; Barbie dolls, 72, 111–12, 113, 114, 187n28; cuteness of, mimicked by children, 15; and death games, 132; "fashion dolls" (French dolls), 111, 132, 187n25; and gender, 187n25; and girls, 111–12; iconicity of, 108, 109, 111; interactive dolls, 113; playing with and animating care, 72, *73*, 74–6; playing with and strangers' care, 69, 71; talking dolls, 112–13; as things and as persons, 108–11; as transitional objects, 61; and the uncanny, 31–2, 126–8; Western ambivalence towards, 102

*dombyra* (Kazakh musical instrument), 13, 47, *48*

*dom rebënka* (baby house), 6, 88

Dostoevsky, Fyodor, 33, 57

Dubuisson, Eva-Marie, 19

Dugarova, Esuna, 35

Durkheim, Émile, 62–3

Durov, Vladimir, 91

Eastern Europe: adoptions from orphanages, 141–2, 143; fiction films depicting children's institutions, 142–3

Ebert, Roger, 141

Edison, Thomas, 112–13

embraces, circle of, 163, *164*

emotional deprivation, 106–7, 121

Enlightenment philosophers, 137

entextualization, 165

Erlan case (Hope House), 134–6, 143–4, *145*

Estrada (Soviet musical genre), 19

estrangement (or defamiliarization), 16, 21, 56, 76. *See also* destrangement

Evreinov, Nikolai, "Storming of the Winter Palace" reenactment, 89

EXPO Astana, 51, 168–9

familiarization techniques, 4, 16–17, 26, 56, 86, 102, 169. *See also* creative chronotope; defamiliarization (or estrangement); intimacy, animation of; intimate familiarizations

families: models of, 39. *See also* kinship

famine, 11, 33, 56, 106, 128

fantasy: and creating worlds beyond children's home, 18–19, 111; and creative chronotope, 4; and frame of play, 152; Kazakhstan's fantasies of futurity, 17; and photography, 42, 43; and political ideologies/social relations, 15–16; and projection, 22

"fashion dolls" (French dolls), 111, 132, 187n25

fatherhood: children in care's lack of closed contact with men, 9, 176n9; Marlin's father as single father, 35, 156, 167, 176n9; Nazarbayev as father figure to state, 10. See also motherhood

Fehérváry, Krisztina, 187n31

feminist scholarship, central Asian, 16

feral children, 126, 137–8, 142, 143, 144, 146, 181n17; "Mowgli syndrome," 138–40

figure, definition of term, 16–17

films: frames, 152; and indexicality, 191n6; portrayal of children's institutions in, 142–3. See also camera; photography

first I, 95–6, 99, 125. See also second I

"fly on the wall" technique, 155

folktales, 13, 37, 182n28, 184n56

"forbidden experiment," 137

fort/da game, 36

foster care, 8, 15, 56–7, 128

Foucault, Michel, 10

"fourth wall," 153

framing: architectural frames, 151; built environment as frame, 165; camera as framing technology, 152, 154; circus ring as frame, 151, 153, 156; double framing, 109, 153; frame of children's play, 47, 48, 71, 109; frames in moving pictures, 152; human bodies as frames, 162; of letters/videos of gratitude, 160–2, 164–5, 167; media frameworks, 151; participation frameworks, 12, 94, 173n22, 174n38; performance frames, 147, 149–50, 153, 178n1; picture frames, 151–2, 166; primary frameworks, 71; psychological frames, 152; social frameworks, 151, 152, 165; and socialization/care, 153; theater as frame on the "real," 31. See also Kashtanka 6 - going home again

freedom, vs. stability, 102–4, 122

French dolls ("fashion dolls"), 111, 132, 187n25

Freud, Sigmund: and Bruno's theory of bonding, 183n38; familiarity and strangeness, 179n22; fort/da game, 36; superego, 181n15; transference, 55–6, 72; the uncanny, 32, 71, 188n4, 188n7

"Friendship of the People" ideology, 58

Gaister, Inna Aronovna, 43

Gell, Alfred, 90, 110

gender: and children's dress/appearance, 7–8; and children's performances of childhood, 86; and children's play, 114; and dolls, 187n25; and feral children, 139; and performance, 178n14, 180n2; and toys, 187n32. See also fatherhood; girls; motherhood; women

"Genie" case, 138, 139, 142

girls: and dolls, 111–12; short hair in orphanages, 8; vulnerability of, 112. See also gender

glasnost, 99

Goffman, Erving, 9, 16–17, 94, 152, 173n22, 179n29

Golding, William, Lord of the Flies, 143

gratitude, letters/videos of, 160–2, 164–5, 167

Greek romance, 30–1

Grice, Elizabeth, 139

griots, 164–5

guest/host relations, 57–8; hospitality, 51, 57

gulag (labour camps), 15, 33, 40–3, 51. See also ALZhIR (Akmolinsk Camp of Women of Traitors of the Country) museum; KarLag (Karaganda Correctional Work Camp) museum

guns: iconicity of as phallic objects, 186n20; toy guns, 111

Hales, Molly, 41, 42

Hansen, Torry, 141, 143

Harmony Lessons (Uroki garmonii) (Baigazin), 143

helplessness, 3, 8, 86, 96

Herodotus, 137

hiding: "nothing to hide," 81–2, 96; "stop hiding behind the puppets," 83–4

Hodges, Jill, 71

Hoffman, E. T. A., 179n22, 188n7

"home" notion, and migration, 50

Homo Sovieticus, 20

hopefulness: and helplessness, 3, 8; hopeful narratives, 5–6, 160; infrastructural/institutional hope, 10; and potential, 79; and projection, 28, 169; and vulnerability, 85, 99

Hope House: author's departure from, 161–2; author's return to, 168–9; building, location and rooms, 6–7; childhood as collective project, 78; children as key to nation's future, 15; children as strangers/guests/hosts, 57; children grouped by age, 7; children held up as future leaders, 21, 68,

94, 133; children seen as "bad subjects," 125; children's performance of *Buratino* dance, 98–9; children's resilience and ways to cope, 133–5; children's use of term "aunt," 58; children's visit to Almaty State Puppet Theater, 14; circus performers' visit, 157, 158; closing of Hope House, 170; concept of temporary institution, 1, 2–3, 6, 9–10, 34–6; created in post-Soviet era, 11; cuteness as childhood aesthetics, 86, 94, 96, 133–4; death of a parakeet, 132–3; destrangement, 54, 56–7; displacement, 21, 28, 34–5; Erlan case, 134–6, 143–4, *145*; fantasy, role of, 15–16, 19; filming lessons and children's play, 150–1, 152, 154–6; filming Marlin's departure, 26, 157–9, *159*, 160–1, 166–7; as a frame, 165–6; framing, socialization and care, 153; framing letters/videos of gratitude, 160–2, 164–5, 167; "Friendship of the People" ideology, 58; gender distinctions and clothes, 7–8; health and medical care, 128; helplessness and hope, 8–9; hopeful narrative, 160; institutional hope, 10; intimate familiarizations, 9; Kazakh language, emphasis on, 5; *Leaders of the Twenty-First Century* (quiz show), 93–4; lesson on expression of time, 37–8, *38*, 39–40; loss/separation and recovery/reunion, 23, 28, 34–40, 46, 51–2; male staff (only guards and drivers), 9; Marlin's 6th birthday, 150–1, 152, 163–4; Marlin's departure, 26, 157–9, *159*, 160–1, 166–7; Marlin's father, DVD for, 156; Marlin's father as single father, 35, 156, 167, 176n9; Marlin's return from sanatorium, 165–6; material comforts and care/kin bonds, 107–8; material comforts and sensory richness, 105–6; materiality and "never offering enough," 102; *Meıırım* Festival of Children's Creativity, 96–8; memory, loss and children's play, 46–50, *48*; "nothing to hide," 81–2, 96; parents and relatives, 6, 8, 10, 14, 34–6, 81; performance, techniques and ideologies of, 14–15; performance and pedagogy, 92–4; performances and aesthetics of childhood, 96; performances by children and professional entertainers, 80–1, 83; playing with author ("the children fix me"), 69, *70*; playing with dolls and animating care, 72, *73*, 74–6; playing with dolls and creative reinvention, 12; playing with dolls and strangers' care, 69, 71; power relations through affective means, 10;

properly performing subject as goal, 20–1; security cameras, 155; socialization and cameras, 154–5; Soviet animation programmes, 182n28, 182n29; staff categories and roles, 9; staff getting little credit for their work, 26; staff not replacing children's mothers, 38–9, 56, 59, 67–8, 77, 107, 122; staff's relationships with children, 59–61, 62, 63, 68–71, *70*, 77, 90; state ideology and children's development, 23; support from state and private sponsors, 4, 5–6, 8–9, 10, 14, 81, 96; things (dolls) as things and as persons, 108–11; toy care, 115–18; toys of bad quality, 113–14
hospital. *See* children's hospital
hospitality, 51, 57. *See also* guest/host relations
Hrdy, Sarah Blaffer, 86
humility: of things, 112; of things' creators (puppet makers), 119–21
hunger: in Soviet orphanages, 128; vs. stability, 103–4, 122

I (first I/second I theory), 62, 95–6, 99, 111, 125
iconicity: of children, 4, 22, 107, 153, 171n3; of children's play, 77; of dolls, 108, 109, 111; of guns as phallic objects, 186n20; of indexical link between director and actor, 65; of toys, 47, 49–50, 110, 121, 186n17; of wildness trope for economy and childhood, 140
ideologies: "Friendship of the People" ideology, 58; political ideologies, 15; state ideologies, 23. *See also* childhood, ideologies of; childhood aesthetics
images: of children, 153–6; digital sharing of, 154
imprisonment, 11, 15, 18, 28. *See also* deportations; gulag (labour camps)
indexicality: children as indexical icons, 4, 153; and cuteness of children, 171n3; gun as indexical icon of phallus, 186n20; indexical link between director and actor, 65; and language, 18; in photography and films, 191n6; and presupposing statement, 179n15; tension between real and represented, 173n30, 191n7; and toys, 117, 186n17; and wildness trope for economy and childhood, 140
individual: and society, 166; Western conception of, 20
individuality, vs. universality, 133
inequality, structural violence of, 140, 153
innocence, 87, 96, 136–7, 140, 188n35

institutionalization. *See* children's institutions

institutions: power and affect, 10; total institutions, 9, 10, 96. *See also* children's institutions; Hope House

*internat* (boarding school), 6, 10, 35, 97

intersubjectivity, 20, 32, 86, 90, 91, 110, 166

intertextuality, 18

intimacy: "diasporic intimacy" concept, 76; "minor intimacies" concept, 75. *See also* intimacy, animation of

intimacy, animation of: concept, 4, 17, 19–21; destrangement, 4, 21–2, 53–8; displacement, 4, 21, 27–30, 34–5; projection, 4, 21, 22, 28

intimate familiarizations, 9, 17

intimation, 56, 62

Jakobson, Roman, 44, 191n6

Jentsch, Ernst, 31–2, 56, 188n4, 188n7

Johnson, Barbara, 44

*kandas* (compatriots), 50, 58

KarLag (Karaganda Correctional Work Camp) museum, 15, 40–1, 42, 43, 51, 57

*Kashtanka* (Almaty State Puppet Theater): author's reasons for choosing as focus, 5; displacement as defining moment, 21; implicit political message, 22, 104; Kashtanka puppet, 12; overview of chapters analysing story, 23–6; production problems, 169; rehearsal crisis, 119–21, 162–4, *164*; unconventional production, 14, 65–6. *See also* "Kashtanka" (Anton Chekhov); *Kashtanka* entries by chapter; puppetry

"Kashtanka" (Anton Chekhov): based on Vladimir Durov's anecdote, 91; interpretations of story, 1–2; lines narrated to audience, 27, 34; memory as main theme, 46; rehearsal scene going for hours, 78; return to first master and dream vs. memory, 169; return to first master and freedom issue, 103; rich smells and textures, 106, 112

*Kashtanka* 1 - getting lost: chapter overview, 23; displacement, 27–8; displacement and deportations/imprisonment, 28; displacement and Hope House children, 28; displacement and puppetry, 28–30; Kashtanka as Greek romance hero, 30–1; Kashtanka at the doorstep, *28*; Kashtanka at the doorstep as a puppet, *29*; *Kashtanka* production, description of scenes, 27, 30–1, 34, 52; "Kashtanka" story, extract from, 27; Kazakh steppe as empty/boundless, 31, 32, 33–4, 46, 51; letter to Mamochka (ALZhIR museum),

44–5, *45*; memory, loss and Hope House children's play, 46–50, *48*; memory and settler colonialism, 46; reworlding Kazakhstan, 50–1; separation/loss and reunion/recovery at Hope House, 28, 34–40, 46, 51–2; separation/loss due to deportations/imprisonment, 28, 40, 50–1; Soviet gulag and memorial museums, 40–5, 51; theater as frame on the "real," 31; theater/stage as a world, 31; the uncanny and nonhuman others, 31–2; violence and puppetry, 32; violence and repressed nomadism, 32–3; women's roles and shortage of preschools, 35

*Kashtanka* 2 - meeting a stranger: chapter overview, 23–4; destrangement, 53–4; destrangement and attachment/psychoanalysis, 55–6, 57; destrangement and deportations/imprisonment, 57–8; destrangement and Hope House children, 54, 56–7; destrangement and the uncanny, 56; Hope House staff's attitudes towards children, 59–61, 62, 63, 77; hospitality and guest/host relations, 57–8; Kashtanka meets a stranger, *54*; *Kashtanka* production, description of scenes, 53, 54–5, 58, 64–5; "Kashtanka" story, extract from, 53; manipulation and puppetry, 62–3; manipulation and Winnicott's transitional object, 61–2; not-mothers and minor intimacies, 75; power and stranger as master, 58; strangeness, acting and projection, 63–4; strangers' care and adoption, 68; strangers' care and play at Hope House, 68–9, *70*, 71; "strange situation" in attachment theories, 66–7, 75; *svoi* and belonging, 65, 75; technique of deanimation, 64; *tëtka* and renaming of dog, 65; transference and animating care with dolls, 72, *73*, 74–6; unconventional (not "Soviet") production, 65–6

*Kashtanka* 3 - jumping through hoops: chapter overview, 24; childhood and cuteness, 78–9, 85–9, 94, 98, 100; childhood and helplessness, 86, 96; childhood and hopefulness, 79, 85, 99; childhood and innocence, 87, 96; childhood and nostalgia, 99; childhood and potential, 79, 86, 100; childhood and vulnerability, 79, 85, 86, 89, 96, 98, 99–100; children and adults' ideologies of childhood, 79–80; children dance in tutus, *82*; children's upbringing as public affair, 84–5; cuteness and *Cheburashka*, 87–9, 99; gander and cat rehearse, *79*; *Kashtanka* production, description of scenes, 78;

"Kashtanka" story, extract from, 78; performance and children, 80–3, 85–6; performance and pedagogy, 78, 92–4; performance animated by internal forces, 86; performance of *Buratino* song by Hope House children, 98–9; performances of children at Hope House, 96; performances of children at *Meiırım* Festival, 96–8; performers/viewers relationship, 89–92; puppet artists-turned stage characters, 83–4; puppetry, pedagogy and Soviet animation, 87; puppetry and first I/second I theory, 95–6, 99; puppetry and socialization, 91, 92; puppets make a pyramid, *80*; traps (acting/art as) and bonding, 90, 96

*Kashtanka* 4 - getting comfortable: chapter overview, 24–5; concept of "materiality," 101–2; freedom/hunger vs. stability, 102–4, 122; Kashtanka as universal protagonist, 103–4; *Kashtanka* lies on her mattress, *102*; *Kashtanka* production, description of scenes, 101, 112; *Kashtanka* production's political message, 104; "Kashtanka" story, extract from, 101; material comforts and ALZhIR museum letter, 104–5; material comforts and care/kin bonds at Hope House, 107–8; material comforts and sensory richness at Hope House, 105–6; no replacement for a mother's love, 107, 122; objects (dolls) as things and as persons, 108–11; objects, overpowering agency of, 111–14; Olzhas tucks Spider-Man into bed, *118*; orphanages as sites of emotional deprivation, 106–7; puppet makers at Almaty theater, 119–21, *120*; toy care at Hope House, 115–18; toys, surprising use of by children, 113, 114; toys and children compared, 121–2

*Kashtanka* 5 - losing a friend: chapter overview, 25; death and children, 131–2; death of a parakeet at Hope House, 132–3; death rates and hunger in orphanages, 128; dolls and death games, 132; feral children, 126, 137–8, 142, 143, 144, 146; feral children and "Mowgli syndrome," 138–40; feral children issue and Erlan case, 143–4, *145*; fiction films on children's institutions, 142–3; figure of demonic child, 136–7; *Kashtanka* production, description of scenes, 123, 125, 126, 128, 146; Kashtanka runs from a broom, *124*; "Kashtanka" story, extract from, 123; Maral loses the gander puppet, *124*; *Orphan* horror film, 140–1; orphans from Eastern Europe and American adoptions, 141–2, 143; Pulcinella show at children's hospital, 128–32, *130*; resilience of Hope House children (Erlan case), 133–6; stigmatization of institutionalized children, 136–7, 140–1; the uncanny and death, 125, 127, 144; the uncanny and marginally human children, 125–6, 144; the uncanny and puppets/dolls, 126–8

*Kashtanka* 6 - going home again: chapter overview, 25–6; circulation of children, 156–7; frames of performance, 149; framing and art (picture frames), 151–2, 166; framing and artists' embraces at rehearsal, 162–4, *164*; framing and built environment, 165; framing and filming at Hope House, 150–1, 152, 166–7; framing and letters/videos of gratitude, 160–2, 164–5, 167; framing and ritual mourning, 165; framing devices and social relations, 151, 165; framing devices/types and socialization/care, 151–3; going back home (author's departure from Hope House), 161–2; going back home (Marlin's departure from Hope House), 157–9, *159*, 160–1, 166–7; Hope House as a frame, 165–6; images of children and filming at Hope House, 153–6; images of children and Kazakh customs, 154; images of children and nostalgia, 154; images of children and vulnerability trope, 153–4; *Kashtanka* makes her debut, *148*; *Kashtanka* production, description of scenes, 147, 149, 153, 156, 166–7; "Kashtanka" story, extract from, 147; photographs/videos and mitigation of absence, 149–50

Kazakh folktales, 13, 37, 182n28

Kazakh language: bilingual (Kazakh/Russian) programming at puppet theater, 4–5, 12; Kazakh state's trilingual language policy, 58

Kazakh legends: *mambet*, 184n58; *mankurt*, 99

Kazakh musical instruments: *dombyra*, 13, 47, 48; *qobyz*, 46

Kazakh poetry, *aitys* (competitive Kazakh poetry), 19

Kazakh puppets (*orteke*), 13, 91

Kazakhstan: adoption, 8, 15, 68, 179n28; childcare issues, 35; childhood, customs/rituals around, 154; childhood, public nature of, 84–5; Committee Protecting the Rights of Children, 15; consumer/media products and cuteness, 87; demonstrations and repression (2022), 169; deportations/imprisonment during Soviet era, 11, 15, 18,

Kazakhstan (*continued*)
28, 33, 50, 57–8; famine during Soviet era, 11, 33, 56, 106, 128; fantasies of futurity, 17; fertility decline, 35; "Friendship of the People" ideology, 58; government welfare for single mothers, 186n12; gulag (labour camps), 15, 33, 40–3, 51; hospitality/host, 51, 57, 58; income disparity, 6; kin networks, 56–7, 67–8; languages (Kazakh and Russian), status/use of, 4–5, 12, 58; multiethnic/ multilingual populations, 58; nomadism, state repression of, 32–3; *oralman* (returnees) and *kandas* (compatriots), 50, 58; orphanages during 1930s famine, 33, 128; orphans, number of (1934), 56; reworlding Kazakhstan, 50–1; and Russia since Russia's 2022 invasion of Ukraine, 185n5; shrines and sacred sites, 107; Soviet and Russian legacies, 4–5; Soviet animations, celebration of, 87; "Spiritual Revival" (*Ruhani Jañgyru*), 5; steppe as "empty" space, 31, 32, 33–4, 46, 51; Strategy Kazakhstan-2050, 85; trilingualism, 58; Unity Day (May 1), 192n16; Virgin Lands campaign during Soviet era, 51. *See also* Almaty (formerly Alma-Ata); Astana; Nazarbayev, Nursultan
Khruschev, Nikita, 35
kinship: kin bonds, 107; kin networks, 56–7, 67–8; kinship systems and exchange of women, 192n14; kinship terms/names, 65, 72; and society vs. individual, 166. *See also* families
Kleist, Heinrich von, 30, 32, 127, 131
Koch, Natalie, 41
Korowai people, 136
*kul'turnost'*, 20
Kung Fu Panda, 15

labour camps. *See* gulag (labour camps)
Lancy, David F., 136
language: bilingual (Kazakh/Russian) programming at puppet theater, 4–5, 12; and indexicality, 18; innateness of, 137, 138; Kazakh state's trilingual language policy, 58
*Leaders of the Twenty-First Century* (quiz show), 93–4
Leblanc, Marie-Angélique, 142
Lemon, Alaina, 178n1, 185n7, 189n16
Lorenz, Konrad, 86
loss: due to deportations/imprisonment, 28, 40, 50; and framing/ritual mourning, 165; and migration, 150; and nostalgia, 99; and

recovery at Hope House, 23, 28, 34–5, 36–7, 51–2. *See also Kashtanka* 1 - getting lost; separation
Luria, Alexander, 44–5

MacDougall, David, 18
Malaya, Oxana, 138–9, 142, 146, 190n27
*Mamkin Dom* (Mama's House), 45
*Mamochkino kladbishche* (Mothers' Cemetery), 45
manipulation, 61–3. *See also* control
*mankurt* (Kazakh legend), 99
marionettes, 11. *See also* puppetry
Marlin case (Hope House): 6th birthday, 150–1, 152, 163–4; DVD for his father, 156; going back home, 26, 157–9, *159*, 160–1, 166–7; return from sanatorium, 165–6
mask, and acting, 64
mass spectacles. *See* spectacle
master: master-animal bond, 65; stranger as master, 58
materialism, dialectical, 16
materiality: ambivalence of notion, 101–2; and attachment, 55; and care, 89, 101–2, 107; and imagined outside, 9; and sentiment, 8, 100. *See also Kashtanka* 4 - getting comfortable; objects
Mazzarella, William, 49, 173n29, 179n20
"me and not-me," 16, 61, 110
media: media frameworks, 151; media products and cuteness, 87; media technologies/objects and children, 21, 113, 187n22; representations of pain, 17
*Meiırım* Festival of Children's Creativity, 96–8
memorial museums, 15, 23, 40–5. *See also* ALZhIR (Akmolinsk Camp of Women of Traitors of the Country) museum; KarLag (Karaganda Correctional Work Camp) museum
memory: and Chekhov's "Kashtanka" story, 46, 169; infantile amnesia, 46; and loss/ separation, 34, 36–7; and nostalgia, 99; and reconnection, 169–70; and settler colonialism, 46
Meyerhold, Vsevolod, 16, 63–4, 76, 127, 183n37, 184n47
migration: and "home" notion, 50; and missing/loss, 150
Miller, Daniel, 112
Milne, A. A., *Winnie the Pooh*, 88
miniatures, 41

"minor intimacies" concept, 75
missing, and migration, 150
Montagu, Ashley, 137–8
Mori, Masahiro, 126–7
Moscow Puppet Theater, 87
motherhood: Hope House staff not replacing children's mothers, 38–9, 56, 59, 67–8, 77, 107, 122; mother and not-mother, 75; mother-child dyad, primacy of in question, 39; mother-child relationship in attachment literature, 55, 66–7, 75; mother-child relationship in Winnicott, 61–2; single mothers, 6, 8, 35, 186n12; Soviet idealization of, 56; Soviet revalorization of, 35; working-class mothers, 187n22. *See also* fatherhood
mourning, and loss/framing, 165
Mowgli: character in Kipling's *The Jungle Book*, 189n21; "Mowgli children," 138–40, 142, 190n27
Mueggler, Erik, 165

Nakassis, Constantine V., 180n2, 187n33
Nasritdinov, Emil, 150
National Geographic Channel, *Is It Real?* (2007 episode on feral children), 138, 190n27
Nazarbayev, Nursultan: with children on billboards, 85; May 1 as Unity Day, 192n16; *oralman* (returnees) policy, 50; paternalistic leadership, 3; referred to as "Papa," 10; stability over freedom, 3–4, 104; stepping down, 169
Nazarbayev, Sara, 10
*News of Kazakhstan*, "Children—Future of the World," 85
nomadism, 32–3
nonsocialization, 137, 138
*No One's Child* (*Ničije dete*) (Vuk Ršumović), 142–3
nostalgia, 22, 41, 99, 121, 154, 184n58
*Nu, pogodi!*, 69, 182n28

objectification, 84, 89, 98, 165
objects: agency of, 12, 111–14; anthropomorphism of, 89; passive vs. production-oriented objects, 183n33; as things and as persons, 108–11; transitional objects (Winnicott), 61–2, 110–11, 117. *See also* materiality
Obraztsov, Sergei V., 87, 181n10
*oralman* (returnees), 50. *See also* kandas (compatriots)
*Orphan* (2009 horror film), 140–1

orphanages: and attachment theories, 67, 71; carers addressed as "Mom," 39; children, uniform treatment of as dehumanizing, 133; children grouped by age, 7; children seen as "bodies," 61; children's gender and dress/appearance, 7–8; as depicted in Eastern European fiction films, 142–3; Eastern European orphanages, adoption from, 141–2, 143; and emotional deprivation, 106–7; and feral children, 142; and hopeful future, ideologies of, 5–6; and loss issue, avoidance of, 37; low status work, 172n16; mortality rate during 1930s famine, 33, 128; orphans, number of (Kazakhstan, 1934), 56; orphans, performances from (*Meiırım* Festival), 96–8; orphans, stigmatization of, 67, 106, 136–7, 140–1, 186n10; orphan's vulnerability trope, 98; power, affect and subject formation, 10; prisoners' children sent to, 44–5; "social orphans" notion, 8; Soviet orphanages, 22, 56, 60, 106, 128; and "total institution" concept, 9; UNICEF's stance on, 191n35; in United States, 128. *See also* children's institutions; Hope House
*orteke* (Kazakh puppets), 13, 91
Ospanov, Bakhit, 97
*ostranenie* (defamiliarization/estrangement), 16. *See also* defamiliarization (or estrangement)

pain, media representations of, 17
pedagogy: and performance, 78, 92–4; and puppetry, 12, 87
Peirce, Charles S., 171n3
performance: and care, 180n2; and children, 80–3, 85–6; and competence, 86, 92, 144; and cuteness, 85–6; frame of, 147, 149–50, 153, 178n1; and gender, 178n14, 180n2; and ideologies of childhood, 96–8; and mask/strangeness, 63–4; and pedagogy, 78, 92–4; performers/viewers relationship, 90–2; and projection, 18, 64; Soviet performance genres, 83; and spectacle, 19–20, 89–90; techniques and ideologies of, 14–15; theatricality vs. performativity, 93
Petrushka (carnival puppet), 87, 91, 129
photography: and animation, 42–3; and fantasy, 42, 43; and indexicality, 191n6; and institutional control, 42; and mitigation of absence, 149–50; mug shots, 42, 43. *See also* camera; films
pity, "politics of pity," 153

play: children's play, frame of, 47, 48, 71, 109; children's play and gender, 114; children's play and iconicity, 77; frame of play and fantasy, 152; and projection, 18
pleasure, and power relations, 10
"politics of pity," 153
possession, and puppetry, 63
potential, 4, 79, 86, 100, 125, 144. *See also* competence
power: and affect, 10; and agency, 22; and animation, 62; and guest/host relations, 58; and objectification, 84; and pleasure, 10; and stranger as master, 58; and subject formation, 10. *See also* control
prisons. *See* gulag (labour camps)
projection: adults' projections on children, 11; and animation of intimacy, 4, 21, 22, 28; and fantasy, 22; and hope, 28, 169; Kazakhstan as empty space for grand projections, 34; and performance/acting, 18, 64; and play, 18; and puppetry, 16, 22
proscenium, 55, 64
psychoanalysis: substitutability/transference, 55–6. *See also* Freud, Sigmund
Pulcinella puppetry, 63, 128–32, 181n10
puppetry: and agency of objects, 12; and animation of intimacy, 19; and bonding, 90–1; Bunraku-style puppets, 11, 126–7; and children, 89–90, 91–2; and death, 131–2; and defamiliarization/estrangement, 16; and destrangement, 22; and disembodiment, 21; and displacement, 28–30; and first I/second I theory, 62, 95–6, 99; government puppet theaters, 5, 11, 87; hand puppets, 11; Kazakh puppets (*orteke*), 13, 91; and manipulation, 62–3; marionettes, 11; and pedagogy, 12, 87; and possession, 63; and projection, 16, 22; Pulcinella puppetry, 63, 128–32, 181n10; puppet artists-turned stage characters, 83–4; rod puppets, 11; and socialization, 12, 91, 92, 102; Soviet puppetry, 13, 87, 91, 185n4; tabletop puppets, 11; and the uncanny, 31–2, 126–8; and universalization, 103–4; and violence, 32, 63. *See also* Almaty State Puppet Theater

*qobyz* (Kazakh musical instrument), 46
queer scholarship, central Asian, 16, 32

Raibaev, Serik, 57
Reactive Attachment Disorder, 141
recovery, and loss at Hope House, 23, 28, 34–5, 36–7, 51–2

Reeves, Madeleine, 175n3, 176n25
residential institutions. *See* children's institutions; *detdom* (children's home); *dom rebënka* (baby house); Hope House; *internat* (boarding school); orphanages
resonance, 49, 62, 179n20
responsibility, and agency, 97–8
returnees (*oralman*), 50. *See also* compatriots (*kandas*)
reunion, and separation at Hope House, 2–3, 9, 34–40, 46, 51–2
robots, 31, 32, 86, 126–7
Rosenthal, Miriam K., 67
Rousseau, Jean-Jacques, 181n17, 189n21
Ršumović, Vuk, *No One's Child (Ničije dete)*, 142–3
Russia: adoption of children by US citizens, 140–1, 143; invasion of Ukraine (2022), 185n5; occupation of Crimea (2014), 104, 185n5. *See also* Soviet Union
Russian folktales, 37, 184n56
Russian language: bilingual (Kazakh/Russian) programming at puppet theater, 4–5, 12; Kazakh state's trilingual language policy, 58
Rutter, Michael, 71

Sats, Natalia, 58
scaffolding (in children's learning), 109
Schenkkan, Nate, 150
Schieffelin, Bambi B., 183n43
second I, 62, 95–6, 99, 111, 125. *See also* first I
Semipalatinsk (East Kazakhstan), 33–4, 57
sensory room, 36, 105–6
"sensory traps," 86
sentiment: and animation, 62; and materiality, 8, 100; and photographs, 42
separation: due to deportations/imprisonment, 28, 40; and reunion at Hope House, 2–3, 9, 34–40, 46, 51–2. *See also* loss
settler colonialism, 46
"sharenting," 154
Shklovsky, Viktor, "Art as Technique," 16
showing/hiding. *See* hiding
shrines/sacred sites, 107
Silvio, Teri, 19, 174n38, 180n7
Simmel, Georg, 57, 76, 151, 152, 166
Singh, Joseph Amrito Lal, Reverend, 138, 142
Slaboshpytskiy, Myroslav, *The Tribe (Plemya)*, 142, 143
Sloterdijk, Peter, 181n15, 183n38, 185n2, 189n11
social aesthetics, 18

socialization: and cameras at Hope House, 154–5; and *Cheburashka*, 88–9; and framing, 153; and imitation/repetition routines, 78, 92; improper/incorrect socialization, 22, 125, 126; lack of and "Mowgli children," 139; nonsocialization, 137, 138; and puppetry, 12, 91, 92, 102
"social orphans" notion, 8
Sontag, Susan, 42, 43
Soviet Union: abortion, recriminalization of, 35; animation, 5, 87, 182n28, 182n29; *byt* (everyday life) vs. *dusha* (soul), 185n1; child-rearing in early Soviet era, 22, 35; children as symbols of state paternalism, 85; children's culture and cuteness, 78, 87; children's upbringing as public affair, 84; circus, 91; consumer culture in late Soviet era, 113; Estrada musical genre, 19; famine, 11, 33, 56, 106, 128; force deportations and imprisonment, 11, 15, 18, 28, 33, 50, 57–8; "Friendship of the People" ideology, 58; *glasnost*, 99; gulag (labour camps), 15, 33, 40–3, 51; *Homo Sovieticus*, 20; *kul'turnost'*, 20; mass spectacles, 19, 89; motherhood, idealization of, 56; motherhood, revalorization of, 35; "Mowgli children" (incl. Oxana Malaya case), 138–40, 142, 190n27; orphanages, 22, 56, 60, 106, 128; *perestroika*, 190n29; performance genres, 83; puppetry, 13, 87, 91, 185n4; purges, 51; "wild capitalism," 140; women's role, 35. *See also* Kazakhstan; Russia; Ukraine
spectacle, and performance, 19–20, 89–90
"Spiritual Revival" (*Ruhani Jañgyru*), 5
stability, vs. freedom, 102–4, 122
Stalin, Joseph, 11, 28, 35, 51, 85, 113, 178n13
Starewicz, Ladislaw, 127
Stasch, Rupert, 136
steppe, as "empty" space, 31, 32, 33–4, 46, 51
Stewart, Kathleen, 19, 175n1
Stewart, Susan, 41
stigmatization, of children in orphanages/institutions, 67, 106, 136–7, 140–1, 186n10
stop motion animation, 127
"Storming of the Winter Palace" reenactment, 89
stranger, the: ambiguous role of, 2, 66; as master, 58; as potential source of anxiety, 53–4; Simmel's definition, 57, 76; "strange situation" in attachment theories, 66–7, 75. *See also* destrangement; estrangement (or defamiliarization); *Kashtanka* 2 - meeting a stranger

Strategy Kazakhstan-2050, 85
subject formation, and power, 10
substitutability, 55, 56. *See also* transference
suspended animation, 1, 13, 26
Suyarkulova, Mohira, 146
Švankmajer, Jan, *Alice*, 127
*svoi* ("our own"), 65, 66, 75, 149, 162, 166, 179n23

Tamagotchi toy pets, 74
*tëtka* ("auntie"), 58, 65, 149
theater: alienation theories, 31, 173n24; "fourth wall," 153; frame of performance created by, 153; as frame on the "real," 31; theater/stage as a world, 31; theatricality and the real, 83; theatricality vs. performativity, 93. *See also* performance
things: humility of, 112. *See also* materiality; objects
Tikhonova, Ekaterina, 143
Tizard, Barbara, 71
Tokayev, Kassym-Jomart, 50, 169, 185n5
Tolstoy, Aleksei, *The Golden Key, or the Adventures of Buratino*, 98
Tolstoy, Leo, 99
Toren, Christina, 20
total institutions, 9, 10, 96
totemism, 62–3
toys: bad-quality toys, 113–14; branded toys, 113; children's surprising use of, 113, 114; comparison with children, 121–2; and gender, 187n32; iconicity of, 47, 49–50, 110, 121, 186n17; and nostalgia, 121; Tamagotchi toy pets, 74; toy care, 115–18; toy guns, 111. *See also* dolls
*Toy Story*, 115
Toziya, Vardan, *Amok*, 143
transference, 55–6, 72
traps: acting and art as, 90; baby faces as "sensory traps," 86; right trap to secure adults/carers' support, 96
*The Tribe* (*Plemya*) (Myroslav Slaboshpytskiy), 142, 143

Ukraine: protest movement (2013–14), 104; Russia's invasion of (2022), 185n5; Russia's occupation of Crimea (2014), 104, 185n5
the uncanny, 31–2, 56, 61, 71, 125–8, 144
UNICEF, 15, 68, 84, 191n35
United Nations Convention on the Rights of the Child, 192n15

United States (US): adoption and foster care vs. orphanages, 128; adoption of Eastern European children, 140–2, 143, 185n7; milk carton movement, 153–4; parents' worries about child predators, 153–4
universality: vs. individuality, 133; and puppetry, 103–4
Uspensky, Eduard, *Krokodil Gena y ego druz'ya*, 88

Vaucanson, Jacques de, 74
*The Velveteen Rabbit* (Margery Williams). *See* Williams, Margery
ventriloquists, 21, 181n10
Victor of Aveyron, 139, 189n21
violence: and objectification, 84, 98; and puppetry, 32, 63; state repression of nomadism, 32–3; structural violence of inequality, 140, 153. *See also* deportations; gulag (labour camps); imprisonment
Virgin Lands campaign, 51
vulnerability: beyond childhood, 132; and competence, 96, 98–9; and cuteness, 79, 86, 89, 98, 100, 125, 144; of girls, 112; and hopefulness, 85, 99; and images of children, 153–4; of toys, 121
Vygotsky, L. S., 181n15, 186n15, 186n17

wildness: "wild capitalism" concept, 140; wildness trope for economy and childhood, 140. *See also* feral children
Williams, Margery, *The Velveteen Rabbit*, 115, 188n38
Winnicott, D. W., 61–2, 110–11, 117
wolf, adopting baby chick, musical about, 141
The Wolf and the Kid Goats, 1–2, *2*, *3*
Wolof griots, 164
women: and consumer culture, 187n22; role of in Soviet Union, 35; trafficking of, 192n14. *See also* ALZhIR (Akmolinsk Camp of Women of Traitors of the Country) museum; gender; girls; motherhood
Woolard, Kathryn A., 75
worlding, 19, 31; reworlding Kazakhstan, 50–1

Yanukovich, Viktor, 104